EDUCATING FOR A WORLDVIEW

Focus on Globalizing Curriculum and Instruction

Edited by
Larry Hufford
Teresita Pedrajas

University Press of America,® Inc.
Lanham · Boulder · New York · Toronto · Plymouth, UK

Library of Congress Control Number: 2006930588
ISBN-13: 978-0-7618-3583-7 (paperback : alk. paper)
ISBN-10: 0-7618-3583-0 (paperback : alk. paper)

*Dedicated to the memory
of Maxine Dunfee*

Table of Contents

Preface

The essays included in the volume have been selected from papers and lectures presented at the 11th Triennial Conference of the World Council for Curriculum and Instruction (WCCI) held in Wollongong, Australia.

The WCCI is a transnational educational organization committed to advancing the achievement of a just and peaceful world community. The WCCI is an NGO of the United Nations, UNESCO: B Status, on the roster of the Economic and Social Council. The first WCCI Conference was held in England in 1974. Since then conferences have been held in Turkey, the Philippines, Canada, Japan, the Netherlands, Egypt, India, Thailand, Spain and Australia.

The theme of the 11th Triennial Conference was "Educating for a Worldview: Focus on Globalizing Curriculum and Instruction." The first essay is a keynote lecture given by Konai H. Thaman, holder of the UNESCO Chair in teacher education and culture at the University of South Pacific. Konai explores the theme of globalization and education from a Pacific perspective and argues that both are western cultural constructs that, like colonialism, were imposed on Pacific societies over a century ago but are not seen to be natural and inevitable in nations which do not have much control either over their education or globalization. Indigenous educators, environmentalists, and cultural conservationists see both education and globalization as tools for cultural, political and economic oppression with negative consequence.

Rose Wu, founder and director of the Hong Kong Christian Institute, is Hong Kong's leading feminist theologian, a grassroots community organizer for the rights of immigrant women working as domestic labor and one of the key organizers of the democracy movement in Hong Kong. Rose's thesis is that the purpose of education in the Confucius, Mencius, Aristotle context has been transformed into education to prepare labor for global capitalism. She describes the Civil Society Education Project in Hong Kong. This is an effort to provide an alternative grassroots education with the goal of creating sustainable societies.

Larry Hufford's Alice Miel Lecture is a personal journey of becoming a peace educator. Hufford's thesis is that one becomes a peace educator through lived experiences. His journey has taken him to countries at war, transitioning out of war or conflict and to very poor countries in search of root causes of hatred and violence in humankind. Hufford calls on us to create communities based on covenants rather than social contracts.

Professors Huber and Warring are experts in multicultural education. Their essay explores strategies for critically analyzing home and school, teacher and student cultures. Peter Heffernan of the University of Lethbridge, Canada discusses the need to oppose "centrism", for example, egocentrism, ethnocentrism, Anglocentrism, etc. He analyzes language instruction and presents a strong case for linguistic diversity.

Judith Johnson discusses the critical role technology can play in humanizing the global village. From the macro to the micro, Judith analyzes an engineering course for Japanese universities that will illustrate a positive, integrative use of technology as a humanizing force.

Michael Higgins of Yamaguchi University, Japan has created a new phonetic alphabet called "The Sound Approach." His research shows that those trained in The Sound Approach did significantly better in sight reading/pronunciation of foreign languages than those not trained.

Jean Benton and Sandra McWilliams discuss a consortium of three European and three United States universities that joined to develop a curriculum for student teachers to better prepare them to work successfully with children at risk of failing in school. Shared global concerns in education on underachievement, especially with children of migrant laborers, led to this project.

Noorjehan Ganihar of Karnatak University, India advocates teaching citizenship education that promotes global citizens and global responsibilities. Marilyn Higgins of Yamaguchi Prefectural University, Japan analyzes models of peace education from Cream Wrights' four kinds of peace education: prevention, construction, mitigation and reconstruction to Toh Swee Hin's Buddhist methodology for teaching and living peace.

Geetha Vitus of Karmela Rani Training College, India writes that global education is vital to understanding social justice issues. She proposes that global education be taught in a manner that will lead students to become life long learners. Thus, she emphasizes the need for links between formal and non-formal education. Alice Asim of the University of Calabar, Nigeria discusses the crisis in Nigeria's schools as a result of a "brain drain" to Europe and North America. Thus, she questions the quality of preparedness of many of Nigeria's teachers. Her solution is to use information technology (IT) and the Internet to strengthen teacher preparedness.

H.M. Shailaja of Karnatak University, India, grapples with a positive definition of peace education. Positive approaches to defining peace are vital if humankind is going to succeed in creating a global culture of peace.

Kathleen Conway discuses a "Teacher Work Sample" and the portfolio as effective means of preparing pre-service teachers to have a greater appreciation of cultural diversity.

In the final essay, Ritsuko Saito of the University of Wollongong, Australia and Noriko Ishizuka of Doshisha University, Japan analyze the educational possibilities of online chat communication between teachers in different countries that cross cultural and curricula boundaries. The authors conclude that both teachers and students can benefit from CMC (cross mediated communication).

Acknowledgements

Special thanks are in order for all who labored to make the 11th Triennial Conference of the World Council for Curriculum and Instruction in Wollongong, Australia a success. The work of Estela Matriano, Jen Burnley, Carole Capparos, Teresita Pedrajas, Sue Fan Foo and all those who volunteered made the Conference a wonderful experience for the participants. Ira Gandasaputra, Eduardo Gonzalez and Randell Laughlin graduate assistants of Larry Hufford supplied the technical work for the manuscript.

CHAPTER ONE

Education and Globalization: A View from Oceania

Konai H. Thaman
UNESCO Chair in teacher education & culture
University of the South Pacific

INTRODUCTION

Let me begin by thanking the organizers for inviting me to participate in this most important gathering. I also wish to acknowledge the indigenous nations of Australia and pay tribute to those who are the traditional owners of the land on which we happen to be gathering at this time. I was humbled when asked to present at this conference since I regard the perspective that I bring as a minority view. However it is good to share perspectives especially on important themes such as globalization and education because these are issues that many people have been grappling with for a long time.

It is also important for people to whom globalization "is done" to have a view. Please allow me to share this poem with you, one that I wrote while attending a conference on educational reforms in Pacific Island Countries (PICs) a few years ago.

today your words are empty
sucking dry the brown dust
left by earth and sky
patches politely parched
with no water flowing
from the mountain top
scars burn on my soft skin
leaving my bandaged heart
to endure the pain
of your tying me
to yourself
(Thaman, 1993:7)

The poem expresses for me the impact colonialism and more recently globalization have had on education and ultimately the lives and cultures of Pacific Island people, something that made the preparation of this address both easy and difficult. Dependence. Independence. Interdependence. Education. Globalization. For me, these are English words with complex meanings that evoke different images depending on where and who you are. So please allow me now to share with you the sense in which I shall be using the terms 'education' and 'globalization'.

DEFINITIONS

Education is worthwhile learning, which can be organized and institutionalized as in formal education; or organized but not institutionalized as in non-formal education; or unorganized and not institutionalized, as in informal education. Globalization refers to an intensification of worldwide relations linking one part of the globe with other parts in ways that what happens in one place is shaped by events occurring in other distant places (Held, 1991). Globalization is a product of the emergence of a global economy, expansion of transnational linkages between economic units, creating new forms of collective decision-making, development of intergovernmental and quasi-supranational institutions, intensification of transnational communications and the creation of new regional and military orders. The process of globalization is often seen as blurring national boundaries, shifting solidarity's within and between nation-states and deeply affecting the constitutions of national and group identities (Held, 1991). Today I plan to share with you some of the difficulties and concerns that many educators in our region have in trying to understand education in PINs in the context of a globalizing world.

It is fitting that we are meeting here in Australia because of the significant role that Australia continues to play in the overall development of many PINs, through assistance, both financial as well as humanitarian. As a Pacific Islander this conference is also important because Australia, together with Europe and the USA are generally seen by most Pacific Island people as nations that are major players in global processes, many of which negatively impact upon their lives and futures. For example, it has been estimated that Australia has the highest per capita level of greenhouse gas emissions in the developed world (27% higher than the amount produced by American citizens) and while Pacific Island Countries are not responsible for global warming and sea-level rise they are amongst those most at risk from its negative impacts (FT 20/6).

My own personal perspective of both education and globalization has been influenced by the same educational processes that most of you have gone through. However, I have also been influenced by my socialization within a particular cultural history and context, together with continued residence in the Pacific island region (Oceania) rather than in Europe or U.S.A. or Australia, where most of the ideas and theories about education and globalization have originated and are regularly debated in educational institutions as well as the mass media. Brumble and Torres (2000), for example, have edited a major book discussing the connections between globalization and education and some of the implications for educational policy while others have suggested that globalization is making the study of education as a disciple, more complex.

In much of the writing on globalization and education there are the inherent assumptions about the nature of society as well as the nature of personhood, as well as certain universal values such as social justice, democracy and human rights. For example, globalization is said to be responsible not only for depressed economies but also for the apparent weakening of nation states. It is estimated for example, that about 60% of world trade take place between the headquarters of multinational corporations (MNC's) without the intervention of states. In this context, globalization is seen as a threat to the fulfillment of one of the most important tasks of nation states, that of educating their citizens. And as you all know, globalization is also closely associated with the development of New Information & Communication Technologies (ICTs), that has resulted in the high speed movement of mass capital from one financial centre to another and today, experts say, global financial markets continue to dictate national economic policies, impacting not only on trade and industry but also nations, people, their cultures, and their education (Torres, 2002).

THE PAST

In discussing globalization and education in Oceania, we are mindful of the past when the most important force in the region has been that of colonialism, a force that some cynics suggest, is continuing under the guise of globalization. For nearly two hundred years we have grown to depend on and learn from Europeans, and the English and French languages together with their associated philosophies and ideologies continue to influence what many of us consider worthwhile to teach and learn as well as the way we think, organize ourselves and relate to one another. It is only recently that some of us have begun to question and interrogate these ideas in the process of trying to understand and theorize our own education.

Many of our societies are small and scattered and most people continue to be involved in subsistence agriculture, hunting, tool making, food gathering and generally just looking after themselves. Most rural people learn what is essential for their survival and protection and the continuation of their cultures, and work is usually related to where they are placed in relation to others. Their indigenous system of education ensure that future generations acquire the types of knowledge, skills and values that are needed for cultural survival and continuity.

In this context, teachers and learners share both a physical environment as well as a cultural system of meanings, practices and institutions. Education is embedded in an eco-cultural environment which not only determined the content and processes of education but also set the standards by which successful learning was judged and/or assessed. When a new mode of teaching and learning in the form of school is introduced, the relationship between its cultural characteristics and that of learners' families and communities become problematic. Experts tell us that in order for learners to be successful in achieving the objectives of the school curriculum, there should be continuity between the two systems of learning – home and school. But for most Pacific students this is not possible because of the need for schools to pass on foreign, specialized knowledge, in ways that are also foreign (Serpell, 1997).

SCHOOLING AGENDA

In most PINs today formal education corresponds to that which prevails in Western, liberal, and industrialized nations where schools are normally seen as having three major agendas: an economic, a cultural and a pedagogic agenda. The idea is that schools would help learners to develop morally and intellectually by expanding their knowledge and understanding of their cultural heritage. This would empower future generations to develop culturally, manage their environment and generate greater wealth for their societies. We know of course, that in many parts of the world, and from the perspectives of countless students, schools have actually failed. In most PINs the school's economic and cultural agendas often come into conflict as the curriculum continues to reflect and transmit the cultures of other people. The school's pedagogic agenda often assumes (wrongly) that there is a certain degree of agreement about appropriate ways and means of preparing students for life's major responsibilities.

As teachers or instructors many of us perceive and carry out our work in ways that reflect our own personal beliefs and values as well as a notion of what education is and our role in that process. However, few of us regularly stop and ask questions such as: What am I doing here and why am I doing it? Whose knowledge and values am I communicating to students/people? Who's cognitive and philosophical theories are being emphasized? Or, whose agenda is being fulfilled? The answers to some of these questions may help us to have a clearer perception of what our role as educators actually is and whether we are moral agents or forced laborers in the education factories of a particular time and place. Only if we consciously reflect upon our work would we be able to better locate ourselves in different contexts including historical, personal, communal and professional. Pacific educators such as myself often experience both moral and epistemological dilemmas because many of us, like the majority of our students, continually face the conflicting emphases of the education that we are supposed to deliver and the education which we received as members of particular cultural groups (Thaman, 1988).

DIFFERENT EDUCATION

Pacific Island societies have cultural histories that are more than three thousand years old. These were sustained and maintained by their own epistemologies and ways of seeing the world and their place in that world. Each group developed particular knowledge systems that formed the bases of the education of group members for the sake of cultural survival and continuity. During the last century and a half and especially in the last fifty years, mainly European knowledge systems have interacted with Pacific societies and helped change not only their social, political and economic structures, but also the way people see themselves and their societies. The degree to which this transforming process, now more commonly referred to as globalization, influences the way we Pacific islanders think and see the world, would, in my view, depend on our ability to clarify for themselves the differences between our received wisdom (from their formal education) and the wisdom of the cultures in which we were socialized and from which we learned.

Today if we view formal education in Oceania with critical eyes, we would see differences between the goals of the school curriculum and those defined by social and cultural groups with which many school children identify. The areas of religion and language are perhaps the most obvious but there are others, including those relating to gender and culture. For example, how can the social and emotional orientation of a Ni Vanuatu secondary school girl be harmonized with the developmental goals of a school curriculum designed primarily by male curriculum experts from England or Australia? Or, how can Pacific Island students reconcile the values cultivated by their schooling in a metropolitan country with the demands of allegiance to their village or cultural group? In this context it is possible to surmise that the greater the discrepancy between the goals of the culture of a student's socialization and that of formal education, the wider is the gap that needs to be bridged in order for the student to achieve the outcomes of formal education.

REFORMING EDUCATION

In the Pacific region the push towards Education for All and Lifelong Learning has been largely due to direct and indirect pressure from the international community and development agencies involved in various forms of reforms and restructuring, reforms that are ostensibly aimed at ensuring that Pacific governments and people become better citizens by embracing the values of democracy, freedom, human rights, good governance and so forth. These agencies, interestingly enough, have their origins and/or headquarters in those very same countries that once ruled Pacific Island societies despite the rhetoric of Jomtien that decision-making and policy processes in the South would no longer be prescribed by external agencies from the North. On the other hand, the rhetoric of modernizing island governments about stakeholder involvement in education has largely remained just that, with the views of parents and civil society largely ignored.

In many PINs as in other developing nations, the international drive to improve human life including providing education for all, has resulted in many communities around the world experiencing quite staggering amounts of change. For small, vulnerable island nations rapid and frequent change has been the rule rather than the exception. Teachers and pupils are often the ones who bear the brunt of educational changes over the last three decades, particularly in the school curriculum. Consultants often come from Western parts of the globe to advise on what types of changes are needed. Different reform projects often demand different things from the same people resulting in what I have called the 'Pacific amoeboid syndrome', where people keep on changing themselves and their perceptions in order to suit the particular demands of superiors and/or financing agencies, who usually have their own agenda. Many local counterparts do not even ask questions preferring to go along with what is proposed by overseas consultants because that is the politest and easiest approach to take.

While writing about educational change, the Director of the Geneva-based International Bureau of Education (IBE) suggested that change strategies, approaches and methods needed to take into account the perceptions of (the) actors in the educational process. He went on to say that this was best done by first analyzing the particular social or cultural representation that actors in the educational process have about the exercise of democracy, human rights and the life of a citizen, in order to define the educational strategies and subsequently to measure the importance of the outcomes concerned (Tedesco, 1997:1).

Unfortunately many people, including those in the forefront of educational reforms, have neither heeded nor taken seriously such an important suggestion. In fact, in most PINs it is simply ignored. Educational reforms of the type to which we have been subjected in the past three decades, took little or no account of Pacific people's representation of the educated, ideal citizen, or the main outcome of Pacific indigenous education and knowledge systems. These systems include structures and processes of storing and transmitting knowledge, skills and values, deemed necessary for the purposes of cultural survival and continuity. Educational reformers both from outside and from within our region have not acknowledged Pacific people's indigenous education and knowledge systems, systems that continue to operate side by side with the modern school based education system (Teaero, 2003; Bakalevu, 2003).

PACIFIC EDUCATIONAL IDEAS

Conceptual analyses of Pacific indigenous educational ideas reveal systems of learning and teaching underpinned by cultural values the most important of which were human relationships and social responsibility. The ideal person in most Pacific cultures was one who knew what to do and did that well. This implied the ability to know one's relationships to other people and how to nurture these according to cultural norms and expectations. Learning was aimed at gaining important knowledge, skills and values and using these in positive ways in order to maintain and nurture these different relationships. This would help people grow and become useful members of their communities. Relationships were also important in defining persons as well as communities (Nabobo, 2003; Liligeto, 2003; Taufeulungaki, 2003). Although school learning affected the indigenous conception of the ideal person and has incorporated success in school, many Pacific communities continue to regard the maintenance of good inter-personal relationships as a key indicator of wisdom. As one of my informants told me when I asked her about her notion of an educated person, "it does not matter, she said, whether you have a PhD, what matters most is that you use that degree to help you meet your obligations to your family and community'. This representation of the 'educated' person continues to be pervasive in most Pacific communities (Thaman, 1988; 2002).

In Tonga for example, the educated citizen is one who is poto – one who knows what to do and does it well. *Poto* is achieved through the appropriate and beneficial use of *'ilo* – defined by Tongans as knowledge, skills, understanding and values that a person acquires through the process of *ako* or learning. Among indigenous Fijians, similar notions exist. The closest equivalent of *poto* is *vuku* or *yalovuku*, which is the culmination of learning or vuli aimed at the acquisition of useful knowledge skills and values or *kila ka* (Nabete, 1997). And in Solomon Islands, among the Lengo, a person of wisdom is manatha; s/he is a person who, through nanau (learning) obtained ligana (wisdom), which is seen as vital for living and surviving in Lengo society (Vatamana, 1997).

Pacific indigenous education systems are still functional in most Pacific societies today especially in rural and remote communities where worthwhile learning occurs under the guidance of elders and specialist teachers. Important knowledge, skills and values are transmitted through a variety of means including myths, legends, dance, poetry, songs, proverbs and rituals. Through observation, listening, imitation, participation and some direct instruction, young people obtain the necessary knowledge, skills and values of their cultures, elders, other adults and sometimes their peers. Learning is practical and directly related to shared values and beliefs. In my own culture, these important values include: include : *'ofa* (compassion), *faka'apa'apa* (respect), *feveikotai'aki* (reciprocity), *tauhivaha'a* (nurturing inter-personal relations), and *fakama'uma'u* (restraint). The achievement of *poto* continues to be measured against such values through people's performance and behaviour in different social contexts.

Poto persons or their equivalents are those who know who they are and understand their social relationships and responsibilities. Failure to maintain social relationships and/or contribute to the welfare of one's group is an indicator of poverty and failure to successfully learn this often reflects negatively on teachers who include family members as well as community elders. Wealth is most indigenous Pacific societies is gauged not by how much money one has but by how well one keeps *vaa/wah*, metaphorical, (inter-personal and relational) spaces, the disturbance or destruction of which often leads to unpeaceful and inappropriate behavior. Knowing and maintaining good inter-personal relationships is the responsibility of everyone in the community and one is considered wealthy if one maintains good relationships and meet social obligations. Unfortunately this major feature of Pacific societies is under threat from proponents of a different type of wealth –capital accumulation that often threatens to destroy the *vaa* and ultimately important relationships. The value of *Vaa*, in my view, needs to be promoted, perhaps even globalized and emphasized in the curriculum of formal education as a way of addressing interpersonal and inter-group conflicts. It may create relevance in the school curriculum, widely seen by many as too abstract and unrelated to people's social realities.

ASKING QUESTIONS OF EDUCATION

During the past two decades, Pacific educators have begun to interrogate the concept of education itself especially curriculum content, pedagogy and assessment methods and the values that underpin them. We know that throughout the history of schooling, the curriculum has emphasized what other people have deemed important based on their perceptions of what a good, pious and economically productive citizen ought to be. In almost all educational reforms and restructuring with which I am familiar, reformers rarely ask how Pacific peoples conceptualize wisdom, learning and knowledge, nor wonder if the values inherent in and propagated by these development projects were shared by the people whose lives were meant to be improved as a result of these projects. Instead, what happens is the wholesale importation of practices and values under the guise of human resource development, enlightenment, cash employment, good governance, human rights, freedom and democracy, etc. in the hope that at the end of the reform period, people will change. Few realize the ideological and philosophical conflicts associated with differing perceptions of most of these ideas, leaving many Pacific people confused and at times angry. Kabini Sanga writing about Solomon Island education concluded that the extent to which school represented the multiple cultures of the Solomon Islands is minimal as the officially sanctioned values are those of the school structure, the approved curriculum and the teaching profession and not those of the cultures of teachers and students. This is the paradox that exists in all PINs which the majority of teachers as well as learners continue to face, and provides a challenge for educational reformers. Today, Pacific Island leaders are calling for a balance in education whereby future generations can learn about themselves and their cultures for the sake of developing strong cultural identities *at the same time* remain part of a bigger, globalizing world without being obliterated by it. Pacific people are now required to learn to live with both the individualist values of schools and the market place and the socially oriented values of their cultures and communities.

The global market ideology is now pervasive in all formal sectors of PINs including education, and it is transforming even its most ardent opposers. Many educational managers and leaders now believe that education is a commodity to be sold rather than something that is provided by nation states for their citizens. Developed neighboring states such as Australia and New Zealand, do not hide the fact that they need to be more proactive in marketing their educational services in the Asia/Pacific region. Such emphases on market-driven economies and educational development have made issues such as cross cultural transfer, globalized curricula and appropriate learning strategies critical as globalization threatens to blur cultural diversity and educational services become increasingly standardized. Apart from rising sea levels, the globalization of education may be the biggest threat to the survival of Pacific societies and cultures.

Today an increasing number of Pacific educators are questioning the value assumptions upon which both education and globalization continue to be based, ones that often claim cultural neutrality. But we know that the cultural neutrality of education, as well as globalization, is neither possible nor desirable, and that partisan beliefs and values like other beliefs and values, are embedded in their own cultural curriculum and agenda (Taylor, 1975). Pacific values need to underpin Pacific education in order for Pacific young people to learn about their responsibilities to themselves and to others. Interestingly many international education advisors and consultants who work in the Pacific too often object to the teaching of values and beliefs that might appeal to customs or traditions or religious authority, yet they are surprised when their own arguments cut little ice with those who insist upon limits to critical rationality itself because *they* take their own ideological axiom for granted (Vine, 1992:178).

Pacific educators know that they have the task of mediating the interface between different cultural systems of meanings and values that exist in our region. The stimulus for this mediation comes from our professional role, which mandates intensive interaction with children as well as the parents whose children they are to educate. Educators, however, would need to understand the differences and commonalties among various cultural perspectives, as often the points of conflict are communicated to them indirectly by the behavior of the students as they commute between the world of home and that of formal education. Furthermore, they would need to find ways of integrating different themes of the various cultures that have contributed to their own professional development. This is important because the current educational picture that we are seeing today is neither clear nor sound. We know that an increasing proportion of Pacific school students are not achieving at high school levels and a recent study by the ADB concluded that primary and secondary schools throughout the region are ineffective and of poor quality (ADB, 1977).

Improving the quality of education in general and of students' educational outcomes in particular is part of a move towards addressing the education crisis many PINs are facing. This is in addition to problems of social and cultural breakdown, environmental destruction, land alienation and landlessness, malnutrition and poor health, violent crime, corruption and spiritual impoverishment, unheard of just thirty years ago. This crisis is particularly worrying in the larger island countries where modernization has resulted in mass migration to towns and cities and where many citizens, especially the young, have not learned the values and wisdom of their cultures but the values of modern, urbanizing cultures, the ones that dominate the school curriculum, not to mention the mass media and new information superhighways. Values of individualism and self-promotion are what young people are bombarded with daily, a far cry from the communal values of compassion, respect and responsibility for one another that underpinned indigenous education systems where service to the group and ultimately the community and nation was seen as more important than self-service. Add to these, values that are entrenched in formal studies at university, that is, of modern subjects such as accounting and financial management, economics, administration, computing science and technology, and you end up with many urban, profit-conscious men and women who have lost touch with the earth, their communities and with each other.

A PACIFIC EDUCATION VISION

A couple of years ago, Ministers of Education from PINs agreed on a Pacific Education Vision. This vision reflected the general aim of development in the region, the successful harmonization of the indigenous and the international, the dissolution of the current dissonance between the two and the creation of a seamless blend that is uniquely Pacific. They endorsed the Dakar Framework for Action to which many PINs are signatories and which asserts that education is a fundamental right and the key to sustainable development, peace, and stability within and among countries and, thus, an indispensable means for effective participation in the societies and economies of the 21st century, which are affected by rapid globalization. The (Pacific) Vision encompasses that which was already defined by the world community but it also responds to the larger vision of Pacific countries and peoples which include the maintenance and enhancement of their own distinctive values, social, political economic and cultural heritages and the development of the capacities that could create a balance between these and those promoted by globalization. In other words, the Vision is for an education that not only assures the survival and continuity of Pacific cultures but also for their preparation to become equal partners with other members of the global community.

This would mean a Pacific region where people would benefit from the good things that modern life brings but where young people are able to learn and benefit from their own cultural values and beliefs, knowledge and understandings, and wisdom; where teachers use culturally appropriate methods of teaching, including teaching in a language that students can understand, and recognizing the importance of context-specific learning.

I believe that the way in which PINs will respond to this new Vision would depend to a large extent on the resilience and strength of their cultures. Anthropological research has shown that the different responses of Pacific culture to foreign colonization in the 19th and 20th centuries were a function of cultural difference. Before European contact, they suggest, Pacific people were aware of cultural difference, defined by people's behavior and performance rather than biology, the determining factor of ethnicity. Culture therefore will remain an important factor in Pacific responses to education as well as to a globalizing world – a world where social development is being de-emphasized and economic development (by IMF, World Bank, ADB and other donors) is driving the vision and mission of PINs (Pacific Plan). This trend is worrying some of us, given the fact that social development depends on human quality and cultural resources, in the form of cultural knowledge, skills and values. The global market-driven education that is the result of globalization and currently being embraced and advocated in our region by many, tends to devalue human quality and marginalia Pacific cultures; and as I mentioned earlier, marginalizing culture will reduce Pacific people's ability to respond to the forces of globalization.

I acknowledge that broadening the outcomes of formal education to include the development of strong cultural identities and focusing on social and cultural development would mean targeting all those involved in the education process.

At our university, we are targeting teachers, teacher educators, education managers and curriculum planners. Other organizations such as the Pacific Resources Centre as well as many local NGOs are focusing mainly on the non-formal sector. Over the last five years, university, staff and students have conducted research and written about their indigenous education systems, particularly notions of learning, knowledge and wisdom, and how these are reflected in various vernacular languages. Last year, *Educational Ideas from Oceania* was published jointly by the UNESCO Chair and the university's Institute of Education (USP). It contains essays authored by Pacific islanders on the educational ideas of various Pacific cultures. The book is being used as a text by educational institutions in our region as well as overseas. Early this month, the Pacific Association of Teacher Educators met at the National University of Samoa to re-think teacher education, especially the teacher education curriculum. And in 2006, we will be hosting an international conference on Pacific Epistemologies which we hope will result, among other things, in the production of teaching and learning resources about ways of knowing and knowledge of Pacific peoples for the use of our students and anyone else who might be interested. And finally, Pacific epistemologies including knowledge systems and pedagogies, have been added to a list of research priority areas for institutional funding by the university - a milestone in our struggle for cultural and cognitive democracy in the Academy.

This year we launched PRIDE, the EU/NZ funded Pacific Regional Initiatives for the Delivery of Basic Education Project which deals with early childhood, primary and secondary education, as well as technical and vocational education and covers both formal and non-formal sectors. PRIDE seeks to improve the quality of basic education in the fifteen PINs by strengthening their capacity to plan and deliver quality education through formal and non-formal means. A key outcome of the Project will be the development of strategic plans for education in each country. The Project also will assist countries to implement monitor and evaluate their plans, providing capacity building activities for educators at national, sub-regional and regional levels. PRIDE is being implemented and managed by the Institute of Education at the USP. It will seek to implement the Pacific Vision of Education developed by Ministers of Education of the Pacific Island Forum, and contained in the Forum Basic Education Action Plan, that was endorsed in August 2001 (PRIDE brochure, 2004).

In all of the activities that I have described, we are very mindful of the need to guard against overvaluing a romanticized, golden past. We acknowledge that western knowledge systems are now part of Pacific people and societies but my hope is that we would develop and encourage a pluralistic view of knowledge in order to reflect our region's different cultural heritages. This will not only help us to re-claim our education but also to reconstruct the knowledge-generation process we call 'research' (and its associated practices) and move beyond the fascination with ethno-science and other ethno-things, that have no intention of questioning the power relations between various knowledge systems, Hountondji (2002).

But questioning long held beliefs is never easy especially in the Academy. The epistemological silencing and efforts to pre-empt any meaningful discussion and exchange of ideas about indigenous knowledge systems in the Academy and other institutions that privilege Western epistemology continue. These challenges remain real in our attempt to counter the harmful effects of globalization by focusing on Pacific cultures, their value and knowledge systems as a way of providing safety nets for our people and a means of educating for peace and social responsibility. My view is that in our current struggle we will continue to find barriers to our attempts to narrow the ever widening gaps between the formal educational institutions that we have inherited and the societies which they are supposed to serve (Thaman, 2003).

Educating for cultural survival and continuity presupposes shared values and shared futures. However, many Pacific nations themselves have been defined not by Pacific peoples but by others. History, especially colonialism and war created nations and destroyed others, often arbitrarily, dividing people and in some cases, obliterating their collective cultural identities. Understanding Pacific people's notions of culture and identity and how these are negotiated and played out will remain an important pre-requisite for any educational reform that is aimed at local as well as global participation in any kind of modern development.

Educating for cultural survival is also important because of the revolution that is being created by the new (computer) technology. This revolution, like the previous one, is causing havoc in our social relationships, as well as in our social institutions of family, work and school. The dominance of the imperative of the market place in our various education systems, especially our higher education system, ignore any notion of social responsibility causing some to conclude that our educational institutions are preparing students to be individual, undifferentiated units, easily interchangeable in the global marketplace. In Oceania, we need to develop an educational theory that takes our cultures into consideration in order to help us reclaim an education that values human relationships and collectivity rather than machines and individuality.

CONCLUSION

We need a new way of seeing and talking about education and globalization in our region in order to counter hegemonic discourses that continue to challenge us. We also need to find new paradigms of change that emphasize complementarily and interconnectedness rather than duality because our long-standing preoccupation with Western scientific traditions have prevented many of us from the possibility of our developing context specific knowledge (Crossman and Devisch). However, we need to be aware also that we are not returning to a golden age but creating syntheses between local and global explorations of human and societal possibilities. The re-claiming of education for human development and social responsibility in our region is not just about being culturally democratic but also about developing a critical theory of our own (Pacific) knowledge systems. We also need to actively participate in discussions about our own knowledge systems, have time to research, record and disseminate that knowledge and build on their capabilities. This is important because of the high degree of Western bias in all areas of knowledge as reflected in the way many international organizations including universities, tend to see themselves as knowledge banks with many experts and consultants seeing themselves mainly as teachers rather than learners. (Brock-Utne, 2002).

Finally, educating for survival and continuity using Pacific indigenous ideas and frameworks is a good alternative to the homogenizing effects of globalization with its McWorld culture that requires no citizenship, responsibility or accountability. The new global order, based on individualism and privatization totally undermine the collective approach, and is perceived by many as a social liability rather than a social good. The kind of economic reforms and restructuring that is now being forced on most PINs by external financial institutions such as the IMF and the World Bank threatens the growth not only of indigenous social and economic institutions, but ultimately democratic governments because they preach the idea that wealth equals material accumulation rather than the enhancement of social relationships. Perhaps we need to globalize the way Pacific people define wealth in order to provide for a more holistic definition of growth, better human relationships and enhanced social responsibility, for the sake of human survival and continuity.

you say that you think
therefore you are
but thinking belongs
in the depths of the earth
we only borrow
what we need to know

these islands the sky
the surrounding seas
the trees the birds
and all that are free
the misty rain
the surging river
pools by the blowholes
a hidden flower
have their own thinking
they are different frames
of mind that cannot fit
a small selfish world
(Thaman, 1999:7)

REFERENCES

Bakalevu, S. 2003. Ways of mathematising in Fijian society. In Thaman, K. (Ed.), *Educational Ideas from Oceania*. IOE/UNESCO Chair, Suva.

Brock-Utre, B. 2002. The place of indigenous knowledge systems in the post-modern Integrative paradigm shift. In Hoppers, C.O. (Ed). *Indigenous knowledge and the integration of knowledge systems,* NAE, Pretoria, pp. 257-285

Burbules, N. and Torees,C.A. (Eds). 2000. *Education and Globalization: the dialectics of the global and local.* Rowman and Littlefield, Lanham, Maryland.

Crossman, P. and Devish, R. 2002. Endogenous knowledge in anthropological perspective. In Hoppers, C.O. (Ed). *Indigenous knowledge and the integration of knowledge systems*, NAE, Pretoria, pp. 96-128

Held, D. (Ed). *Political Theory Today.* Standford Uni. Press, Stanford, CA.

Hountondji, P.J. Knowledge appropriation in a post-colonial context. In Hoppers, C.O. (Ed), *Indigenous knowledge and the integration of knowledge systems*, NAE, Pretoria, pp. 23-38.

Liligeto, A. 2003. Indigenous education, culture and technology. In Thaman, K.H. *Educational Ideas from Oceania.* IOE/UNESCO Chair, Suva.

Nabete, J. 1997. Fijian vernacular educational ideas. Unpublished paper, USP, Suva.

Nabobo, U. 2003. Indigenous Fijian Educational Ideas. In Thaman, K. (Ed), *Educational Ideas from Oceania,* IOE/UNESCO Chair, Suva.

Taufe'ulungaki, A.M., Benson, C., and Pene, F. 2002. *Tree of Opportunity.* Institute of Education, University

Taufe'ulungaki, A.M. Pacific Education: where to now? 2001. Paper prepared for Forum Education Ministers Meeting, Auckland.

Tedesco, J.C. 1997. What education for what citizenship? *Educational Innovation* 90:1 of the South Pacific, Suva.

Thaman, K.H. 1988. Ako and faiako: cultural values, educational ideas and teachers' role perceptions in Tonga. Unpublished PhD theses, USP, Suva.

Thaman, K.H. 1993. Culture and the Curriculum. *Comparative Education* 29(3):249-260.

Thaman, K.H. 1999. *Songs of Love.* MANA Publications, Suva.

Thaman, K.H. 2002. *Vaa:* a foundation for peace and inter-cultural understanding in Oceania. Paper presented at the UNESCO Conference on inter-cultural education, Jyvaskyla University, Finland.

Thaman, K.H. 2003. *Educational Ideas from Oceania.* Institute of Education, USP, Suva.

Serpell, R. 1993. *The significance of schooling.* CUP, Cambridge.

Vatamana, E. 1997. Lengo vernacular educational ideas. Unpublished paper, USP, Suva.

Vine, I. 1992. Moral diversity or universal values? In Lynch, J., Modgil, C. and Modgil, S. (Eds), *Cultural diversity and the school.* Vol.1, Falmer Press, pp.169-210

Visvanathan, C.S. 2002. Between two pilgrimage and citizenship. In *Indigenous knowledge and the integration of knowledge systems*, NAE, Pretoria, pp. 39-52.

CHAPTER TWO

A Pedagogy for Building a Justpeace Global Civil Society

Rose Wu
Hong Kong Christian Institute

INTRODUCTION

It is a great honor to be invited to be a keynote speaker at the 11th Triennial Conference of The World Council for Curriculum and Instruction. I will share with you my past experiences and reflections on the subject of education as well as my vision of building a global civil society on the principle of just peace. My perspective is that of a practical feminist theologian and educator in Hong Kong.

What is education?

For Aristotle, education was the primary function of the *polis* to provide laws, written and unwritten, that would educate people to become more virtuous citizens, for only such citizens would make a good *polis* possible. Thus, it was not schools that Aristotle initially had in mind when he discussed education but the laws and mores of the whole community. It was the responsibility of citizens, however, to deliberate on the laws and support those that would promote the common good.

Confucius and Mencius asserted the obligation of the educated to be civil servants to offer counsel and service to the emperor. It placed a special duty on the educated elites as they must bear concern for the good of society and guide the ruler in actions in accordance with the Way. According to Confucius, "eagerness to learn" was placed above the potential civil virtue of persons "doing their best for others and . . . being trustworthy in what they say."

Although the philosophies on education of Aristotle and Confucius are biased toward the elites in society, they both reflect the belief that the core meaning of education is to benefit society as a whole. Thus, education at those times was seen as a foundation for building society and the common good.

Unfortunately, our contemporary world has become dominated by the global market economy, and the purpose of education has subsequently become driven toward merely producing people to be part of such an economic system, an economic system which is dehumanizing and diminishes the objective of seeking the common good. Because of this domination, most of the conversation about education is about means, rather than about ends. As a result, the objective of schooling is primarily focused on how to make a living rather than how to make a life.

To change this attitude and rediscover the aim of education to promote the common good for today's global society, we must re-examine the impacts of mainstream economic theory and rhetoric and examine its consequences for education.

As we look around the world, we cannot deny that the global family is experiencing a fundamental crisis, a crisis in the global economy, global ecology, and global politics. Hundreds of millions of people in Asia as well as the rest of the world increasingly suffer from unemployment, poverty, hunger, disease, and the disintegration of their families. Our environment is mercilessly being raped for short-term profit. More and more countries are shaken by corruption in government and business. Hope for a lasting peace among nations slips away from us. It is increasingly difficult to live together in harmony in our cities and villages because of social, racial, ethnic, and religious conflicts. Even neighbors often live in fear of one another.

We thus face a number of major challenges. How do we, for instance, develop and promote an alternative value system and worldview that will act as a counterweight to neo-liberal values? In what way can education provide a glimpse of hope for the future of humanity?

In the following presentation, we will first look at the "big picture" of how the global economy works and its impact on human communities. In the second part, I will highlight certain crises which exist in our contemporary education system and will use Hong Kong as an example to illustrate how economic globalization processes influence Hong Kong's education system. Lastly, I will demonstrate how the Hong Kong Christian Institute, or HKCI, participates in reshaping or rebuilding justpeace and a sustainable society in Hong Kong through our Civil Society Education Project.

THE BIG ECONOMIC PICTURE

In the 19th century, laissez-faire theory led some thinkers to conclude that one could not intrude upon the workings of the market. Any attempt to interfere would be to go against nature herself. What proponents of the free market rarely noted was that the rules governing market behavior were not "natural" but had gradually been introduced over the course of several centuries in Europe, North America, and Asia as well as other parts of world.

Robert N. Bellah and other authors of the book *The Good Society* rightly point out that "economic activity is part of a larger social whole; the economy can be completely isolated from politics only in a game." If we look at the Greek origins of the word *economy*, we find it means "management of the household." The functions of economy are embedded in the structure of the larger life of the community and are framed by institutions grounded in law and the mores of society. The phrase further implies that the rules governing production and the provision of goods and services ought to reflect the moral claims of justice that order the polity as a whole (Bellah et al. 1992).

THE NEO-LIBERAL DEVELOPMENT PARADIGM

With the publication of Adam Smith's famous work *The Wealth of Nations* in 1776, the discourse on economy shifted to the blind worship of the theory of laissez-faire, the notion that economic competition is governed by rules outside human control. Since then, the market system has become the sea in which all modern societies must navigate. As the industrial era arrived, Karl Marx viewed market processes with dismay as fair competition eroded, leading to the monopolistic domination of the many by the few; a process that continues today.

In its present form, economic globalization is motivated by the neo-liberal development paradigm, which sees a diminishing role for governments and places the utmost importance on markets to allocate resources efficiently. According to this view, unfettered markets, free trade, and financial liberalization will bring about heightened competition, increased efficiency, and faster economic growth—roughly in that order. Hypothetically, growth would allow developing countries to catch up with developed countries as growth would trickle down to the poor, thereby closing the gap between the rich and poor within countries. Growth, neo-liberalists believe, would even promote equality between women and men (see Dollar and Ghatti 1999).

Policy prescriptions that flow from the neo-liberal doctrine typically include trade and financial liberalization, deregulation, and privatization. These core policies, aimed at efficiency and growth, are promoted primarily by the World Trade Organization (WTO) and international financial institutions (IFIs), such as the International Monetary Fund (IMF) and World Bank, through multilateral trading rules and conditionalities for loan disbursements. In this way, these economic institutions have played a significant role in shaping the macroeconomic policy environment in developing countries.

THE IMPACT OF ECONOMIC GLOBALIZATION ON HUMAN COMMUNITIES

Critics from both the ecumenical and secular world have long recognized that economic globalization is an institutional expression of a mainstream development paradigm, i.e., neo-liberalism (Dickinson 1998 and WCC 2002). As such, economic globalization is not simply a value-neutral, technology-driven, historical process; it is also a neo-liberal political and economic project. However, an almost fundamentalist approach to neo-classical economics in the past 20 years has tended to promote the rigid view that free markets can solve everything. This, unfortunately, is not the case.

What though is the real economic picture?

When we look at the performance of the global economy in the last two decades, at least two features stand out.

Slower Growth and Regression in Human Development:

First of all, global socioeconomic progress has actually diminished in the last 20 years of heightened economic globalization. A study by the Centre for Economic Policy Research (Weisbrot et al. 2002) shows that during the period 1980-2000 growth in gross domestic product, or GDP, and human development achievements (e.g., in life expectancy) have slowed down when compared to the period 1960-1980, a period associated with protective economic policy, and have even deteriorated for many countries, especially for the poorest nations. A summary of the findings is shown in Box 1.

Box 1: The Scorecard on Economic Globalization

- **Growth:** All groups of countries experienced an across-the-board decline in economic growth between 1980-2000 when compared to 1960-1980. The group of poorest countries actually experienced a reduction of 0.5 percent per year in GDP growth in 1980-2000 from an annual growth rate of 1.9 percent in 1960-1980.
- **Life Expectancy:** With the exception of the highest performing group, progress in life expectancy was reduced in all groups of countries during the period of globalization. The slowdown in improvement in life expectancy was more evident for women than for men.
- **Infant and Child Mortality:** Progress in reducing infant mortality slowed down in 1980-2000 compared to 1960-1980 with the middle and worst performing groups experiencing the largest decline.
- **Education and Literacy:** The rate of growth of primary, secondary, and tertiary enrolment and public spending on education saw less growth for most groups of countries from 1980 to 2000 than from 1960 to 1980.

Source: Weisbrot et al. 2002

Growing Inequality:

Second of all, inequality is worsening both between and within countries. A pioneering study by a World Bank economist (Milanovic 2002a) indicates a clear upward movement in global inequality. The global Gini coefficient, a popular measure of inequality, is estimated at 66 percent, meaning 66 percent of the world's population has zero income while the remaining 33 percent enjoy all of the world's income. Notably, the global Gini coefficient of 66 percent is also higher than in any single country. The 1980s and 1990s also witnessed increasing disparity between the rich and poor within both developing countries and developed countries.

What other hidden problems has the neo-liberal market economy created, however?

Exclusion of Non-market Goods and Services:

Perhaps most dangerous of all, the neo-liberal market economy focuses exclusively on goods and services that can be exchanged in the market for a profit. It factors out "non-marketable" goods and services, such as those provided by women's domestic and reproductive labor and subsistence labor in general as well as environmental services, rendering such work statistically invisible and worthless.

A major implication of excluding non-market activities is that non-market costs and benefits are effectively ignored in conventional economic analyses. More concretely, what is typically considered "economically efficient" or low cost may actually represent a transfer of costs from the market to the household and ecological realms such that women's work and the environment are effectively subsidizing economic production (Elson 1991, Shiva 1995). Furthermore, neo-classical economic analysis is geared towards the present, overlooking costs to future generations. Eventually, the costs that are shifted to the "non-market" sphere feed back negatively on the economy as a whole in the medium and long run in terms of losses in labor productivity and environmental problems, among others.

Lack of Analysis of 'Power':

Neo-liberal economic analyses typically take the economic structure (i.e., factors of production) as well as the economic order (i.e., the institutional and organizational framework where economic activities take place) as given and unchanging. One consequence is that the issue of "power"—for instance, in military, political, and technological terms—and how it can influence economic outcomes are not given due consideration in economic analyses, and yet power relations between developed and developing countries, between rich and poor, between men and women, clearly influence economic outcomes.

Neglect of Different Socio-Cultural Contexts:

Finally, the significance of values and attitudes, social conventions, behavioral norms, and cultural mores to economic policy tends to be underestimated, if not completely ignored, by neo-classical economists. According to some observers, this, in effect, presupposes an implicit Western context of the economy. Research, however, indicates that differences in socio-cultural contexts affect economic costs and choices in numerous ways. Because of these hidden problems, mainstream economic theory and rhetoric in favor of economic globalization does not, on balance, seem to relate with the actual life experiences of many people, particularly women and children, in the developing world.

THE CRISIS OF EDUCATION IN THE CONTEMPORARY WORLD

There are three trends of development in education today that are accepted norms that very few people question. The first trend is the predominance of the natural science paradigm in education which claims that its authority is based on objectivity and is independent of morals and values. As a result, ethical reflection about the good life and the good society, drawing on the religious, philosophical, and literary heritage of humanity, is no longer at the centre of higher education.

The second trend is the increasing rationalization of the economy and administrative bureaucracy which is opening up many new technical and managerial middle-class occupations. In this labor environment, students aspire to simply acquire the skills that will allow them to enter these occupations—a phenomenon known as utilitarian individualism. In many respects, the school system in general, and the university in particular, are among the primary institutional embodiments of utilitarian individualism.

The third trend involves advances in economic theory and empirical methods of analysis, developments in organizational behavior, and refinements of managerial technique that have reached the point where non-profit institutions, including colleges and universities, are grown in tandem with the business corporation. For many business leaders, for example, the university is simply one more element in the market.

Through the influence of these trends, education as part of the grand global market system is not so much a separate moral entity as it is a business, and the vitality of any society's economy only rests on high standards of competition, productivity, and consumption.

THE HONG KONG EXPERIENCE

In the past few decades, we have witnessed the almost total phasing out of civic and critical attempts to examine what purpose education serves besides the human resource function as defined by government and business. Here I will highlight two major problems in the education system in Hong Kong which serve as clear illustrations of the crisis in education that I described earlier.

Professional Groups as 'Stakeholders':

The governance of Hong Kong is dominated by "functional constituency," or stakeholder, politics. Among themselves, vested elite interest groups compete but generally enjoy and share special privileges provided by the legal and political framework. The majority of the masses, however, are non-participatory social agents. Worse, the myth of the existence of a "level playing field" is constantly fed to them, confining their focus on ways to improve their own individual financial condition. Education plays a crucial role in embodying and disseminating this myth in which individuals are made to believe there is "fair opportunity" open to them and that they have only themselves to blame for failing to climb the ladder. According to this myth, those who successfully perform in this system need not question the discourse of elite politics, even less the unfair systems that underlie it.

Distorting Knowledge and Learning:

A core issue here is how educators see knowledge and whether their ideas are conducive to the building of reflective epistemic communities. Unfortunately, knowledge taught in modern schools is "globalized" and decontextualized. It prepares children for computational and language skills presumably required by the job market that, in turn, are dictated by the trends of the global market. However, as the global market, including the job market, become increasingly volatile, skills that it require become more and more narrowly defined; students are less and less likely to be exposed to the critical and core aspects of learning. Ironically, the fragmented technical skills which they are urged to acquire often become obsolete even at the very moment they are being drilled on them.

Moreover, the unemployed or underemployed are made to believe that they are "ontological misfits," i.e., they are rightfully banished from this world which follows social Darwinian logic. There is no place for them in communities which aim at "progress," "competitiveness," and "development." All they can do is sell their "competitive advantage" by becoming even cheaper labor.

All in all, knowledge and learning have been distorted to become an interwoven part of this social exclusion project. Hence, no longer are knowledge and learning connected to the products, traditions, and efforts of a collective search for wisdom and lessons of life. Rather, schools nowadays are shamelessly aiming at training students to treat knowledge as commodities they consume at one stage of their lives and expect to yield a return at the next.

With arrogance and the elitist mentality deeply rooted, decision makers in Hong Kong now tend to perpetuate educational policies which are no less "colonial" and non-participatory than they were prior to 1971. English, and now Mandarin, both non-indigenous languages, are elevated to such a high status that it becomes very destructive to genuine learning, which is closely connected to a grounded, critical culture that needs the indigenous language to help nurture it.

Education in Hong Kong will remain an enslaving project as long as the two interlocking features of elitism stay firmly in place. For there to be any significant breakthrough, the political and epistemological conceptions embedded and adopted by society have to undergo drastic transformations. There will be no real change if people are "educated" to remain passive recipients of state- and business-directed and sponsored education programs. Without a civic revolt, educational reforms will only serve the interests of global economic forces and other vested interests even more rigorously than before and will do so under some noble pretexts.

ANOTHER WORLD IS POSSIBLE

Churches have always been interested in economic and development matters—
an interest grounded in the Christian conviction in the sacredness of all creation
and caring for all life. Therefore, if people are being denied their basic needs due
to policies related to economic globalization, this is much more than just an economic issue for Christians but a violation of God's justice. The 1937 World Conference on Church, Community, and State, a forerunner of the World Council of
Churches (WCC), reminds us:

> Individual acts of charity within a given system may mitigate its injustices and
> increase its justice. But they do not absolve the Christian from seeking the best
> possible institutional arrangement and social structure for the ordering of social
> life (WCC 1992).

It is in this vein that WCC advocates "just, participatory and sustainable communities" rather than economic development per se. This model of community
implies the nurturing of equitable relationships between peoples regardless of
gender, class, and race and between people and the environment.

From a faith-based perspective, the overall well-being of people should be
the foremost measure of economic success rather than individual utility maximization, profit maximization, and GDP growth. Similarly, for feminist economists, the starting point is the provisioning of human life rather than the rational,
efficient allocation of resources. Both churches and feminist economists are in
agreement that human wellbeing and fulfillment go beyond measures of consumption and income.

OIKONOMIA AND THE CARING ECONOMY

Ecumenical churches and feminist economists have a broader, richer definition
of "economy" and "economics" that does not make a hierarchical distinction
between the household or subsistence economy and the market economy. Not
incidentally, these words are rooted in the Greek word *oikos*, referring to the
household and its daily operations, and *oikoumene*, or the household of God.

WCC (1992:5; 1998) sees economics as one way of "considering large com-
plexes of social and community realities, including personal relationships and
expectations, the loyalties and senses of priority that govern the processes of
production, distribution, and consumption." It has stated that economic globalization is promoting a competing vision of *oikoumene*, that is, a globalized *oikoumene* of exploitation in contrast with the *oikoumene* of faith and solidarity that
motivates and energizes the ecumenical movement.

In feminist economics, the foremost methodological principle in economic
analyses is based on the understanding that unpaid social reproductive or caring
labor, which is essentially about the maintenance of human life outside of the
market, is a vital part of any economic system, that is, the economy is much
bigger than the production, distribution, and consumption of goods and services

that can be sold in markets. As indicated in the previous parts of this paper, women's negative experiences with economic globalization are rooted in the material and moral devaluing and exploitation of women's reproductive and domestic labor. As one of the measures to address this problem, feminist economists have advocated the inclusion and visibility of the caring economy in all national income accounts and the factoring in of care work in all economic models and analyses.

COMMUNITY, COOPERATION, AND RELATIONALITY

The concept of community is a fundamental one to ecumenical churches. Thus, WCC believes that new economic paradigms should provide a "vision of a global community whose interdependence is not reduced to markets and trade." Moreover, it should "acknowledge a common destiny as co-inhabitants of the one earth for which we all share a responsibility and from which we should all equally benefit." Along these lines, church-based movements are spearheading the development of the concept of an "economy of communion."

Similarly, in the feminist view of the economy, interdependent human actors connected by an intricate web of relationships, rather than the isolated individual, are at the centre of economic analyses. The paradigm recognizes that cooperation rather than competition may often generate the best possible combination of resources and that collective enterprise is likely to reap greater benefit than individual effort. Perhaps at the risk of over romanticizing motherhood, some feminist economists point to mothers' unpaid work as hardly fitting into the neo-classical model of rational self-interest, but there are many other examples from various countries and societies of women coming together to protect and support their communities.

THE ECONOMY AS A REALM OF POWER AND PEOPLE'S PARTICIPATION

WCC and the feminist economics discipline comprehend that the economy is a realm of power. Globalization processes exacerbate economic problems by promoting economic interdependence in the context of tremendous disparities in power between developed and developing countries, between the rich and poor within countries and between men and women. It is also understood that economic power is closely linked to political power, technological power, military power, and so on. According to WCC

(1992:6), "'What Adam Smith called the invisible hand has to be made visible and power relationships have to be revealed."

Likewise, feminist economists have always understood that power relations are a driving force in the economy, from the global level down to the household level, where access to and control of economic resources are often in the hands of rich white men. They recognize that the historical subordination of women may be traced to structures that concentrate power in the hands of a few and perpetuate women's powerlessness, perceived or otherwise, in economic and other dimensions of life that interact with each other. Hence, feminist economists and movements also strongly advocate for the democratization of political and economic decision-making structures and processes so that women can actively participate in defining and implementing economic policies that have a bearing on their lives and the lives of their communities.

EDUCATION FOR CHANGE

In order to transform our contemporary world and our education system, we should first recover a more classical notion that it is the whole way of life that educates. As the authors of *The Good Society* point out, a genuine "education society" means something more than a society with good schools. It means a society with a healthy sense of the common good, with social morale and public spirit, with a vivid memory of its own cultural past. In addition, we should also recover an enlarged paradigm of knowledge, which recognizes the value of science but acknowledges that other ways of knowing have equal dignity. Practical reason, in its classical sense of moral reason, must regain its importance in our educational life. Thirdly, the idea of education for citizenship should be an essential task for building a mutually responsible and inclusive civil society.

A HONG KONG EXPERIMENT

Since the handover in 7997, Hong Kong has suffered from the illusion of the promise of "one country, two systems." To face this new challenge, we, first of all, have to reorient our Hong Kong identity with a new lens, that is, Hong Kong, on one hand, is now part of China. Whatever we do, we will have an impact on the future of China. On the other hand, since China entered the WTO, Hong Kong's future is even more tightly woven to globalization. In order to develop Hong Kong into a more democratic, humane, just, and sustainable system for the future generations of China and Hong Kong, HKCI sees our role in society as being a moral and faith-based catalyst to strengthen civil society to counter the dominant forces of destruction through alliances with other nongovernmental organizations (NGOs) and social and human rights activists.

One concrete example of our witness in Hong Kong was our effort to form the Civil Human Rights Front (CHRF)—a coalition of 52 NGOs in Hong Kong which facilitated mass demonstrations on July 1 last year as well as this year. During these demonstrations, more than half a million people were inspired to come out and walk together in order to defend each other's freedoms and political rights. We are proud that HKCI was one of the seeds of this transformation. From immersing ourselves in the people's movement, Christians and the people became united and mutually empowered. From now on, the people of Hong Kong will never forget this significant event and will remember that when people are willing to stand in solidarity with each other there is always hope to bring about change.

In addition, the staff of HKCI has initiated two new education programs in the past few years.

The first program is an alternative educational resource which reconnects Christian ministry with political and social transformation. The first effort that we have attempted in this area is a social ministry course for seminarians that was launched with the Lutheran Theological Seminary in September 2001. The course includes both theories of practical theology and social ministry as well as field research based on the social, economic, and political context of Hong Kong. The students are asked to articulate a particular social issue as a ministerial concern, and each group of students has to write a research paper. The objective of the course is to enable seminarians to use an integrated approach to doing theology by fusing theory and praxis, action and reflection, culture and theology, church and society, the personal and social, social justice and spirituality. For the next three years, we will invite more seminaries to participate in this joint program and will expand the social ministry program into three series. In addition to the first course mentioned above, we will also include a course entitled Public Policies and Christian Values and a field work program in the summer for seminarians.

The second program is a civil society education project for teenage students. We believe that the future of Hong Kong is in the hands of the future generation.

However, young people in Hong Kong are always seen as a social problem rather than as potential leaders. To counter this prevailing view, we must develop an alternative model of education to allow our young people to think and act critically and responsibly. In the past two years, HKCI and other Christian organizations launched a four-day exposure camp for 26 Form 3 to Form 6 students to introduce them to poverty in our community. In addition to organizing summer camps, we have been successful in transforming this program into a long-term project with some schools in Hong Kong. We eventually want to develop alternative education materials for secondary schools and church youth fellowship groups.

A PEDAGOGY FOR BUILDING A JUSTPEACE GLOBAL CIVIL SOCIETY

Based on our past experience from the above projects, there are six essential characteristics of our pedagogical activities whish I would like to share with you.

Our Pedagogy Is Contextual and Situationally Related.

It gives priority to the contemporary context or situation in which it is involved rather than to other situations, other times, and other places. While historical data, classic texts, and experiences from elsewhere may help in the process of education, our main concern is to explore and contribute to immediate contexts, situations, and practices.

Our Pedagogy Is Socio-Politically Aware and Committed.

Having learned from the powerful example of praxis-based liberationist and feminist theologies that apply the tools of suspicion to theology as well as to the social and political order, we are convinced that our pedagogy should adopt the view from "below," i.e., the perspective of those groups and individuals who experience institutionalized injustice and oppression in such away that their voices are not heard and their interests are ignored.

Our Pedagogy Is Experiential.

It aims to facilitate students to have firsthand exposure of practical situational realities and to release genuine expressions of our feelings and compassion toward our society. It also implies openness to the world and being attentive to the needs of our neighbors.

Our Pedagogy Is Reflective.

Critical reflection on lived contemporary experience is an important starting point for engaging in our praxis-based education. It is by students thinking through and analyzing their own experiences and the issues and situations that they face that the process of practical education actually begins.

Out Pedagogy Is a Transformational Activity.

In both terms of process and outcome, it aims to make a difference to the students in their understanding of society and their commitment to be active agents to transform the contemporary world.

Our Pedagogy Is Based on Trust and Hope.

As people of faith, our hope reflects a trust in the goodness of a God who listens and responds to our communal lament that is a true act of repentance and trust. Hope requires us to have faith in "the other" who is larger than the self. Only through our sense of connecting with "the other"-the larger community, nature, and God-can we grasp a glimpse of hope for life.

What we share in common is the quest for greater solidarity, love, and justice for the most marginalized people of our communities. We share the value that the economy is organized to serve life. When we see lives that are exploited in the name of the market economy, we must cooperate to make changes and seek alternatives for those who suffer from economic exploitation and oppression.

To end my presentation, I would like to share with you the story of a group of high school students with whom the Civil Society Education Project worked. The outcome of this particular project turned out to be an inspiration for many people who were involved in it as it revealed what education can achieve.

The project began three years ago when Frankie Ng, a HKCI staff member, was invited by a high school teacher in Tuen Mun to work with a group of student volunteers at the school. Through discussion, it was agreed that the cooperative endeavor between HKCI and the school would be to clean a beach. While clearing away the debris on the beach, the students discovered that the sand was black. They wondered whether there was a connection between the black sand and the expansion of a nearby incinerator that was being built.

The students also learned that Greenpeace in Hong Kong was starting a project with members of the neighborhood. The students then began to interview the Greenpeace organizer and people in the area. Through these interviews, they learned that the incinerator was damaging the health of the people. Many of the students, in fact, lived in Tuen Mun and were possibly affected as well.

After discussing among themselves what they could do, the students decided to have a school assembly to inform other students about the problem in Tuen Mun and to invite the student body to sign their petition against the construction project-an appeal which resulted in more than 400 signatures. Their next step was to discuss the issue with the Tuen Mun District Council. Through these efforts and others, they were able to get the project suspended. Now, three years later, the project is still suspended.

Since then, five students from this group formed a group called JEPERS and initiated several other projects, such as publishing a series of newspapers about the poverty of young people in Hong Kong, and joining human rights activities with other NGOs.

Afterwards, when we reflected on this experience with the teacher involved with this project, she shared with us that she noticed a variety of positive outcomes. First of all, the students began to see themselves as citizens and to express a sense of caring about the community where they live because of their active participation in the project.

One student who was not a good student academically, she said, regained her confidence in herself through this experience. In conclusion, the teacher said the students had gone beyond what she could teach them; they had taught themselves through what they had done and achieved. It was a lesson not to be learned in a classroom or by reading a textbook but through active participation in issues affecting their life and community.

REFERENCES

Bellah, Robert N., Richard Madsen, William M. Sullivan, Ann Swidler, Steven M. Tipton (1992). *The Good Society*. New York: Random House, Vintage Books.

Beneria, Lourdes (1999). "Structural Adjustment Policies" in Jane Peterson and Margaret Lewis, eds, *The Elgar Companion to Feminist Economics*. Cheltenham and Northampton: Elgar.

Berik, Gtinseli, Yana van der Meulen Rodgers and Joseph Zveglich,Ir. (2002). "Does Trade Promote Gender Wage Equity? Evidence from East Asia." CEPA Working Paper 2002-14.

Dickinson, Richard (1998). *Economic Globalisation: Deepening Challenge for Christians*. Geneva: WCC.

Dollar, David and Roberta Ghatti (1999). "Gender Inequality, Income and Growth: Are Good Times Good for Women." Gender and Development Working Paper Series No. l.

Elson, Diane (1991). *Male Bias in the Development Process*.

Rodrik, Dani and Francisco Rodriguez (1999). "Trade Policy and Economic Growth: A Skeptic's Guide to the Cross National Evidence. NBER Working Paper 7081.

Seguino, Stephanie (2000). "The Effects of Structural Change and Economic Liberalization on Gender Wage Differentials in South Korea and Taiwan." *Cambridge Journal of Economics* 24: 437-459.

Stiglitz, Joseph (2002). *Globalization and its discontents*. World Council of Churches (1992). Christian Faith and the World Economy Today. Geneva: WCC.

WCC (2002). *Economic Globalization: A Critical View and an Alternative Vision Geneva*: WCC.

World Bank (2002). Global Links. Http ://www.worldbank.org

Weisbrot, Mark, Dean Baker, Egor Kraev and Judy Chen (2002). "The Scorecard on Globalization 1980-2000: Twenty Years of Diminished Progress." CEPR Briefing Paper.

CHAPTER THREE

Alice Miel Lecture:
A Personal Journey To Peace Education

Larry Hufford
St. Mary's University

It is an honor to be in a position to give the Alice Miel Memorial Lecture at the 11th Triennial Conference of the World Council for Curriculum and Instruction (WCCI) in Wollongong, Australia. Professor Miel along with other prophetic women and men saw the need for an international, interdisciplinary organization designed to promote multi-and transcultural understanding; respect for international human rights; peace education; conflict prevention and resolution education; gender education; and, ecological education. The goal was to bring together educators on all levels, pre-kindergarten to university to non-traditional adult education, practitioners as well as researchers, in a way that created international networks to help bridge East and West, North and South.

Under Alice Miel's leadership, educators such as Estela Matriano, Maxine Dunfee, Louise Berman, Doris Phipps, Fr. Jaime Diaz, Norman Overly, Shigekazu Takemura, Fayez Mina, Betty Reardon and Piyush Swami have continued to promote the WCCI and its motto of "unity through diversity." Thus, it is not only an honor, but a tremendous responsibility to give the Alice Miel Lecture.

A person is not born a peace educator. Life experiences and learned values lead an educator to promote social justice and nonviolence as a means to resolve conflict. Initially, experiences in my own country, the United States, led me to peace education. As a citizen of the United States in July 2004, I would like to stand before you and declare my country as an example of the prophetic vision of Alice Miel. Unfortunately, I cannot do this. While there are thousands of educators in the United States working to promote the values and goals of Alice Miel, the current neoconservative government is the antithesis of the WCCI vision. Therefore, I shall offer a personal reflection and begin with two of many personal experiences from the 1960s.

As a young civil rights activist in the 1960s, I was run off the road one evening in South Texas (Robstown, Texas). Two men held guns to my head and told me to leave town. What was I doing that so infuriated these men? The year was 1967 and I was registering Mexican-Americans and African-Americans to vote. I was organizing the poor in Robstown to take their community issues to

City Hall, the County Courthouse and to the halls of the State legislature. The Voting Rights Act was not passed by the U.S. Congress and signed into law by President Johnson until 1965. In the State of Texas, from 1902 to 1966, a person had to pay a poll tax to vote. This was a policy designed to keep the poor, especially African Americans and Mexican Americans, from voting. It was not until 1966 that, the United States Supreme Court found the poll tax unconstitutional. As United States' citizens we often forget that our country existed as a nation-state for 190 years before it became politically democratic. Yet, in the year 2000, only 51% of eligible voters chose to exercise this right in one of the country's closest presidential elections. In a 2000 democracy index study of the 50 U.S. states, my state, Texas ranked 45th out of 50.

My first point is that democracy cannot be exported or imposed on a people in a short timeframe. In fact, I reject the language that democracy can be imposed on a people. For democracy to succeed citizens must own the struggle; citizens must understand, believe in and defend basic democratic values and principles, and, citizens must structure their democracy in a manner consistent with their culture and historical reality. The second point is that as a peace educator in the United States I need to be concerned about the health of democracy in my own state and nation.

Another one of my projects in the 1960s, was to try to organize a migrant worker health clinic for farm workers who could not afford private health insurance. The physician who headed the County Medical Society in Corpus Christi, Texas, told me "if you want to practice socialized medicine, I will buy you a one way ticket to Cuba." I did not succeed in creating the migrant health clinic. Health care in the United States remains to this day, a privilege not a right. The United Nations Universal Declaration of Human Rights was adopted in 1948. Article 25 of the UDHR calls for adequate medical care for all and the right to security in the event of sickness. Yet, in the United States today there are over 44 million men and women employed fulltime who do not have health insurance. Today, the state of Texas has the nation's highest number of uninsured children in the United States. In my state of Texas, 22% of children under 18 are not covered by health insurance. As an educator advocating social justice there is much to be concerned about in my own state and nation. The dominant cultural value in the United States is an extreme form of individualism. This prevents citizens from visualizing and understanding issues such as a lack of medical insurance as a form of structural, institutional or systemic violence.

These experiences from the 1960s, along with my growing belief that the war in Vietnam did not meet traditional just war theory developed by ancient philosophers and theologians such as St. Ambrose, St. Augustine, Grotius, Saint Thomas Aquinas, and Francisco de Vitoria, led me to adopt a philosophy of nonviolence and to commit my life's work to doing what one person can to create more justice in my community, nation and world. I believe in grassroots relational democracy, human rights, sustainable economic, cultural, political and ecological development and a diverse global community. I sincerely believe in the WCCI motto "unity through diversity."

Since 1986, I have taken fifteen to twenty students a year to countries in war, e.g., El Salvador, Nicaragua and Guatemala; to countries transitioning from dictatorship to a more open society such as Haiti, Honduras, and Cuba; to countries with ethnic violence such as the Chiapas region of Mexico; and, to poor countries such as Bangladesh, to study rural development in the model of the Indian Nobel Prize in Economics winner, Amartya Sen.

What have I learned from these experiences? I have learned that it is impossible to destroy the human spirit. As the eminent humanist, Norman Cousins stated, "When it is darkest, the stars shine brightest." On every one of these journeys I also realize how little I understand about the human psyche. I have visited mass grave sites in El Salvador and Guatemala, interviewed family members of those disappeared, interviewed torture survivors, child soldiers, women who have witnessed the military assassinate their husbands and sons, as well as husbands and fathers who witnessed soldiers beat and rape their wives and daughters. These experiences have humbled me, as I now understand that I have the potential to commit heinous acts of violence. These experiences mean that I am in an ongoing dialogue with the Divine Spirit. I meditate regularly on what these experiences mean for me. Why have I had these experiences? What does the Divine Spirit want me to do with them? As a peace educator how can I share my transformative experience with students? How can I explain to students the importance of opening one's life to the possibility of being transformed? With all the darkness one finds in the world, how can I as a peace educator be a person of hope, a social justice activist who is constructive not destructive? How can I be a person and educator who is part of the solution to the injustice experienced in the world today? I do not have answers to give students. I do not have answers to give participants of this conference. I reject the idea that I can "give" anyone knowledge, truth or wisdom. What I hope, is that I can be a role model, an exemplar, a person who is a lifelong learner, a person who meditates daily on the metaphysical questions: Who am I? Where did I come from? What is my purpose in life?

My life experiences have led me to ask questions in search of a better understanding of the human psyche and human behavior. Key questions are:

- **What is the root cause of evil?**
  In El Mozote, El Salvador, I interviewed the lone survivor of a massacre at which over 1,000 men, women and children were raped, tortured and murdered, then buried in a mass grave. To listen to this lone survivor, a woman with no formal education, discuss the root causes of evil was very humbling.
- **What is the root cause of hatred and fear?**
  If I do not understand the root cause of hatred and fear, how can I practice or teach love?
- **Is war a force that gives us meaning?**
  Only a false and superficial unity comes from blind patriotism or nationalism.

- **When does religion become evil?**
  One criterion is when one believes that my religion is THE truth instead of A truth.
- **Can we, as a global community, succeed in making the WCCI motto "unity through diversity" a reality? Or, is a "clash of civilizations" inevitable?**
  Jonathan Glover, who directs the Centre of Medical Law and Ethics at King's College, London, writes that three factors seem central when human beings act in an inhuman and evil manner:
  1. There is a love of cruelty.
  2. Emotionally inadequate people assert themselves by dominance and cruelty.
  3. Moral resources which restrain cruelty can be neutralized.
     We see this in today's glorification of war. 40% of U.S adults reacted to the abuse of prisoners in Abu Ghraib by saying that the interrogation techniques were similar to fraternity pranks not human rights abusers. Many of these are adults who watch reality TV where the purpose is to humiliate and emotionally break participants. Peace educators must be at the forefront of the emotional quotient movement. Intelligence/education without emotionally healthy students/citizens can and will lead to authoritarianism.

My personal travels and experiences have taught me that:
- **Where religion is a source of conflict, it must become part of the solution.**
  For example in the Middle East, peace proposals will not work if they are not connected to religion.
- **In the 21st Century, there is no national security, only collective security.**
- **A closed society is inevitably organized in an authoritarian manner.**
- **A transparent society holds itself open to self-criticism and reflection on failure to live up to its fullest potential as a just community.**
- **There is no democratic gene.**
  Democratic principles and values must be learned by each new generation.
- **Foreign aid all too frequently serves the interests of the donors, rather than the interests of the recipients.**
- **Existing international institutions are not up to the tasks of preserving peace or preventing civil strife.**
  It is obvious the UN needs to be reformed, but not on a U.S model. There is a democratic deficit in the current UN structure along with international organizations such as the World Trade Organization.

- **Global collective needs and social justice lags behind because the development of international institutions that would be necessary for their promotion has not kept pace with the development of global financial and economic markets.**
- **The war on terrorism is a metaphor war.**
  Metaphor wars will never be won militarily. Yet, in the U.S. leaders continue to use metaphoric language.
  > E.G., In the United States President Nixon declared a war on drugs. The drug problem, however, is more of a public health issue than a military issue. There is no military solution to the drug problem in the United States.
  > E.G., President Johnson declared war on poverty in the United States. Root causes of poverty have yet to be addressed. There is no military solution to problems of poverty.
  > E.G., President George W. Bush declared war on terrorism. Addressing root causes of terrorism will minimize such acts and the support for them. Terrorism is a crime requiring good intelligence, police work and a transparent, independent judicial system. Implying there is military solution to terrorism ends up creating more terrorists.
- **The core of present day American supremacist ideology is the synthesis of market fundamentalism, religious fundamentalism and the belief that the United States possesses the ultimate political and economic truth.**

Having visited mass grave sites and researched mass involvement in, and support for, such actions I continue to reflect on the question: How can a human being become so full of hate and fear that he or she can support heinous acts of violence? How can university educated leaders create and justify heinous acts of violence such as the Nazi campaign against Jews? After all, Joseph Goebbels, Hitler's key advisor, had earned a PhD in Literature from the University of Heidleberg. How can a person with a doctorate in the Humanities become such a cruel, inhumane human being? How could university educated persons in the U.S. design a plan for the firebombing of civilian populations in Dresden and Tokyo, or, the dropping of atomic bombs on civilian populations in Hiroshima and Nagasaki? What explains the Rwandan genocide? Pol Pot's killing fields? Current atrocities in the Democratic Republic of the Congo? Sudan? Myanmar?

In reflection on the learned nature of hatred, I understand that:
- **One cannot kill without a claim to virtue**
- **Hate is ill will seeking a victim**
- **Hate energizes people**
- **Hatred is a form of death**
  I see this when interviewing perpetrators and victims of crimes against humanity. I look into their eyes and see death.

- **Hate is seeing a stranger in the other**
- **Hate is dehumanizing the other**
  There is a need to avoid caricatures. Educators need to realize hatred can give emotionally insecure children and adults meaning.
- **One can become addicted to hating**
- **The other is always responsible for my hatred**
- **When one hates his brother, he hates himself**
- **Poverty, hopelessness, powerlessness feed hatred**
- **Hatred is a disease.**
  Hatred is a public health issue best addressed and treated by loving, caring family members, healthy neighborhoods/communities and compassionate educators. Many who hate have no family or teachers who truly care about them as children of the Divine Spirit.

In 1982, Irving Janis, a social psychologist, wrote a treatise on group-think. His research demonstrated that groups, like individuals, have short-comings. Groups can bring out the worst as well as the best in humankind. It was the German philosopher, Nietzsche, who wrote that "madness is the exception in individuals but the rule in groups." In real or manufactured crises, group contagion can give rise to collective panic and collective acts of violence. According to Janis, the symptoms of groupthink are:

- **Illusion of invulnerability**
- **Belief in the inherent morality of the group**
- **Collective rationalizations**
- **Stereotypes of out-groups**
- **Self-censorship**
- **Illusion of unanimity**
- **Direct pressure to censure/punish dissenters**
- **Self-appointed mind guards for the group**

These symptoms of groupthink provide an accurate description of the neoconservative foreign policy decision makers in the current Bush Administration. Interestingly, the group leaders of non-state terrorist organizations such as al-Qaeda and the neoconservatives in the current U.S. government share a common language. Both groups believe they have been chosen to "cleanse the world of evil" and both believe they have the responsibility to "create a more peaceful world." Not a world where diversity is appreciated, but one where violence, force and fear create a false and frightening unity.

Journalist Chris Hedges author of the book *War Is a Force That Gives Us Meaning*, wrote that wars today are not "clashes of civilizations," conflicts of ethnic hatred or religious wars. Today's wars, Hedges argues, are manufactured. They are born out of the collapse of civil societies, perpetuated by fear, greed and paranoia. They are run by gangsters who terrorize all, including those they purport to protect.

Lawrence Le Shan in *The Psychology of War* differentiates between "mythic reality" and "sensory reality" in wartime. In sensory reality we see things as they are. Those in combat quickly lose the ability to maintain a mythic perception of war. Hedges notes that wars that lose their mythic stature for the public are doomed to failure, for war is exposed for what it is--organized murder.

As peace educators we are challenged to counter those promoting mythic war, that is, imbuing events with meanings they do not have. For example, defeats become signposts on the road to military victory, enemies are dehumanized so they are no longer human, and we view ourselves as the embodiment of absolute goodness. In mythic war we fight absolutes. We must, for example, defeat evil. War, in this context, is addictive to those fighting it and to those civilians at home promoting nationalism. As peace educators, we must understand that war is often an addiction that exposes the capacity for evil that is within each of us. As peace educators we are obligated to understand how war can dominate a culture, distort memory, corrupt language and infect all of society. We must also understand, as Hedges wrote, that war can give us the meaning and purpose we long for in life. In the midst of war, people realize the trivia that dominates our conversations, while the shallowness of much of our lives becomes apparent.

How can persons throughout our world transcend the darkness I have described? How can the WCCI goal of "unity through diversity" be realized?

The events of September 11, 2001, occurred in the middle of the 10th Triennial Conference of the WCCI being held in Madrid, Spain. On the evening of 9/11 delegates met for a prayer service. At that memorial service there were Muslim and Jewish prayers; Buddhist chants; Hindu, Sikh and Jain prayers; Ba'hai, Chrisitan and indigenous prayers. There was no attempt to have one universally acceptable prayer. There was no attempt to pretend that there was one universal culture. There was, rather, a deep sense of "unity through diversity" felt by all those who were present.

Charles Kimball, a Baptist minister and chairperson of the Theology Department at Wake Forest University recently authored a book titled *When Religeon Becomes Evil*. The five symptoms of religion becoming evil are:

- **absolute truth claims**
  (my religion is the Truth, not a Truth)
- **blind obedience**
  (means I do not respect other faiths)
- **establishing the "ideal" time**
  (end of the world scenarios)
- **saying the end justifies the means**
- **declaring holy war**

While no single religious tradition is exempt from these corruptions, each does have the means to identify and correct such tendencies within its own wisdom tradition.

Jonathan Sacks, Chief Rabbi of the United Hebrew Congregation of Britain, in his book *The Dignity of Difference: How to Avoid the Clash of Civilizations,* states that all faiths need to cross the boundaries of difference, turning their communities outward instead of inward. In other words, Sacks argues that humanity's deepest question is how to turn our post-Babel differences into a source of blessing rather than conflict.

As peace educators our challenge is to move from our stereotyped image of other religions to an understanding of other faith traditions. As those of us who were in Madrid on 9/11 know, images evoke emotion, they do not, of themselves, generate understanding. Media loves images of confrontation, not reconciliation. Peace educators must work to prevent the "image of confrontation" from becoming a "culture of confrontation." Jonathan Swift once observed that we have "just enough religion to make us hate one another but not enough to allow us to love one another."

Western civilization has known five universalist cultures: ancient Greece, ancient Rome, medieval Christianity and Islam, and the Enlightenment. Three were secular, two religious. Each brought gifts to the world, yet each also brought great suffering.

At present, we are living through a sixth universal order: global market fundamentalism. It threatens all things local, traditional and particular. What is needed today is not only a theology and philosophy of commonality, but also a theology and philosophy of the dignity of difference.

The world is not a single machine. It is, as Sacks states, a complex, interactive ecology in which diversity-- biological, personal, cultural and religious—is one of essence. Any reduction of this diversity results in a diminution of the quality of our shared life. Fundamentalism in any form is the attempt to impose a single truth on a plural world. Religions must not merely tolerate one another; they must find positive value in the diversity of the human condition.

Jonathan Sacks promotes the idea that the creation of a new covenant is necessary for peace and justice. Relationships that promote the integrity of the other cannot be based upon economic, political or military power. The use of power is ruled out by the requirement of human dignity. In other words, if you and I are linked because I can force you to do what I want, then I have secured my freedom at the cost of yours. A covenant, however, is the use of language and action to create a bond of trust through the word/action given, the word/action received, the word/action honored in mutual fidelity. As Sacks states, a covenant is not a contract. It is not limited to specific conditions and circumstances. Covenants are relational, that is, they affirm the dignity of difference. I have one kind of relationship with my parents, one with my spouse, my children, friends, employer, members of my faith, nation and world. This complexity of relationships is the nature of real life. It is one key way of recognizing the path to the realization of the WCCI goal of "unity through diversity." Pluralism is a form of hope. We recognize that precisely because we are different, each of us has something to contribute to the shared project of creating more justice and peace.

Covenants are more foundational than contracts. Covenants create societies, social contracts create states. Benjamin Barber, Professor of Civil Society at the University of Maryland, advocates creation of a new covenant through a doctrine of preventive democracy and CivWorld.

In a critique of American society Barber argues that the United States often refers to itself as a model of multiculturalism, yet shows little respect for cultural diversity or religious heterogeneity when they lie outside the American imagination. Barber believes the current Administration is pursuing empire because of fear. Can fear defeat fear? Can a politics of nation-states create a more just world as it contends with more powerful non-state actors, for example, al-Qaeda, OPEC and the World Trade Organization?

The goal of terrorism is to promote and instill fear in people. Yet it is not terrorism, but fear that is the enemy. In the end, fear will not defeat fear. When a militarily powerful nation is governed by fear, it leads to policies of "pre-emptive strike" and "wars of choice." When a nation and people are governed by fear, inaction is not acceptable. Fear's empire leaves little room for democracy. On the contrary, democracy refuses to make room for fear. As Barber concludes, only preventive democracy will prevent terrorism.

Barber's conceptualization of CivWorld (global civic engagement) matches Sacks' idea that covenants create new societies and respect diversity. CivWorld is the creation of new forms of citizen to citizen interaction. It is where persons around the world seek to create new diverse global forms of democratic governance founded on civic cooperation. CivWorld is not "world federalism." It is a foundation, however, for nurturing transnational forms of global citizenship that will lead to "unity THROUGH diversity." Democratic outcomes depend on democratic struggle and the readiness of citizens to wage it. This is true of "CivWorld preventive democracy" on a global scale.

Fear reduces citizens to spectators. Fear is disempowering making individuals who fear helpless. A global citizenship based on CivWorld will build walls around fear. Global civic engagement is real and is already visible. And, it is grassroots democracy in action. As peace educators, it is critical that the root cause of and attraction to hatred be understood. Hatred is learned behavior. Agape love (unconditional) is also learned. As educators we have a responsibility to teach agape love, to live agape love by working nonviolently for greater justice. In every major religion working for justice is the highest form of prayer.

As peace educators we are obligated to apply ethics to analyze history and current world realities so that we can understand a side of human nature often left in darkness. This is essential if we are going to succeed in promoting hope and creating a world with less misery. Teachers on all levels can have children, adolescents, teenagers and adults analyzing issues by applying three alternative ethical theories to real life situations, current events or historical case studies.

- **Rule based ethics (Immanuel Kant)**
- **Utilitarian/consequentialist/ ends-based ethics (Jeremy Bentham)**
- **Care based ethics (Golden Rule found in all major religions).**

It is my belief that education for justice and peace must promote hope not optimism. Optimism is the belief that humankind will inevitably progress to a more just, peaceful world. It is a passive virtue. Hope is the faith that, together, we can create more justice and peace in the world. Hope is an active virtue. Hope requires action from responsible citizens creating new relationships, societies and citizens through covenants, and CivWorld. Hope is preventive democracy. Hope is the path to kinship and understanding of the stranger, empathy with "the other," and the courage to extend a hand across boundaries of estrangement or hostility.

As educators accepting our responsibility to do what one person can do to create "unity THROUGH diversity", let us begin with the creation of, and education for, new covenants. That is, new forms of relational societies and new global grassroots networks that bring life to a new global citizenship rooted in CivWorld. Each one of us must become a personal exemplar of living the dignity of difference that leads to unity THROUGH diversity. One person can make a difference. Alice Miel made a difference and, through the WCCI, continues to positively impact new generations of educators from around the world. Let each of us honor Alice Miel by continuing her life's work. Let each of us live our personal and professional lives in a manner that promotes global unity while respecting a dignity of difference.

REFERENCES

Barber, B.R. (2003). *Fear's empire: War, terrorism, and democracy*. New York: W.W. Norton & Company.

Christopher, P. (1999). *The ethics of war and peace: An introduction to legal and moral issues* (2nd ed.). Upper Saddle River: NJ: Prentice-Hall.

Glover, H. (1999). *Humanity: A moral history of the twentieth century*. London: Jonathan Cape.

Hamburg, D.A. (2002). *No more killing fields: Preventing deadly conflicts*. Lanham, MA: Rowman & Littlefield.

Hanh, Thich Nhat. (1991). *Peace is every step: The path of mindfulness in everyday life*. New York: Bantam Books.

Harris, I.M, & Morrison, M.L. (2003). *Peace education* (2nd ed.). Jefferson, NC: McFarland & Co.

Hedges, C. (2002). *War is a force that gives us meaning*. New York: PublicAffairs.

Janis, I.L. (1982). *Groupthink* (2nd ed.). Boston, MA: Houghton Mifflin Company.

Johnson, J.T. (1999). *Morality and contemporary warfare*. New Haven, CT: Yale University Press.

Kidder, R.M. (1995). *How good people make tough choices: Resolving the dilemmas of ethical living*. New York: Fireside.

Kimball, C. (2002). *When religion becomes evil*. New York: HarperCollins Publishers.

Lang, A.F, Pierce, A.C., & Rosenthal, J.H. (2004). *Ethics and the future of conflict: Lessons from the 1990s*. Upper Saddle River, NJ: Pearson Prentice Hall.

Lifton, R.J. (2003). *Super power syndrome: America's apocalyptic confrontation with the world*. New York: Thunder's Mouth Press/Nation Books.

Lyons, G.M., & Mayall, J. (Eds.). (2003). *International human rights in the 21st century: Protecting the rights of groups*. Lanham, MA: Rowman & Littlefield Publishers.

Owen, N. (Ed.). (2002). *Human rights, human wrongs*. Oxford, England: Oxford University Press.

Owen, W. (1994). The *works of Wilfred Owen*. Harvard Square, MA: Wordsworth Poetry Library.

Sacks, J. (2002). *The dignity of difference: How to avoid the clash of civilizations*. New York: Continuum.

Sampson, C., Abu-Nimer, M., Liebler, C., & Whitney, D. (Eds.). (2003). *Positive approaches to peace building: A resource for innovators*. Washington, D.C: Pact Publications.

Sawin, J.L. (2004). Mainstreaming renewable energy in the 21st century. *Worldwatch Paper*, 169.

Sells, M. (1999). *Approaching the Qur'án: The early revelations*. Ashland, OR: White Cloud Press.

Soros, G. (2004). *The bubble of American supremacy: Correcting the misuse of American power*. New York: PublicAffairs.

Steiner, N., Gibney, M., & Loescher, G. (Eds.). (2003). *Problems of protection: The UNHCR, refugees, and human rights*. New York: Routledge.

Stern, J. (2003). *Terror in the name of God: Why religious militants kill*. New York: HarperCollins Publishers.

Widner, J.A. (2001). *Building the rule of law: Francis Nyalali and the road to judicial independence in Africa*. New York: W.W. Norton & Co.

CHAPTER FOUR

Assessing Culturally Responsible Pedagogy in Student Work Reflections, Rubrics, and Writing: A Global Worldview in the Teaching/Learning Process

Tonya Huber
Wichita State University

Douglas F. Warring
University of St. Thomas

The continual approximation of culturally responsible pedagogy requires deeper levels of reflection and more culturally sensitive awareness and language usage. Pre-service and in-service pedagogists need to transfer the knowledge base about social justice and global interdependence into actions, inclusive of language, behaviors, and practices. How do educators plan and assess curriculum and instruction to support student learning, equity, social justice, and a global worldview in the teaching/learning process?

This paper explores strategies for critically analyzing home and school cultures, teacher and student cultures, and the elements of culture that inform such analysis. Evolved from critical multicultural education (McLaren, 2002) and framed on the "Knowledge Bases for Diversity in Teacher Education" (Smith, 1991, 1998, 2000), these strategies require the participant to dig beneath surface veneers and challenge traditional explanations regarding the curriculum, instruction, and teaching/learning process. As McLaren (1998) explained:

> Why is a critical pedagogy so necessary? Part of the answer is that mainstream pedagogies generally avoid or attempt to obscure the question that should be central to education: What is the relationship between what we do in the classroom and our effort to build a better society. (p. xiv)

A characteristic of multicultural, social reconstructivist, reflective teaching is the teacher's inward focus on his or her own practices and beliefs as well as the outward focus on the social conditions in which these practices are situated (see Kemmis, 1985; Tabachnik & Zeichner, 1991). Both individual (self), as well as institutional (other) issues are thereby reviewed.

Those who advocate a social reconstructionist view [of reflective teaching] certainly acknowledge the importance of subject matter, student understanding, research-based teaching techniques, and an emphasis on the students' interests, thinking and development. Teachers who practice a multicultural, social reconstructionist version of reflective teaching view the substance of other versions through the lens of the larger society. Such teachers realize that without solid subject matter taught using appropriate effective instructional techniques, as well as curricula based on the needs, interests, talents, and learning styles of the children, students will not attain the knowledge base and skills necessary to become active participating members of society. Knowledge, skills, and personal development are not seen as individual ends but as essential components of a wider educational endeavor that helps students become active participants in improving our democratic society. A concern for issues of equity, justice, and human rights in both the teaching and the learning process serves as the backdrop for examining teaching and schooling. (Gillette, 2001)

ELEMENTS OF CULTURE—SELF

A valid heuristic for knowledge, skills, and personal development is found in the consideration of the multi-faceted elements of culture (see Figure 1). Without ongoing critical reflection, many educators study, teach, and assess without full awareness that the students whom they teach perceive the world in radically different ways (see Gardner, 1983; Gilliland, 1995; Guild & Garger, 1985; Huber& Pewewardy, 1990a, 1990b; & Shade, 1989; for the knowledge base on multiple intelligences, modalities, and cultural styles). A learning process that engenders critical reflection on individual identity is one that requires participants to determine the significant aspects of their own cultural identity, locate iconic/symbolic/representative artifacts for each aspect, and then interpret the meaning. Huber (2002, pp. 17-25) has been asking students to prepare Culture Clip Exhibits for more than fifteen years. The guidelines for a 15-week semester course are found in Figure 2, though Clips have been created by students in 2-week intensive international courses, as well as by students enrolled in 4-week summer programs. Table 1 provides a rubric for the project exhibit and written captions.

ELEMENTS OF CULTURE—OTHERS

Maclang-Vicencio (2003) articulated the need for culture-responsive curriculum that, ultimately traverses the transdisciplinal continuum, which goes beyond the disciplinal and multidisciplinal learning areas in order to engage educators in "community-based action projects that provide opportunities to engage in individual and group action in the school and community" (p. 70).
Freire (1969/1989) explained:

To be human is to engage in relationships with others and with the world. . . . Men relate to their world in a critical way. They apprehend the objective data of their reality (as well as the ties that link one datum to another) through reflection—not by reflex, as do animals. . . . Transcending a single dimension, they reach back to yesterday, recognize today, and come upon tomorrow. (p. 3)

The cultural awareness activity "Whose Culture?" provides a heuristic for participants to engage in critical reflection on the components of self, student, home, school, and community culture (see Figure 3) to identify aspects of each that approximate or deter the accomplishment of teaching/learning that is culturally responsible and promotes equitable, just, global worldviews (see Gutek, 1997; Igoa, 1995, Townsend, Clarke, & Ainscow, 1999). As Tabachnik and Zeichner (1991) detailed: A social reconstructionist conception of reflective teaching has a democratic and emancipatory impulse and the focus of the teacher's deliberations is upon substantive issues that raise instances of inequality and injustice within schooling and society for close scrutiny (pp. 8-9).

BRIDGING CULTURES

The works of Paulo Freire (1969/1989), Peter McLaren (1993), G. Pritchy Smith (1998, 2000), Sonia Nieto (1992), Christine E. Sleeter and Carl A. Grant (1999), Jacqueline Jordan Irvine (1990), Joseph Tobin, David Wu, and Dana Davidson (1989), and other critical pedagogists committed to social justice and "humaneness" (Smith, 2004) must be "actioned as pedagogies and not merely focused on curriculum" (McMaster, cited in Huber, 2002, cover). John McMaster, Faculty of Education, Pedagogics and Cultural Studies, University of Southern Queensland, advocates, "One of the errors we have made in the past, I believe, is that we have failed to interrogate what culturally diverse pedagogies may look like . . . a primary tool for preparing beginning teachers, for vastly complex educational settings" (cover). What learning experiences facilitate the development of culturally sensitive and responsible pedagogists? How do educators facilitate their students' understanding of the cultural genocide that has been a part of United States education, what Joel Spring terms deculturalization?

Deculturalization is one aspect of a strange mixture of democratic thought an intolerance that permeates American history. The concept of deculturalization demonstrates how cultural prejudice, racism, and religious bigotry can be intertwined with democratic beliefs. Deculturalization combines education for democracy and political equality with cultural genocide.

> Deculturalization is the educational process of destroying a people's culture and replacing it with a new culture. (p. 3; emphasis added by the original author)

Perhaps Roger I. Simon (2000) has best detailed the need for a critically reflective approach to teaching about the cultural collisions and tragedies that have birthed the present moment:

an approach to the past in relation to its absolute discontinuity from the time of the present . . . this form of remembrance holds to historical memories as traces of another's time that may disrupt my own. On such terms, remembrance becomes a practice that supports a learning from the past that is a fresh cognizance or discovery that unsettles the very terms on which our understandings of ourselves and our world are based. In its most powerful form, such remembrance initiates forms of learning that shift and disrupt the present, opening one to new ways of perceiving, thinking, and acting. (p. 13)

As President of the World Council for Curriculum and Instruction (WCCI), Larry Hufford (2003) reminded members:

> Globally speaking, these are dark times. We, as global citizens, face issues such as unilateral militarism, empire, state and stateless terrorism, global poverty, failed and failing states, narcotrafficking, trafficking in persons, child labor and child soldiers, gender equity, ecological insecurity, ethnic, racial and religious conflicts. . . .A more just global community is not historically or theologically determined. I, along with others, must create it. That is, I must be involved in my community, locally, nationally, and/or globally, in an effort to daily model humaneness along with a personal commitment to justice and peace. As educators, it is not enough to teach peace. Each of us is obligated to be an exemplar, a role model of personal commitment to cross cultural/gender understanding, nonviolence, respect for an ecological balance and to confronting human created structural/silent violence that keeps people poor and oppressed. In short, educators must model civic engagement. (1-2)

WHOSE CULTURE?

The "Whose Culture?" field-based learning cultural awareness experience (see Figure 3 and Table 2) targets multiple outcomes, a primary one being the reflective immersion in a cultural activity that places the participant in a *minority* position, one in which as many aspects of culture as possible are unknown to the participant. The professor with explanation of how the event/activity meets requirements must approve the experience. Frequent sites are the many places of worship afforded in a Metro area. Consistently, participants report the mutual respect and regard these cross-cultural religious encounters engender. As Don Whitson (2004), a pre-service teacher reported:

> Master Thich Thien Hanh (Presiding Monk) at the Bu'u-Quang Buddhist Temple invited me to join the other participants for the afternoon meal that followed the ceremony in which we had just participated. I sat down on the floor in the traditional Vietnamese style and enjoyed a food/culture extravaganza. More importantly, the experience was an event with prayer before and after eating. It was a meditation practice (silence was observed during eating) to fully engage in the act of nourishment and all that it brings to the being and senses. It was a time to reflect and pay respect to the spirits. It was many things, but for me it was a time of acceptance, friendship, and internal re-evaluation from a people who spoke a different language, engaged in a different religion, enjoyed different meal customs, and looked and behaved a little differently than myself (a 50-ish white male whose experience with the Vietnamese culture prior to this

event had been my military service in 1970). But, through all the differences, we enjoyed each other's company, laughter, and a shared meal—both physical and spiritual food. We ended the experience with mutual respect, understanding each other a little better on our cultural awareness journey. (p. 3)

Ruth Schott's (2004) cultural awareness experience was, perhaps, one of the most challenging of her cohort. Independently, as a pre-service teacher in her junior year of college, without peers or team members, she immersed herself in a Muslim religious ceremony. Her reflections were enthusiastically shared with her colleagues:

> I attended Islamic *Jummauh* prayer at the Muslim Community Center in Wichita Not only did I witness rituals and prayer services that were foreign to me, I also had the opportunity to experience what it would be like to be covered like Muslim women. A couple of very friendly Muslim women put the *Hijab* around my head completely covering my hair and then put a piece of lovely silk lavender cloth over the entire lower half of my body due to the fact I was wearing a knee-length skirt. Even though the Islamic religion has very distinct rules and rituals that the Muslim community must follow, I found myself in a very peaceful, calm, loving, family environment. The doors to the community center were left open so the wonderful warm breeze and air filled the prayer area. The prayer service was an entirely new experience for me. I especially enjoyed (what I would describe as) the beautiful, musical Arabic chanting used to recite the prayers. The fluid motion of the prayer service was very soothing. The man who led the prayer would chant in Arabic for a while, and then the people would bow. He would chant some more, then the people would kneel with their heads and hands touching the floor, then they would sit, then kneel again, followed by only the men reciting what sounded like a brief, low musical reply back to the leader of the prayer. The people would then stand, bow, and kneel again during certain points in the prayer. This activity seemed to repeat itself over a ten-minute period.
>
> In my entire lifetime I have never experienced anything remotely like the *Jammauh*. Coming from an upper-middle-class Christian upbringing, there was absolutely no resemblance to any type of Christian worship service I was used to. In my experience of the Christian religion, it is customary to get dressed up for church, and I don't think one would be allowed in the church service without shoes on. Men, women and families all worship together--there is no separation of the sexes. Nursery school and children's bible classes are provided for the youngsters. There is no such thing as nursery school or children's prayer school for Islamic youth during the *Jammauh*. The churches I have attended along with the church that I am attending now do not provide food after the service, and I have never in my life eaten an entire meal with my fingers!
>
> Even though the *Jammauh* was a completely foreign experience to me, I felt extremely comfortable and at peace during my time there. I was stunned to be welcomed with such warmth and hospitality by the people of the Muslim Community Center.

The testimonies of Whitson and Schott resonate the experiences of their colleagues and uphold Hufford's (2003) admonition that the Golden Rule exists in every religion.

Most of us are persons of faith. Thus, we share a belief that each individual on earth has within a spark of the Divine. At the last WCCI Triennial in Madrid, Spain, participants were in shock as events of 9/11 unfolded. On the evening of 9/11 participants met to pray for understanding and a just, peaceful response. There were Hindu, Sikh, Buddhist, Jewish, Muslim, Christian, Baha'i prayers and chants. As persons of faith, each of us is called to oppose those of our particular faith who would turn our faith tradition into a movement of hatred and evil. Every major world religion has a Golden Rule and messages of cooperation, community and service to others; not simply charity, but a service that nonviolently challenges structural violence and structural sin. Every major world religion has a strong peace message. (p. 2; see, also, Hufford, 2000, pp. 180-181)

Teachers who discover these common aspects of religious beliefs are better prepared to work effectively with the diversity of beliefs and religions represented in America's classrooms. As Whitson (2004) concluded:

It is necessary that the teacher's perception, is just that, the teacher's perception. We as educators have to crawl out of our skin and occasionally wear the skin of our students. I can never be enculturated beyond my own individual culture, but I can be acculturated, acquiring deeper understandings of other cultures. This is not free--not free from harassment, not free from the investment of resources, not free from challenges, and not free, in general, from negative arenas. But usually great things are not free. The knowledge base built in considering diverse populations from all perspectives will create a classroom that is better equipped and managed, able to facilitate instructional methods that are universally beneficial and that model an inclusive approach and attitude. . . . These additional cultural tools will enable the author/teacher to design and implement a curriculum and instruction that is promising for all students. Many threads connect us, but the one that is most common is that we are all human beings. One of the characteristics of humankind should be a sense of being humane and actively showing concern for others. Teachers being human and humane accomplish that. This journey is not about the teacher. This learning experience is for the most important participant in the educational journey, the student. (pp. 21-22)

IDENTIFYING THE PARAMETERS DEFINING DIVERSITY

What is needed is a culturally sensitive and responsible pedagogy for all students to maximize learning in American education. Culturally responsible pedagogy is not color-bound or language-specific but subsumes all diversities to ensure sensitivity to and responsibility or all learners. (Huber, Kline, Bakken, & Clark, 1997b, p. 131). The faculty teaching the foundation courses at Wichita State University in 1991 adopted this holistic orientation. G. Pritchy Smith's (1991) "Knowledge Bases for Diversity in Teacher Education" provided the unifying framework for the three different courses and shared field experience (see Table 3). The faculty updated the knowledge bases when they were published by the American Association of Colleges for Teacher Education as *Common Sense about Uncommon Knowledge: The Knowledge Bases for Diversity* (Smith, 1998) and again when Smith (2000) expanded the original 13 to 15 (see Table 4 for the current knowledge bases). As Smith explained, "the need for teachers to understand culture and understand the individual learner as a unique cultural being intimately connects avant-garde methods of critical inquiry with the knowledge bases for diversity in teacher education" (p. 27).

Recognition of the knowledge bases has evolved into a pivotal aspect of each major assignment for these faculty and students. The applicable parameters must be identified on the cover sheet for each major project across the four courses in the Core I, foundations-level courses, Introduction to Diversity: (a) Exceptionalities, (b) Cultural Issues, (c) Human Development, and (d) Field Experience.

WRITING TO LEARN CULTURE

Culturally Responsible Pedagogy in the teaching/learning process often requires substantial rewriting, but, more importantly, substantial rethinking--the kind of thinking that requires time to revisit the deep wells of memory, personal experience, and personal belief in order to extract a clearer picture of the personal meanings the writer intends and the extrapolated meanings that readers can subsequently take away from the reading and apply to their own lives, circumstances, and work with curriculum and instruction. When properly guided, the effect of the thinking and reflective process on procedure and application is central to learning, equity, and social justice. This is in addition to the time required to absorb and assimilate ideas uncovered initially, in reading and study, unearthed during critical inquiry, and finally, embedded in the feedback and commentary from peers, faculty, and other readers.

At the point that students pick up a pen or strike a key, they become very vulnerable. The editing/revising/ feedback process makes the writer even more vulnerable while issues of social justice and global diversity compound the issues. We are aware--as professors, editors, reviewers, authors, and lifelong learners ourselves--that writing is an extremely vulnerable process, especially when one is discussing something that is of deep personal meaning and significance. As Myers (1984) detailed:

> Writing to learn is not learning to write. But the emphasis of writing to learn is on learning content, not the writing skills themselves, although writing skills are likely to improve through practice. In this approach writing is a vehicle for clear and logical communication. It is process in which thinking—the organization, evaluation, and synthesis of knowledge—is essential.

One of the major elements that distinguishes a piece of work as one of scholarly merit is that the writing of the scholar evidences not only an awareness and understanding of the choices inherent in the writing process, but also a willingness to hold those choices up for public scrutiny, and an ability to articulate, explicate, and defend the choices made with regard to both facets of the work. Doing so is evidence of deep engagement with the critical inquiry process and has the secondary effect of lending credibility to the work.

Elliot Eisner (2002) clarified the importance of reflection: "Self-reflection on one's own teaching, though important, is seldom sufficient. . . . We often simply don't know what we are unaware of. It is a phenomenon that permeates parenting and friendships as well" (pp. 56-57). Social reconstructionist reflection is a critical component of the process of developing and assessing culturally responsible pedagogy in pre-service and in-service teacher work.

Table 1. Culture Clips Rubric for Feedback

Exemplary	Target	Accomplished	Not Accomplished
Developed comprehensive analysis of 12-15 aspects of individual culture in captioned clips/artifacts	Developed comprehensive analysis of 12 captioned clips/artifacts	Provided 10-12 captioned clips	Provided captions and/or clips
Caption statements include 4 clearly labeled sections: (a) a definitive or representative title, (b) the date defining the clip, (c) the element(s) of culture, and (d) a reflective statement on the significance of the clip to individual culture	Included in each caption statement (a) a title, (b) a date defining the clip, (c) the elements of culture, and (d) a reflective statement	Communicated important information in caption format	Communicated information as isolated pieces
Caption reflective statements include application of program content from a total of more than 6 parameters of the knowledge bases for diversity	Caption reflective statements include application of program content from at least 6 parameters of the knowledge bases for diversity	Caption reflective statements incorporated issues of diversity	Caption reflective statements identified diversity topics

Worked collaboratively and professionally during the exhibit to communicate effectively using meaningful display of artifacts/clips, a complete caption for each clip, a cultural circle and a current photo (if culturally appropriate)	Worked collaboratively and professionally during the exhibit to present major points using a display of artifacts/clips, a complete caption for each clip, a cultural circle, and a photo	Interacted at the exhibit using clips and captions	Presented information at the culture clips exhibit
Applied APA professional writing standards in expression of ideas, format, and style	Applied APA professional writing standards	Applied aspects of APA writing standards	Presented project as a student product

Note: For this assignment, the rubric categories are weighted as follows: Exemplary=20, Target=15, Acceptable=12.5, Unacceptable=11. If a component is missing, the score is zero.

Evaluation of _____   Total Points: _____ /100

Table 2. Whose Culture? Field Experience Requirement

	Exemplary	Proficient	Acceptable	Not Acceptable
Description of Cultural Awareness Event	Detailed description of the event, including (a) date, location, and name of activity, (b) purpose of event, (c) participants in the event, (d) explanation of how this activity introduced you to a cultural group different from your own	Description of the event, including (a) date, location, and name of activity, (b) purpose of event, (c) participants in the event, (d) explanation of how this activity introduced you to a cultural group different from your own	Description of the (a) event, (b) purpose of event, (c) participants in the event, (d) how this activity introduced you to a cultural group different from your own	Consideration of event description and explanation of how this activity introduced you to a cultural group different from your own
Analysis of Elements of Culture	Interpretation of more than 10 elements of culture, including, at least 2 surface and 8 deep, with supporting documentation (e.g., notes, programs, photos, artifacts)	Interpretation of at least 10 elements of culture, including 2 surface and 8 deep with documentation (e.g., notes, programs, photos, artifacts)	Application of at least 10 elements of culture	Consideration of elements of culture
Curriculum Resource Evaluation	Detailed and documented responses to all required curriculum resource evaluation components	Documented responses to curriculum resource evaluation components	Documented responses to the majority of curriculum resource evaluation components	Cursory consideration of components
School Environment Evaluation	Detailed and documented responses to all school environment components	Documented responses all school environment components	Documented responses to the majority of school environment components	Cursory consideration of components
Family and Home Culture	Detailed and documented responses to all family and home culture components	Documented responses to all of the family and home culture components	Documented responses to the majority of family and home culture components	Cursory consideration of components

Reflection and Analysis of Elements of Home and School Cultures	Specific identification and analysis of the intersecting elements of home and school cultures, including visual analysis and integration of major core readings	Specific identification of the intersecting elements of home and school cultures, including visual analysis and references to major class readings	Identification of the intersecting elements of home and school cultures including visual analysis	Cursory consideration of elements of culture and implications regarding professional knowledge base development
Application of APA Writing Guidelines	The entire document is word processed and includes headers and consistent pagination; professional grammar, spelling, punctuation, and word usage; consistent with APA guidelines, including double spacing, in-text citations, and references to major core readings	The document is word processed and includes headers and pagination; professional grammar, spelling, punctuation, and word usage; including double spacing, in-text citations, and references to major class readings	The document is word processed and includes headers and pagination; professional grammar, spelling, punctuation and word usage; including double spacing and in-text citations	Inconsistent application of professional writing standards

Note: For this assignment, the rubric categories are weighted as follows: Exemplary=20, Proficient=15, Acceptable=10, Not Acceptable=0. A total rubric score of 100 or above with no aspect scored as zero is required. An exemplary submission includes: Title page and paper with references and support documentation, a copy of the FER requirements (from the Road Map) goals and parameters analysis, evidence of approval, and this rubric.

Approval of Activity_____ Date Approved _____
Name _____Date Submitted _____

Table 3.　Smith's Knowledge Bases for Diversity [1]

Parameters	Guiding Principals
I. Foundations of Multicultural Education	a review of international, legal, and historical, theory, research, and practice undergird the study and practice of multiculturalism
II. Sociocultural Contexts of Human Growth and Development in Marginalized Ethnic and Racial Cultures	child-rearing, social interaction, gender role identification, parenting, responsibility, cultural/developmental scripts, and other psycho-socio-cultural patterns affect the way people learn and respond to reading
III. Cultural and Cognitive Learning Style Theory and Research	cultural cognitive styles and multiple intelligences research, combined with a thorough understanding of learning style theory, enables the teacher to maximize instruction
IV. Language, Communication, and Interactional Styles	recognizing cultural styles related to speech patterns, verbal and nonverbal interactions, and inter-relationship patterns
V. Essential Elements of Culture	studying ancient through contemporary history of cultures highlights common features and distinctive differences of deep culture characteristics that help the educator better understand the individual child or student
VI. Principles of Culturally Responsive Teaching and Culturally Responsive Curriculum Development	analyzing the language, concepts, principles, practices, theory and research on teaching responsive to, and responsible for cultural issues in the explicit, implicit, and null curricula including cultural synchronicity, congruity, continuity, correspondence and cultural scripts
VII. Effective Strategies	strategies, policy, and practice can produce positive effects for previously low-achieving students
VIII. Foundations of Racism	issues of racism, slavery, genocide, prejudice, bias, stereotyping, and discrimination and their effects on micro-and macrocultures
IX. Effects of Policy and Practice on Culture, Race, Class, Gender, and Other Categories of Diversity	determining the impact of the differential effects of policy and practices on race, class, gender, and culture regarding such issues as teacher expectations, ability grouping and curriculum tracking studies, desegregation and integration studies, discipline, and suspension/expulsion and drop out/push out factors
X. Culturally Responsive Diagnosis, Measurement, and Assessment	*replacing* of the traditional view of intelligence as a physical substance, a measurable, entity, and a subsequent focus on measurable, easily quantifiable constructs focusing on linguistic and logical-mathematical intelligences and culture-specific norms
XI. Socio-cultural Influences in Subject-specific Learning	planning with recognition of cultural influences on specific school subjects

XII. Gender and Sexual Orientation	knowledge about gender differences and the impact of sexual orientations, both the students' own and those of family members, on students
XIII. Experiential Knowledge	lived and supervised clinical experiences that include personal cross-cultural and multicultural lifestyle experiences and supervised demonstration of culturally responsive teaching in clinical school settings with culturally diverse student populations and professional knowledge about how teachers teach effectively and responsibly in multicultural classrooms representing diversity issues, particularly from action research, ethnography, case studies, and educational anthropology
XIV. Foundations of Identifying and Teaching Special Needs Students	preparation of regular education teachers to identify and respond sensitively and appropriately to students' special needs, an aspect of teacher education that typically occurs only for those candidates certified as special education
XV. Foundations of International and Global Education	analyzing global and international education beyond introductory comparative education which often contributes to the provincialism of teachers in the United States

[1]While the parameters define and organize the knowledge bases for developing culturally responsible pedagogy, they transcend the theoretical to visibly emerge in curriculum development. Adapted from G. P. Smith, 1991, 1998, 2001 (Huber, 2002, p. 42).

Table 4. Parameters of the Knowledge Bases for Diversity in Teacher Education by Course

Parameters of the Knowledge Base	CI[1]	E[2]	HD[3]	FE[4]
1. Foundations of multicultural education	X			X
2. Sociocultural contexts of human growth and development in marginalized ethnic and racialctures	X	X	X	X
3. Cultural and cognitive learning style theory and research	X	X	X	X
4. Language, communication, and interaction styles	X	X	X	X
5. Essential elements of cultures	X			X
6. Principles of culturally responsive teaching and culturally responsive curriculum development	X	X		X
7. Effective strategies	X	X		X
8. Foundations of racism	X	X	X	X
9. Effects of policy and practice on culture, race, class, gender, and other categories of diversity	X	X		X
10. Culturally responsive diagnosis, measurement, and assessment	X	X	X	X
11. Socio-cultural influences in subject-specific learning	X	X		X
12. Gender and sexual orientation	X	X	X	X
13. Experiential knowledge	X	X	X	X
14. Foundations of identifying and teaching special needs students	X	X		X
15. Foundations of international and global education	X		X	X

[1]**CI** = Cultural Issues; [2]**E** = Exceptionalities; [3]**HD** = Human Development; [4]**FE** = Field Experience

Figure 1. Elements of Culture[1]

SURFACE CULTURE
(observable)

1. Arts	(traditional and contemporary music, visual and performing arts, and drama)
2. Folklore	(folk tales, legends, and oral history)
3. Food	(food and culinary contributions)
4. Heroes/Personalities	(historical, contemporary, and local figures)
5. History	(historical and humanitarian contributions, and social and political movements)
6. Holidays	(patriotic holidays, religious observances, and personal rites and celebrations)

DEEP CULTURE

1. Ceremony and Celebration (what a person is to say and do on particular occasions)

    A. What is the purpose (e.g., political, seasonal, religious, didactic?)
    B. Which are especially important for children and why?
    C. What cultural values do they intend to inculcate?
    D. What aspects of socialization/enculturation do they further?

2. Communication

    A   What languages and varieties of each language are used in the community? By whom?
       When? Where? For what purpose?
    B. Which varieties are written, and how widespread is knowledge of written forms?
    C. What are the characteristics of "speaking well," and how do these relate to age, sex, context,
       or other social factors? What are the criteria for "correctness"?
    D. What roles, attitudes, or personality traits are associated with particular ways of speaking?
    E. What range is considered "normal" speech behavior? What is considered a speech defect?
    F. Is learning a language a source of pride? Is developing bilingual competence considered an
       advantage or a handicap?
    G. What is the functionality of the native language in the workplace or larger environment?

H. What gesture or postures have special significance or may be considered objectionable?
    What meaning is attached to direct eye contact? To eye avoidance?
I.   Who may talk to whom? When? Where? About what?

3. Courtship and Marriage (attitudes toward dating, marriage, and raising a family)

4. Eating Customs and Rules

A   What is eaten; in what order; and how often?
B.   What foods are favorites; what taboo; what typical?
C.   What rules are observed during meals regarding age and sex roles within the family, the order of serving, eating, utensils used and appropriate verbal formulas (e.g., how, and if, one may request, refuse, or thank)?
D.   What social obligations are there with regard to food giving, preparation, reciprocity, and honoring people?
E.   What relation does food have to health? What medicinal uses are made of food, or categories of food?
F.   What are the taboos or prescriptions associated with the handling, offering, or discarding of food?

5. Education

A.   What is the purpose of education?
B.   What kinds of learning are favored (e.g., rote, inductive)?
C.   What methods of teaching and learning are used at home (e.g., modeling and imitation, didactic stories and proverbs, direct verbal instruction)?
D.   Do methods of teaching and learning vary with recognized stages in the life cycle; with the setting; or according to what is being taught or learned?
E.   What is the role of language in learning and teaching?
F.   Is it appropriate for students to ask questions or to volunteer information? If so, what behavior signals this? If not, what negative attitudes may it engender?
G.   What constitutes a positive response by a teacher to a student? By a student to a teacher?
H.   How many years is considered normal for children to go to school?
I.   Are there different expectations by parents, teachers, and students with respect to different groups; in different subjects; or for boys vs. girls?

6. Aesthetics (the beautiful things of culture: literature, music, dance, art, architecture, and how they are enjoyed)

A. What is considered beautiful?
B. What are important works of art? artists? buildings?
C. What dances are performed at celebrations?

7. Ethics and Discipline (how a person learns and practices honesty, fair play, principles, moral thought, etc.)

8. Family Ties (how a person feels toward his or her family, friends, classmates, roommates, and others)

A. Who is in a *family*? Who among these (or others) live in one house?
B. What is the hierarchy of authority in the family?
C. What are the rights and responsibilities of each family member? Do children have an obligation to work or to help the family?
D. What are the functions and obligations of the family in the larger social unit? To the school? To its individual members?
E. What is the relative importance of an individual family member vs. the family as a whole? What is the degree of solidarity or cohesiveness in the family?

9. Health and Medicine (how a person reacts to sickness, death, soundness of mind and body, medicine, etc.)

A   Who or what is believed to cause illness or death (i.e., the *germ theory* vs. the supernatural or other causes)?
B. Who or what is responsible for curing?
C. How are specific illnesses treated? To what extent do individuals utilize or accept *modern* medical practices by doctors and other health professionals?
D. What beliefs, taboos, and practices are associated with menstruation and the onset of puberty?
E. What are beliefs regarding conception and childbirth?
F. What beliefs or practices are there with regard to bodily hygiene (e.g., bathing frequency and purpose)?
G. If a student were involved in an accident at school, would any of the common first aid practices be unacceptable?

10. History, Traditions, and Folk Myths (attitudes toward heroes, traditional stories, legendary characters, superstitions, etc.)

A   What individuals and events in history are a source of pride for the group?
B. To what extent is knowledge of the group's history preserved?
C. In what forms and in what ways is it passed on?

    D. To what extent is there a literate tradition of the history of the group (e.g., written history, and knowledge of written history within the group itself)?

    E. To what extent are traditions and historical events reflected in aphorism and proverbs?

    F. Do any ceremonies or festive occasions re-enact historical events?

    G. How and to what extent does the group's knowledge of history coincide with or depart from scientific theories of reaction, evolution, and historical development?

    H. To what extent does the group in the United States identify with the history and traditions of their country of origin?

    I. What changes have taken place in the country of origin since the group or individual emigrated?

    J. For what reasons and under what circumstances did the group or individuals come to the United States (or did the United States come to them)?

11. Kinesics and Interpersonal Relationships (forms of non-verbal communication or reinforced speech, such as the use of the eyes, the hands, and the body)

    A. Is language competence a requirement or qualification for group membership?

    B. How do people greet each other? What forms of address are used between people in various roles?

    C. Do girls work and interact with boys? Is it proper?

    D. How is deference shown?

    E. How are insults expressed?

    F. Who may disagree with whom? Under what circumstances?

    G. Are mitigating forms used?

12. Grooming and Presence (the cultural differences in personal behavior and appearance, such as laughter, smile, voice quality, gait, poise, hair style, cosmetics, dress, etc.)

    A. What clothing is typical? What is worn for special occasions? What seasonal differences are considered appropriate?

    B. What significance does dress have for group identity?

    C. How does dress differ for age, sex, and social class?

    D. What restrictions are imposed for modesty (e.g., can girls wear shorts, or shower in the gym)?

    E. What is the concept of beauty, or attractiveness? How important is physical appearance in the culture? What characteristics are most valued?

    F. What constitutes a compliment and what form should it take (e.g., in traditional Latin

American culture, telling a woman she is getting fat is a compliment)?
G. Does the color of dress have symbolic significance (e.g., black vs. white for mourning)?

13. Life Cycle

A. What are the criteria for the definition of stages, periods, or transitions in life?
B. What are attitudes, expectations, and behaviors toward individuals at different stages in the life cycle?
C. What behaviors are appropriate or unacceptable for children of various ages? How might these conflict with behaviors taught or encouraged in the school?
D. How is language related to the life cycle?
E. How is the age of children computed? What commemoration is made of the child's birth (if any) and when?

14. Natural Phenomena

15. Ownership (attitudes toward ownership of property, individual rights, localities, beliefs, etc.)

16. Precedence (what are accepted manners toward older persons, peers, and younger persons)

A. Who has authority over whom? To what extent can one person's will be imposed on another? By what means?
B. How is the behavior of children traditionally controlled, to what extent, and in what domains?

17. Rewards and Privileges (attitudes toward motivation, merit, achievement, service, social position, etc.)

18. Rights and Duties (attitudes toward personal obligations, voting, taxes, military service, legal rights, personal demands, etc.)

19. Religion (attitudes toward the divine and the supernatural and how they affect a person's thoughts and actions)

A. What is considered sacred and what secular?
B. What religious rules and authority are recognized in the community?
C. What is the role of children in religious practices? What are they supposed to know or not to know about the religion?
D. What should an outsider not know, or not acknowledge knowing?

    E.   What taboos are there? What should not be discussed in school; what questions should not be asked; what student behaviors should not be required?

    F.   Are there any external signs of participation in religious rituals (e.g., ashes, dress, markings)?

    G.   Are dietary restrictions to be observed, including fasting on particular occasions? Are there any prescribed religious procedures or forms of participation if there is a death in the family? What taboos are associated with death and the dead?

20. Roles (what positions in the social grouping are available to members)

21. Sex Roles (how a person views, understands, and relates to members of the opposite sex and what deviations are allowed and expected)

22. Space and Proxemics (attitudes toward self and land; the accepted distances between individuals)

    A   Is there a seasonal organization of work or other activities?

    B.   What is acceptable presence or grouping of individuals (e.g., do children stay with adults and listen or go outside)?

    C.   How do individuals organize themselves spatially in groups (e.g., in rows, circles, around tables, on the floor, in the middle of the room, around its circumference)?

    D.   What is the organization of the home (e.g., areas allotted to children or open to children,
appropriate activities in various areas of the home)?

    E.   What geo-spatial concepts, understandings, and beliefs exist in the group or are known to individuals?

    F.   What is the knowledge and significance of cardinal directions (North, South, East, West)? At what age are these concepts acquired?

    G.   What significance is associated with different directions or places (e.g., heaven is up,
people are buried facing west)?

23. Subsistence (attitudes about providing for oneself, the young, and the old, and who protects whom)

24. Taboos (attitudes and beliefs about doing things against culturally accepted patterns)

    A.   Are particular behavioral prescriptions or taboos associated with the seasons (e.g., not singing certain songs in the summertime or a snake will bite, not eating oysters when there is an R in the name of the month)?

25. Time (attitudes toward being early, on time, or late)

    A.   What beliefs or values are associated with concepts of time? How important is punctuality? Speed of performance when taking a test?

    B.   Is control or prescriptive organization of children's time required (e.g., must homework be done before watching TV, is bedtime a scheduled event)?

    C.   Is time a monochromic or polychromic concept?

26. Values (attitudes toward freedom, education, cleanliness, cruelty, crime, etc.)

27. Work and Play (attitudes toward the relationships between work and play or free time)

[1]Adapted from Gonzales, 1978.

Figure 2. Culture Clips Guidelines

Week 1 (or Day 1)
1. Study the elements of surface culture (see Figure 1).
2. Reflect on meaningful aspects of your culture for each of the 6 elements identified as surface culture.
Due Week 2
3. Place a picture of yourself (if culturally appropriate) in the center of a piece of paper/posterboard (at least 11"x17") or on a technologically generated web (using legal size paper or larger). Include your name on this visual representation.
4. Select at least one clip (artifact/symbol/icon/representation/ picture) to represent the surface element of food and arrange/attach the clip on your exhibit.
5. Write a caption for your clip. Each caption must include at least the following 4 clearly labeled sections: (a) a definitive or representative title, (b) the date defining the clip—not the date it was captioned, (c) the element of culture, and (d) critical reflection--interpretation of possible implications for your role as a culturally sensitive and responsible educator—this separates *student activity* from the behavior of a reflective pedagogist who seeks opportunities to grow professionally. At least one specific reference to the knowledge base is required for each caption. Reference the citation and begin a reference page.
Due Week 3
6. Repeat steps 4-5 to create a clip and caption for a holiday. Add the necessary information to your reference list and continue to do so with each new entry.
7. Using technological skills, create a cultural identity circle that considers at least the following microcultural group identifiers for yourself: ethnicity, race, gender, language, religion, creed, age, exceptionalities, sexual orientation and preference, socioeconomics, regional/geographic origins and connections. Base your analysis on the present and include percentages that equate to 100% of your identity. An example of a cultural identity circle is provided by Gollnick and Chinn (2002, p. 21) in *Multicultural Education in a Pluralistic Society* (6th ed.).
Due Week 4
8. Repeat steps 4-5 to create a clip and caption for two elements of surface culture: heroes/personalities and history.
Due Week 5
9. Repeat steps 4-5 to create a clip and caption for the remaining two elements of surface culture: arts and folklore.
Due Week 6
10. Submit the 6 surface elements of culture captions. Clips should not be submitted. These will be returned with feedback.
Week 7
11. Discussion of caption feedback.
Due Week 8
12. Repeat steps 4-5 to create a clip and caption for a self-selected deep element of culture.

Weeks 9-14

13. Develop comprehensive analysis of 10 elements of deep culture in captioned clips. Insure that captions include application of program content and parameters of the knowledge bases for diversity.

Due Week 14

14. Culture Clips Exhibit—Work collaboratively and professionally during the exhibit to communicate effectively using meaningful display of artifacts/clips, a complete caption for each clip, a cultural identity circle, and a current photo (if culturally appropriate). Exhibits are enriched by samples of your food element of culture or by other experiential aspects or take-aways for the guests who peruse your exhibit.

Figure 3. Whose Culture?

Consider: Enculturation is the process of learning one's own culture, influenced by home and family. Acculturation is the process of learning aspects of a culture other than one's own, influenced by schools and society. How does the relationship between the school culture and home culture impact learners? It is critical to maximizing educational effectiveness for those involved in the educational process to recognize the culture(s) of their classrooms, programs, and institution, and how these may conflict with the traditional or home culture or learners participating in that acculturative process.

Attend an activity that introduces you to a different ethnic group with which you are not already familiar. Select an activity in which you will be the minority. Your event must have the approval of your instructor. Based on observations and questions, determine the culture for a specific learner. Select a learner who is significantly different from yourself. Responses should reflect the perspective of the interviewee, not the assumptions of the interviewer.

Review a resource from the school in which you are observing. Ideally, select a text that is used by all members in the class. Complete a curriculum resource evaluation regarding all items pertinent to the item under review. Provide specific examples documented by page numbers, frequency counts, and/or passage documentation. If a question is not applicable (NA), provide an explanation telling why. Credit will not be given for single-word responses.

Observe an educational setting–the site at which you are observing in this Core. Describe the setting with specific attention to the questions regarding the school environment. Again, documentation matters.

Reflect on all of this information and present a reflective interpretation in narrative accompanied by a visual/graphic, software-generated representation (e.g., concept map, Venn diagram, bar graph, table) that documents the analysis.

SCHOOL CULTURE

Curriculum Resource Evaluation

1. Bibliography (APA format) of resource.
2. Type of resource being reviewed (text, film, video, module, curriculum unit, other)
3. Level considered most appropriate by author(s) or school district and/or developer: Early Childhood, Primary, Intermediate, Middle School, High School, General, Adult
4. Is the resource current? Copyright date alone does not indicate content currency.
5. Which visibly different groups or people are depicted in this material?

6. How are various groups depicted? In what roles? Be specific as to gender and ethnicity, physical abilities, age, frequency of appearance, and context of appearance.
7. Does the content present contributions written and/or edited by different ethnic groups? Does the content present multiple perspectives?
8. How might the book affect the image of a visibly different group of people? Consider both macro and microcultures.
9. Does the resource include illustrations that realistically portray the events involved?
10. Is the content material integrated (no added sections for special groups)?

School Environment

1. Do the bulletin boards, posters, photographs, maps, and other visible curriculum materials reflect ethnic diversity? If so, how?
2. Do the calendars in the school include information about ethnic minorities, women, and outstanding Americans of minority groups?
3. Do the foods that are served in the school cafeteria reflect ethnic diversity? If so, in what ways?
4. Does the classroom or school library include an ample number of books about American ethnic groups for all grade levels? If so, have the books been evaluated for their sensitivity to ethnic groups?
5. Do the school assemblies and extra-curricular activities reflect the ethnic diversity of American life? If so, to what extent?
6. What behaviors are rewarded? Aggressiveness? Obedience? Conformity? Achievement? Competition? Other behaviors?
7. What rewards or punishments are used to accomplish these behaviors? Who administers these?
8. What values are promoted?
9. How are parents encouraged to participate?

FAMILY AND HOME CULTURE[1]

1. How many generations has the family lived in the United States?
2. What ethnic heritage does the family claim?
3. What are the social roles of each family member (financial support, child-care, . . .)?
4. What is the family structure? What members make up the structure?
5. What is the educational background of the family? What is the attitude toward education?
6. How is "leisure time" spent?
7. What is the role of religion?
8. What non-verbal communication styles are evident?
9. What language(s) is/are spoken?
10. What values are taught?
11. What does the diet consist of? Eating times? Eating behaviors?

12. How are gender roles defined?
13. What is the attitude of family members toward the school program and faculty?
14. How often have family members visited the school site? What type of atmosphere did they report finding?
15. What, if any, chores and responsibilities are assigned to the children?

[on letterhead]
INFORMED CONSENT DOCUMENT

DESCRIPTION OF CULTURAL ACTIVITY: The purpose of this activity is to provide the Wichita State University student with the opportunity of exploring the complexities of home and school cultures by observing in schools and engaging in an activity and discussion with a school student and/or the student's family. This is an assignment for a Multicultural Foundations class and aims to provide students with additional information about people in *real world* contexts. Fictitious names will be used in the case study, and it will not be used for any other purpose than for a class report comparing home and school cultures.

The student observer will ask to participate in an activity, interaction, or discussion with you, your child, and/or your family. None of the activities should be intrusive into your family's privacy; the objective is to understand the student in the context of his/her family and in his or her culture. This is not intended, nor will it be used, as any kind of evaluation. It is an assignment for the student to understand the relationship between textbook information, school environment, and the active world of an individual student and family.

POTENTIAL DISCOMFORT: There may be some initial discomfort in allowing an outsider into family activities; however, most participants have relaxed after a short period with the pre-professional student observer, and have had no other uncomfortable feelings or thoughts.

POTENTIAL BENEFITS: By allowing the pre-professional student observer to participate in family activities and to observe a school student in the context of family life, you will be helping to prepare a future teacher with an understanding of the complexity of development and of the differences there are in families and individuals and in their interactions with each other.

CONSENT: I have fully explained to the individuals the nature and purpose of the activity, potential discomforts, and possible benefits involved in participation in the case study.

_____   _____   _____   _____
Instructor's   Date   Student Observer's   Date
Signature   Signature

I have been satisfactorily informed of the procedures described above. I know that the instructor (978-3322) and student will be available to answer any questions that I may have. I know that I may withdraw participation in the project at any time. I have received a copy of this form.

_____   _____
Participant's or Participant's Parent's Signature   Date

REFERENCES

Bennett, Christine I. (1990). *Comprehensive multicultural education: Theory and practice* (2ⁿᵈ ed.). Boston: Allyn and Bacon.

Freire, Paulo. (1969/1989). *Education for critical consciousness.* New York: Continuum.

Gardner, Howard. (1983). *Frames of mind: The theory of multiple intelligences.* New York: Basic Books.

Gillette, Maureen D. (2001). It's got to be in the plan: Reflective teaching and multicultural education. In Carl Grant, & Mary Louise Gomez (Eds.), *Campus and classroom: Making schooling multicultural* (2ⁿᵈ ed., pp. 349-365). Upper Saddle River, NJ: Merrill Prentice-Hall.

Gilliland, H. (1995). *Teaching the Native American* (3ʳᵈ ed.). Dubuque, IA: Kendall/Hunt.

Gollnick, Donna M., & Chinn, Philip C. (2002). *Multicultural education in a pluralistic society* (6ᵗʰ ed.). Upper Saddle River, NJ: Merrill Prentice-Hall.

Gonzales, F. (1978). *Mexican American culture in the bilingual education classroom.* Unpublished doctoral dissertation, The University of Texas at Austin.

Guild, P. B., & Garger, S. (1985). *Marching to different drummers.* Alexandria, VA: Association for Supervision and Curriculum Development.

Gutek, Gerald L. (1997). *American education in a global society: Internationalizing teacher education.* Prospect Heights, IL: Waveland Press.

Huber, T. (1993). *Teaching in the diverse classroom: Learner-centered activities that work.* Bloomington, IN: National Educational Service.

Huber, T. (1996). Social and Multicultural Foundations of Education, Wichita State University, a program review. In Mary M. Merryfield (Ed.) *Making connections between multicultural and global education: Teacher educators and teacher education programs* (pp. 102-103). Washington, DC: American Association of Colleges for Teacher Education (AACTE).

Huber, T. (2002). *Quality learning experiences (QLEs) for ALL students.* San Francisco, CA: Caddo Gap Press.

Huber, Tonya, Frank M. Kline, Linda Bakken, & Frances Clark. (1997a). From traditional teacher education to culturally responsible pedagogy: Moving a graveyard. In Carl A. Grant (Ed.), *Proceedings of the National Association for Multicultural Education, 1995* (pp. 182-208). San Francisco: Caddo Gap Press.

Huber, Tonya, Frank M. Kline, Linda Bakken, & Frances Clark. (1997b). Transforming teacher education: Including culturally responsible pedagogy. In J. E. King, E. R. Hollins, & W. Hayman (Eds.), *Preparing teachers for cultural diversity* (pp. 129-145). New York: Teachers College Press.

Huber, Tonya, & Cornel D. Pewewardy. (1990a). A review of literature to determine successful programs for and approaches to maximizing learning for diverse learners. *Collected Original Resources in Education* (CORE), *14*(3).Birmingham, West Midlands, United Kingdom: Fiche 1 D05.

Huber, Tonya, & Cornel D. Pewewardy. (1990b). *Maximizing learning for all students: A review of literature on learning modalities, cognitive styles, and approaches to meeting the needs of diverse learners.* (ERIC Document Reproduction Service No. ED 324289).

Hufford, Larry. (2000). Integrating ethics into international relations curricula. *Journal of Interdisciplinary Education, 4*(1), 179-189.

Hufford, Larry. (2003). A message from the president: Bright shining stars. *International Journal of Curriculum and Instruction, 5*(1), 1-2.

Igoa, Christine. (1995). *The inner world of the immigrant child.* New York: St. Martin's Press.

Irvine, Jacqueline Jordan. (1990). *Black students and school failure; policies, practices, and prescriptions.* New York: Praeger.

Kemmis, S. (1985). Action research an the politics of reflection. In D. Boud, R. Keough, & D. Walker (Eds.), *Reflection: Turning experience into learning* (pp. 139-164). London: Croom Helm.

Maclang-Vicencio, Evelina. (2003). Exploring the concept of integration in the basic education curriculum of the Philippines. *International Journal of Curriculum and Instruction, 5*(1), 65-75.

McLaren, Peter. (1998). *Life in schools: An introduction to critical pedagogy in the foundations of education.* New York: Longman.

McLaren, Peter. (2002). Marxist revolutionary praxis: A curriculum of transgression. *Journal of Critical Inquiry Into Curriculum and Instruction, 3*(3). 36-41.

Nieto, Sonia. (1992). *Affirming diversity: The sociological context of multicultural education.* White Plains, NY: Longman.

Schott, Ruth. (2004, April). *Jummauh* prayer at the Muslim Community Center. Paper presented in Multicultural Education, C&I 711, Wichita State University, Wichita, KS.

Shade, Barbara, J. R. (Ed.). (1989). *Culture, style, and the educative process.* Springfield, IL: Charles C. Thomas Publisher.

Sleeter, Christine E., & Carl A. Grant. (1999). *Making choices for multicultural education: Five approaches to race, class, and gender* (3rd ed.). Upper Saddle River, NJ: Merrill.

Simon, Roger I. (2000). The paradoxical practice of *zakhor*: Memories of "What has never been my fault or my deed." In Roger I. Simon, Sharon Rosenberg, & Claudia Eppert (Eds.), *Between hope and despair: Pedagogy and remembrance of historical trauma* (pp. 9- 25). Lanham, MD: Rowman & Littlefield Publishers.

Smith, G. Pritchy. (1998). *Common sense about uncommon knowledge: The knowledge bases for diversity.* Washington, DC: American Association of Colleges for Teacher Education.

Smith, G. Pritchy. (2000). Relationships among Knowledge Bases for Diversity in Teacher Education: Critical Pedagogy, Critical Inquiry, and Story. *Journal of Critical Inquiry Into Curriculum and Instruction, 2*(3), 26-30.

Smith, G. Pritchy. (2004, April 2). *Speaking Out On Assessment of Multicultural Competences and Outcomes: Some Cautions.* Keynote address presented at the National Conference on Assessment of Multicultural/Diversity Outcomes, Kansas City, MO.

Spring, Joel. (2000). *The intersection of cultures: Multicultural education in the United States and the global economy* (2nd ed.). Boston: McGraw Hill.

Spring, Joel. (2004). *Deculturalization and the struggle for equality: A brief history of the education of dominated cultures in the United States* (4th ed.). Boston: McGraw Hill.

Tabachnik, B. R., & Zeichner, K. M. (1991). Reflections on reflective teaching. In K. M. Zeichner & B.R. Tabachnik (Eds.), *Issues and practices in inquiry-oriented teacher education* (pp. 1-21). London: The Falmer Press.

Tobin, Joseph J., David Y. Wu, Dana H. Davidson. (1989). *Preschool in three cultures: Japan, China, and the United States.* New York: Yale University Press.

Townsend, T., P. Clarke, & M. Ainscow. (1999). *Third millennium schools: A world of difference in effectiveness and improvement.* The Netherlands: Swets & Zeitlinger.

Whitson, Don. (2004, February 22 & April 5). *Physical and spiritual food at the Bu'u-Quang Buddhist Temple.* Paper presented in Multicultural Education, C&I 711, Wichita State University, Wichita, KS.

Whitson, Don. (2004, April). *Surface and deep culture elements.* Exhibit and paper presented in Multicultural Education, C&I 711, Wichita State University, Wichita, KS.

Wichita State University College of Education. (2004). *Introduction to diversity: Guide to Core I, CI 311*. Wichita, KS: Author.

Zeichner, Kenneth M. (1996). Teachers as reflective practitioners and the democratization of school reform. In K.M. Zeichner, S. Melnick, & M. L. Gomez (Eds.), *Currents of reform in pre-service teacher education*. New York: Teachers College Press.

CHAPTER FIVE

Globalizing Curriculum and Instruction by Encouraging a Breaking Away from Hegemonic Discourse

Peter J. Heffernan
University of Lethbridge

"It's like being in love: you say, this is the material with which I want to spend my time." – *Alistair MacLeod* (Canadian novelist and short story writer)

INTRODUCTION

In its mission statement, the WCCI includes the words: "[The] WCCI is a transnational organization committed to advancing the achievement of a just and peaceful world community." And in the preamble to its constitution, the WCCI states:

> "As educators in the world community, we have responsibility to ensure that education contributes to the promotion of equity, peace and the universal realization of human rights. To this end, [we] . . . should strive to facilitate in every person the development of 1) a comprehensive sense of respect – of self, others and the environment and 2) the capacity to participate at all levels of world society from local to global."

We also read in the WCCI constitution that it has as its purposes "to stimulate and facilitate collaboration on cross-cultural and transnational endeavors . . ., [to] encourage more humane, tolerant, and peaceful approaches for ecological sustainability and global unity through diversity, . . . [and] to employ education as a vehicle for the promotion and realization of human rights."

These are lofty, worthy, ideals. I read and interpret them from the perspective of a bilingual, intercultural educator. And from that perspective, I can see that they lean towards valuing diversity and away from the promotion of hegemony of any kind.

This paper revisits these ideals and invites self-critical analysis of our academic research and publishing and other forms of scholarly dissemination as curriculum researchers and leaders, engaging with one another as we are in the context of the WCCI. It invites us to reflect on strategies to counter the twin phenomena of hegemony and its natural sidekick — "centrism" in any of its forms, whether they be egocentrism, ethnocentrism, Anglocentrism, and so forth. I contend that such reflection should begin in academics' own house first and in looking at our daily situations and practices, so as to avoid the well-known problem of assigning blame for their perpetuity on others, of assuming as an underlying premise of our work that egocentrism, ethnocentrism, Anglocentrism and such are localized elsewhere. On this, Van Dijk (1994c: 275) has written: "Racism, ethnocentrism, anti-Semitism and nationalism are not limited to the realms of politics, the media, employment or housing, nor to the minds and practices of the less-educated, the arch-conservatives or the bigots. In many, sometimes subtle, forms these systems of dominance and inequality may be expressed and enacted anywhere in society, not least among the elites. Also in academia."

This writer has tackled the problem elsewhere (Heffernan, 1995; 2002; 2003) and continues to do so in his ongoing research on Anglocentrism in education, publishing and dissemination of research work. This research is axiological, aligned with a socio-political, action-research paradigm in the tradition of such individuals as Paulston (1980), Martel (1999) and Skutnabb-Kangas (2000) and with the theoretical work of proponents of critical pedagogy (e.g., Pennycook, 1990), for whom reflexivity is the watchword. Only a summary overview of the findings will be reported directly here.

ANGLOCENTRISM AND THE HEGEMONY OF ENGLISH-LANGUAGE DISCOURSE

Linguists report that an estimated 80 percent to 90 percent of papers in scientific journals are written in English, up from 60 percent in the 1980s (Montgomery, in *Associated Press*, 2004:2). One hears those numbers routinely relative to publication and other forms of dissemination of research in many disciplines, including Education. For me, a second language and intercultural educator, it seems logical, however to think that at last in my field of curricular specialization, even when recognizing that English is the most taught second language in the world today, publication and other dissemination patterns might differ from this broader norm, perhaps even significantly.

To determine this, I have examined the language-of-publication and the language-of-referential-discourse patterns in a representative sample of second language reviews for significant publication periods over the past decade to decade and a half. This systematic review for which the methodology is discussed in detail in Heffernan (2003), has unearthed startling findings and a challenge for the field.

THE RESULTS

Tables 1-3 present a summary of this research project's early results of the study of language choice in Canadian publications: the *Canadian Modern Language Review* (CMLR*), NOTOS: Journal of the Intercultural and Second Language Council,* and the *Journal of the Canadian Association of Applied Linguists* (a more detailed presentation, analysis and interpretation of these results can be found in Heffernan, 2002).

Table 1. Language of Publication of Articles in the CMLR, NOTOS and the Journal of the CAAL

Journal and Years Analyzed	Total Articles	Articles in English	Articles in French	Articles in Languages other than English and French
CMLR 1990-1999	304	219 (72.0%)	85 (28.0%)	0 (0%)
Notos 1999-2002	33	30 (90.9%)	2 (6.1%)	1 (3.0%) ·
Journal of CAAL 1994-2001	79	31 (39.2%)	48 (60.8%)	0 (0%)

Table 2. Language of Bibliographical References in Articles Published in English in the CMLR, NOTOS, and the Journal of the CAAL

Journal and Years Analysed	Bibliographical References in English	Bibliographical References in French	Bibliographical References in Languages other than English and French
CMLR 1990-1999	5,885 (92.6%)	391 (6.2%)	78 (1.2%)
NOTOS 1999-2002	223 (91.0%)	1 (0.40%)	21 (8.6%)
Journal of CAAL 1994-2001	818 (93.8%)	51 (5.8%)	3 (0.4%)

Table 3. Language of Bibliographical References in Articles Published in French in the CMLR, NOTOS, and the Journal of the CAAL

Journal and Years Analysed	Bibliographical References in English	Bibliographical References in French	Bibliographical References in Languages other than English and French
CMLR 1990-1999	1,596 (63.2%)	921 (36.5%)	7 (0.30%)
NOTOS 1999-2002	18 (72%)	7 (28%)	0 (0%)
Journal of CAAL 1994-2001	568 (50%)	562 (49.5%)	5 (0.50%)

With the exception of the *Journal of the CAAL*, there is a net tendency towards publication of articles in English, even though the audience of all three journals is predominantly teachers of languages other than English, especially French. It is noted too that the referential discourse in English-language articles is skewed dramatically towards other English-language scholarship, while in the French-language articles this is more balanced, indeed more attuned with the reality of intellectual and cultural diversity in Canadian and world scholarship. This reading of the findings was corroborated by Wright, one of the extremely few Anglo-Canadian academics teaching and conducting research in a French-Canadian university, who wrote: "When it comes to research, French-language universities have an edge because they have reference works in both languages. Researchers are exposed to a variety of ideas, whereas in English Canada, the Anglo-Saxon tradition is dominant "(cited in Trudeau-Reeves, 2004).

The following tables 4-6 present a summary of my related findings with respect to three specialist international publications: the *International Review of Applied Linguistics in Language Teaching* (IRAL), *Language Learning: A Journal of Research in Language Studies* (L.L.), and *Foreign Language Annals* (again, a more comprehensive review of these results can be found in Heffernan, 2003).

Table 4. Language of Publication of Articles in IRAL, Language Learning and Foreign Language Annals

Journal and Years Analyzed	Total Articles	Articles in English	Articles in French	Articles in Languages other than English and French
IRAL 1990-1994	50	48 (96.0%)	2 (4.0%)	0 (0%)
L.L. 1995-2002	78	78 (100%)	0 (0%)	0 (0%)
F L Annals 2000-2002	120	120 (100%)	0 (0%)	0 (0%)

Table 5. Language of Bibliographical References in Articles Published in English in IRAL, Language Learning and Foreign Language Annals

Journal and Years Analyzed	Bibliographical References to English Publications	Bibliographical References to French Publications	Bibliographical References in Languages other than English and French
IRAL 1990-1994	1.441 (90.1%)	70 (4.4%)	80 (5.5%)
L.L. 1995-2002	4,280 (98.2%)	29 (0.70%)	50 (1.1%)
F L Annals 2000-2002	3.375 (96.8%)	45 (1.3%)	68 (1.9%)

Table 6. Language of Bibliographical References in Articles Published in French in IRAL, Language Learning and Foreign Language Annals

Journal and Years Analyzed	Bibliographical References to English Publications	Bibliographical References to French Publications	Bibliographical References in Languages other than English and French
IRAL 1990-1994	17 (50%)	17 (50%)	0 (0%)
L.L. 1995-2002	N/A	N/A	N/A
F L Annals 2000-2002	N/A	N/A	N/A

The reported results, with respect to special Canadian second language publications is more evidence of English language publications even though the target audience of these reviews includes a majority of teachers of languages other than English. Almost 100% of the articles published in these reviews are published in English; the scholarship referred to tangentially therein is almost exclusively other English-language scholarship; and the very limited publication of two articles in a language other than English, French in both cases, incorporates quite strikingly more balanced, representative, diversity-valuing referential discourse.

Now, it will be argued that English is the 'lingua franca' of academic discourse. Indeed, am I not being like the doddering fool out of touch with reality ensconced in my Ivory Tower or like the crazed dog barking up a wrong tree? As a researcher and academic, I did ponder these points and questions (which, in fact, have been raised). And at the end of this reflection, I decided to persist and analyze also the related patterns in specialist publications with language-specific audiences for whom the specific languages are languages other than English.

Tables 7-9 which follow present a summary of my findings for this research in two representative language-specific publications with wide subscription bases: the *French Review* and *Hispania*, which target French and Spanish/Portuguese and educators, respectively.

Table 7. Language of Publication of Articles on Pedagogy in the French Review and Hispania

Journal and Years Analyzed	Total Articles	Articles in English	Articles in French	Articles in Spanish/ Portuguese
French Review 2000-2002	45	40 (88.9%)	5 (11.1%)	N/A
Hispania 2000-2002	31	25 (80.6%)	N/A	4 / 2 (12.9%/(6.5%)

Table 8. Language of Bibliographical References in Articles Published in English in the French Review and Hispania

Journal and Years Analyzed	Biblio – References to Publications in English	Biblio – References to Publications in French	Biblio. – References to Publications in Spanish/ Portuguese	Biblio. - References to Publications in other Languages
French Review 2000-2002	663 (80.9%)	154 (18.8%)	-	3 (0.30%)
Hispania 2000-2002	307 (89.2%)	-	37 (10.8%)	0 (0%)

Table 9. Language of Bibliographical References in Articles Published in French and in Spanish or Portuguese in the French Review and Hispania

Journal and Years Analyzed	Biblio. - References to Publications in English	Biblio. - References to Publications in French	Biblio. - References to Publications in Spanish/ Portuguese	Biblio. - References to Publications in other Languages
French Review 2000-2002	69 (38.1%)	108 (59.7%)	-	4 (2.2%)
Hispania 2000-2002	85 (51.8%)	-	75 (45.7%)	4 (2.5%)

In the language-specific reviews with language-specific audiences whose language of concern is a language other than English, paradoxically (see Postovsky, 1975, Edge, 1996 and Frantz, 1996) the majority of articles are still published in English. Additionally, the pattern of respect for linguistic, cultural and intellectual diversity in the referential scholarly discourse holds: those articles published in English in both the *French Review* and *Hispania*, the high majority of articles in both instances, refer overwhelmingly to other English-language scholarly works; those articles published in French, Spanish or Portuguese refer in a much more balanced representative way to the diversity of intellectual discourse in those languages, in English and in other languages.

What is any curriculum and instruction leader, particularly one who is also a specialist in second language/intercultural education to make of all of this? Many academics will simply suggest, in their best North American vernacular: "Get with the program, buddy." Or, if the primary objective is scientific discovery which is purportedly ideologically neutral, with respect to the language of research dissemination and of referential discourse: "What's the difference what language is used?" Even some academics sensitive to bilingualism and multiculturalism and who are proficient themselves in at least two languages (e.g., Wright, cited in Trudeau-Reeves, 2004: 19) bristle when people attribute general intellectual differences of opinion arising periodically between English- and French-Canadians, for example, to their differing backgrounds. This researcher, on all of these positions, begs to differ. Clearly, as he has found in Heffernan (1995), the language of publication and of referential discourse makes all the difference. This is so because language modifies curriculum and textbook writers' as well as researchers' cultural prisms such that they are in fact enabled, indeed empowered, to adjust perspective, uncover political and ideological biases, and unlock collective memories and values cherished in one language/culture and often literally written off in another.

INTERPRETATION AND DISCUSSION

In my research, I have come across no other even relatively basic quantitative studies such as mine, focused particularly on the language of academic discourse in applied linguistic journals. Even well-intentioned writers, expressing personal opinion or reporting on qualitative work in which they have engaged, appear to be misled. For example, Van Dijk's (1998: 435) wish to "make an effort to go beyond the monolingual hegemony of the English language in academic publishing, by making use of discourse data and scholarly literature from various languages, countries and academic traditions" is tempered by other observations he has made. "We have taken for granted that English is the dominant academic language of our age . . . . There may be occasional expressions of discontent with this kind of cultural imperialism but in practice and forced by circumstances, even the most severe critics of this situation also write in English — at least if they want to be heard all over the world" (Van Dijk, 1997: 291), for which, in way of examples, he cites Tove Skutnabb-Kangas and Lees Hamelink.

In way of reaction, Schmitz (2000: 283), while acknowledging that "most international journals" are written and published in English, adds: "But the adverb 'most' must not lead us into believing that the few that do publish in languages other than English are not important. A good example of a scholarly periodical that accepts articles in English, French or German is the *International Review of Applied Linguistics in Language Teaching* (IRAL)." Yet, Schmitz too has no quantitative data on this or any other applied linguistic journals' actual practice.

Likewise Flowerdew, who conducted interviews between 1996 and 1999 with eleven journal editors of leading international journals in applied linguistics, reports: "For those journals that were not limited to publishing papers on the English language, the non-native speakers' (NNS) contribution was seen as vital in providing research into languages other than English" and "60-70 percent are about other languages" (2001: 143). Yet, in the article, Flowerdew does not include the interview protocol used nor does he provide any quantitative data relative to NNS contributions with which to compare the editors' self-reporting perceptions of their publications' practices, nor indeed does he define the term, NNS, which is fundamental in his study. His research is related in theoretical terms to work in the last couple of decades on issues of power relationships, differential access and the social construction of knowledge in applied linguistics and in scholarly discourse generally, dealing with the participation or not of whom (and in what language) in the academic conversation and dealing with such notions as "the centre" and "the periphery." However, like most applied linguistic researchers, he essentially ignores the issue of the language of publication of articles and of their related referential discourse, thereby apparently inadvertently buying into Anglo-dominance, if not Anglo-exclusivity, in publishing. As well, in his treatment of the notions of "the centre" and "the periphery" (they are not his), he is oddly acritical regarding this unusual dichotomy.

It is not this researcher's intent to elongate this unduly nor does he pretend he is able to articulate as eloquently as the original authors the passion of the debate he has discovered on this issue (which, in any case, he has reviewed elsewhere). For WCCI readers intrigued by and wishing to explore the issue further, suffice it to mention, along with these studies already cited above, a sample of the related works of Ammon et al. (2001), Bahktin (1984), Bakewell (1992), Blanco (1981), Bourdieu and Macquart (2001), Calvé (1993), Crystal (2000), Davis (2001), Dorian (1981), Eggington (1995), Hansen (2001), Hedderich (1999), Mazrui and Mazrui (1992), Phillipson (1985), Phillipson and Skutnabb-Kangas (1985), Picard (2002), Robins and Ullenbeck (1996), Salskov-Iversen et al. (2000), Seljak (2003), Swaan (1998a, 1988b), The Lethbridge Herald (1998), Van Dijk (1994b, 1994c), Watson (1992), and Wells (1999).

Nor is it this researcher's intent in this paper to analyze in detail and interpret all of the results appearing in the table presented earlier (this has been done already in Heffernan 2002, 2003). Rather, let us simply show that good intentions alone will not change practices respecting Anglo-exclusivity in research publication. Nor will publication policies and practices which apparently suppress rather than promote and celebrate diversity of linguistic and cultural expression.

In way of examples, how does one explain the apparent disconnect between the *CMLR*'s stated mission and editorial goals and its practice? The *CMLR* mission statement (Board of Directors, *CMLR*, 1995: 4-5) reads: "The Canadian Modern Language Review has evolved . . . to a Canada-wide bilingual, refereed scholarly publication of national scope and international repute" and lists as one of its distinctive features "regular publication of a substantial number of articles in each of English and French, as well as articles written in other languages." Yet, this review did not publish one article in the decade of practice studied (Table 1) in a language other than English or French, with almost 75 percent of its articles published in English, though the majority of its readers teach French and many also teach other languages.

In the other two Canadian publications studied, *NOTOS* has largely mirrored the *CMLR*'s practices in this vein. Only the *Journal of the CAAL* has recognized it's principally French-teaching leadership and published more in accord with that linguistically. This is in keeping with its publication policy to include "a variety of articles in French and English," which appears in its "Guidelines for Authors of Articles" in each issue.

The international journals are more problematic in this regard. Both *Language Learning* and *Foreign Language Annals* are silent in their authors' guidelines and mission statements about language of publication. *IRAL*, based in Europe, states specifically (on the inside front cover of each issue) that "The languages of publication are English, French and German," though "non-native speakers are expected to have their manuscript checked by a native speaker" as "papers in faculty English, French or German will be rejected." The proviso-like nature of this invitation appears to work as intended. Notwithstanding *IRAL's* statement, like its two other international counterparts studied, it also publishes almost 100 percent of its articles in English.

Both journals with a language-specific focus, the *French Review* and *Hispania*, include statements about language of publication policy. In the case of the French review, it reads: "Contributions may be in English or French, but contributors are very earnestly urged [sic] to use the language in which they can write more effectively . . . Perfect legibility is essential, especially with articles or quotes in French. The typesetter is not expected to know foreign languages . . ." (appearing in the "Guide for Authors" in each issue). This invitation is unusual, reminiscent in other contexts of the back-handed compliment. It is redolent of a kind of professional myopia, sociolinguistic pathology and extremist pragmatism of the sort where the tail wags the dog. In way of result, as shown in Table 7, the *French Review* anomalously published almost 90 percent of its articles in English in the period reviewed. Its predominantly English-published articles (Table 8) mitigated this result somewhat with approximately 20 percent of their bibliographical references to languages other than English, mainly French. Its French-published articles' bibliographical lists (Table 9) reflected the kind of referential discourse balance characteristic of French-language articles, where applicable, published in all the journals reviewed in this project.

In the case of *Hispania,* the language of publication policy reads: "*Hispania* invites submission of original, unpublished articles . . . having to do with Spanish and Portuguese . . . Articles may be in Spanish, Portuguese or English; however we encourage authors to submit in Spanish and Portuguese" (appearing in the "Guide for Authors" in each issue). This invitation exhibits an altogether different tone and intent. It also garners significantly different results. The proportion of articles published in Spanish and Portuguese, as Table 7 shows, rises to almost 20 percent. More significantly, though, even if the 80 percent of articles in English continued here too in their referential discourse to be dominated by English biographical references (almost 90 percent, as Table 8 shows), the higher proportion of articles in Spanish and Portuguese in this review also showed a much more balanced English/Spanish/Portuguese referential discourse (Table 9) having been arrived at therein. This is not to suggest, however, that the review *Hispania* has achieved nirvana in this respect; vigilance and consciousness-raising will need to continue to be watchwords for its editors, contributors and readers too.

In way of analogy, as Canada's Commissioner of Official Languages Dyane Adams discovered, with a debate (Fallis 2004, Martin 2004, *National Post* 2004) which raged recently in one of Canada's self-described national newspapers, the *National Post*, she had been forced to take an editorial upbraiding for having had the temerity to make the sociolinguistically sound argument that, while the issue of English/French balance in the composition of the Canadian civil service has been addressed, the fact of francophones continuing to use English or feeling they have to use English mainly in designated bilingual workplaces remains to be addressed. Virtually any and all sociolinguistic research conducted over the past three to four decades dealing with power relationships between dominant and minority language speakers would contend she is on the right path and justified in her raising this concern.

FURTHER OBSERVATIONS AND CONCLUSIONS

There are limitations and ongoing directions of this research on which I have reported elsewhere (Heffernan, 2003). So, I state again that I will not unduly elongate this paper by going into these here. Rather, I will attempt now to connect the issues reported on in this study in quite specific ways to the WCCI, to this triennial conference, and to the theme guiding our reflections and which indeed is the raison d'être for our assembling here in Wollongong. Though my research focuses constructively and critically on language-of-publication policy and practices within a specific curricular field, the issues raised are pertinent to all curriculum and instruction leaders.

We are the World Council for Curriculum and Instruction. This conference's theme is: "Educating for a world view: Focus on globalizing curriculum and instruction." As well, I revisit our association's fundamental aims to "encourage more humane, tolerant, and peaceful approaches for ecological sustainability and global unity through diversity, . . . [and] to employ education as a vehicle for the promotion and realization of human rights," among which the UNESCO includes linguistic rights.

In its interpretation and actualization of the above, the WCCI might opt with some for a view that a policy of bilingualism or of multilingualism leads to a decline in so-called "cohesionism" (Jedwab, 2003) within society and within institutions. Proponents of this position might also argue that, "where multilingualism characterizes the bottom [sic] of the world's societies, monolingualism seems to be the rule at the top" (Van Dijk, 1997: 292). Yet, as Watson (1992) points out, no causal relationship has been shown between linguistic diversity and economic development, though such a link is indeed generally made between illiteracy and underdevelopment and non-literacy languages and poor economic development. And it does seem that non-literary languages are doomed to remain so if one or only a few languages dominate the world's publications scene. All the same, yet others will argue that English dominance is a legacy of history and of the current global politico-economic context and that we throw in the towel. In this vein, Singh (1998: 301) states: "It is quixotic on the part of academics to even think of resisting these influences. It would also be an ostrich policy to ignore the reality of British/American English being the dominant academic language."

In my mind, this sort of thinking represents a kind of brow-beating into so-called "manufactured consent." To wit, it misses the point or acts in the way of a rhetorical 'reductio ad absurdum.'

To argue or warn against Anglocentrism, if not Anglo-exclusivity, in publications and in other forms of dissemination of research results is not simply idealistic posturing of the linguistic Greenpeace sort. To proponents of respect for linguistic diversity in education, Anglocentrism whether triumphalist or unconscious is of as much concern as is, for example, the curricular perpetuation of exclusively patriarchal values and of androcentric behaviors and outlooks in children, which has been raised so effectively as a fundamental issue by feminist scholars (Seljak, 2003). Similarly, scholars concerned with racial equity argue that education's bigger hidden curriculum presents Eurocentric or so-called "white" values – and easy of knowing and interpreting the world – as normative or superior to those of other cultures (Banks, 1995).

Like these other critical scholars, proponents of linguistic diversity also question, for instance, "the use of English terms such as 'tribe,' 'primitive,' 'animism,' 'underdevelopment,' 'illiteracy' – which often refers to inability to read in the Latin script – and others which give the overall impression of a 'civilized' North and a less than civilized South" (Mazrui and Mazrui, 1992: 96). In a broader examination of the issue, they view action such as the exclusion of scholarship in languages other than English as being tantamount to inferiorization and marginalization. As Van Dijk (1994a: 276) has stated: "There is one form of ethnocentrism that is often disregarded, also in more liberal or progressive academic circles, namely the nationalism, regionalism, provincialism, linguicism, if not parochialism, of the data and scholarly literature used and referred to in many academic books, journals and articles." In a sense, he has thereby reversed the equation. The inadequate or the willingly complicit torchbearers of Anglo-conformism in worldwide Academe and publishing industries, posturing as the ones with the upper hand or as the keepers of the one-right-linguistic-way are exposed for their intended or unconscious narrowness of vision and purpose; the downtrodden keepers of secrets and spreaders of messages in the world's diversity of languages are implicitly recognized for their cosmopolitanism, their sophistication, their balance, their breadth of perspective. Indeed, ignoring theories, methods, data and results of scholars working outside the English-speaking triumvirate of Anglo-Irish, Canado-American and Australasian traditions is "a form of scholarly and cultural chauvinism which at the very least diminishes the relevance and generality of our findings, and in any case contributes to the reproduction [à la Bourdieu] of prevailing forms of cultural and academic hegemony" (Van Dijk, 1994a: 276).

Do we as curriculum and instruction leaders from around the world let the tail wag the dog? Does accepting that English is an academic 'lingua franca' preclude our also actively endeavoring to include reference to scholarship in other languages emanating from other cultural traditions? Does recognizing the need to accommodate those who read only in English mean catering exclusively to this want of linguistic development in such individuals? Does intellectual laziness and lack of curiosity about other linguistic and cultural traditions' work and thinking trump our need for far-reaching searching for truth and understanding? Do we simply acquiesce robotically to the market and the presumed forces which define it and which apparently dictate language of publication? Do we do any or all of these things or do we instead adopt the old-fashioned criticism of solidarity, make it work among us as curriculum and instruction leaders from all parts of the world, and consciously take on the challenge of promoting linguistic diversity bringing it to the centre of our values as the WCCI?

The risk is not too great. Scholars worldwide and coming from many traditions have already debunked purported "research" alleging inferiority attributed to Blacks, to Aboriginals and to women, among others. Changing linguistic atti-

tudes and practices relative to academic scholarship and curriculum writing is
also possible, certainly desirable, and worth the effort.

Working to "encourage more humane, tolerant and peaceful approaches for
ecological sustainability and global unity through diversity" need not be only
wishful thinking linguistically. As pointed out in Skutnabb-Kangas's (2000)
voluminous tome on this topic, societies (and, by extension, we might also suggest associations) which overtly value and protect biodiversity logically and
consistently also overtly value, protect and promote human diversity in all its
forms – including its most fundamental linguistic form.

Some practical suggestions come to mind for the WCCI. Reserve space in
WCCI journal publications for at least one or two article(s) per issue in some of
the languages of wide access. Likewise, publish occasionally a translation in
English of an article originally submitted and published in a language other than
English. Include brief summaries in three or four languages of wide access of
articles published in English and in other languages. Include reviews of books
published in languages other than English by specialists who know these languages in order to introduce WCCI readers tangentially to scholarship and theo-
rizing anchored in these linguistic/cultural traditions. Develop language-specific
networks within the WCCI. Include language-specific sections in languages of
wide access for papers presented at WCCI conferences. No snub is intended.
This paper is reflective, critical and conscious-raising. With that stated, avoid
admonitions in future calls for papers for WCCI conferences, which read (high-
lighted in bold letters, which was the case for the 2004 triennial conference:
"ALL PAPERS ARE TO BE SUBMITTED IN ENGLISH."

It is this paper's intent to make friends, to widen the WCCI network, and to
make it more inclusive, linguistically and otherwise. It invites WCCI members
and readers to reflect openly and to avoid presupposing 'accusation' that is
deemed to be too political or rhetorical rather than scientific. As scholars such as
Flyvbjerg (2002) and Jensen (2003), not to mention the inimitable and indomi-
table Chomsky, have noted, effective intervention by outspoken seekers of "best
practices" and of equity in the social world, and one might even say more particularly in the world of scholars, is rife with danger, a delicate matter, but still
worth the doing.

Van Dijk's (1994c: 436) thinking about the role of critical analysis of discourse practices warrants repeating here:

> "It is one (necessary) task to study pronouns, discourse coherence, conversa-
> tional strategies or politeness phenomena, among a multitude of other struc-
> tures and functions of text and talk. It is a more complex and a more demanding
> task to study these properties of 'text' in relation to 'context,' that is, as a con-
> dition or function of cognitive, social, cultural and political structures and proc-
> esses. However, it is a daunting, but truly multidisciplinary, challenge to finally
> examine how this 'text In context' contributes to the reproduction and demise
> of such complex structures as the systems of social domination. Those who pull
> off that job adequately are approaching the ultimate scholarly aim, namely not
> only of understanding the world . . . but also of changing it."

I conclude where I began. In my life and in my professional world, my love is languages because of the world rich in diversity to which they have exposed me. Like me, I am sure any and all who read this would take cause with our love being neglected, overlooked, shunted to the side, treated shabbily. By many estimates, the world's 6,500 languages existing today will be reduced to a few hundred by 2100. Like a lover, my heart rends at the thought of these things. And to those who might ask me: "But is it a happy place you inhabit?", I respond with the nurturing cradling of the Canadian poet and novelist MacLeod discussing in his case his relationship to his literary work: "It's like being in love: you say, this is the material with which I want to spend my time" (*Maclean's*, 2003:41).

REFERENCES

Ammon, U., K. J. Mattheier and P. H. Nelde. Lingua francas in Europe – except English. *Sociolinguistica: International Yearbook of European Sociolinguistics 15*. Tübingen: Max Niemeyer Verlag, 2001.

Associated Press. English Won't Dominate as World Language. *MSNBC News*, February 26, 2004: 1-3.

Bahktin, M. *The Dialogic Imagination*. Austin, TX: University of Texas Press, 1984.

Bakewell, D. Publish in English or Perish? *Nature 356*. (1992): 648.

Banks, J. A. Multicultural Education: Historical Development, Dimensions and Practice. In J. A. Banks (Ed.) *Handbook of Research on Multicultural Education*. New York: MacMillan (1995): 3-24.

Blanco, G. M. Beyond the Bilingual Classroom: Increased Use of L1 in Professional Activities. *Focus: Thought-Provoking Papers in Bilingual Education*. Rosslyn, VA: National Clearinghouse for Bilingual Education, 1981.

Board of Directors, *Canadian Modern Language Review*. Mission Statement. *Canadian Modern Language Review* 52, no. 1 (1995): 4-6.

Bourdieu, P. and L. Wacquant. New Liberal Speak: Notes on the New Planetary Vulgate. *Radical Philosophy* 105 (2001: 2-5.

Calvé, P. Pour enseigner le français . . . en français. *La revue canadienne des langues vivantes* 50, no. 1 (1993): 15-29.

Crystal, D. *Language Death*. Cambridge: Cambridge University Press, 2000.

Davis, W. *Light at the Edge of the World: A Journey Through the Realm of Vanishing Cultures*. Toronto, ON: Douglas & McIntyre, 2001.

Dorian, N. *Language Death*. Philadelphia, PA: University of Pennsylvania Press, 1981.

Edge, J. Cross-Cultural Paradoxes in a Profession of Values. *TESOL Quarterly* 30, no. 1 (1996): 9-30.

Eggington, W. G. English: Everyone's Rock at the Centre of the World? *Journal of Asian Pacific Communication* 6 (1995): 139-151.

Fallis, R. Just Say 'Non.' *National Post*, Toronto, Ontario, Canada (April 5, 2004): A-11.

Flowerdew, J. Attitudes of Journal Editors to Nonnative Speakers' Contributions. *TESOL Quarterly*, 35, no. 1 (Spring 2001): 121-150.

Flyvbjerg, B. Making Social Science Matter: Why Social Inquiry Fails and How It Can Succeed Again. (Translated by Steven Sampson). Cambridge: Cambridge University Press, 2002.

Frantz, A. Seventeen Values of Foreign Language Study: *ADFL Bulletin* 28 (1996): 44-49.

Hansen, L. Language Attrition: The Face of the Start. N. M. McGroarty (Ed.) *Annual Review of Applied Linguistics* 21 (2001): 60-73.

Hedderich, N. When Cultures Clash: Views from the Professions. *Die Unterrichtspraxis* 32, no. 2 (1999): 159-164.

Heffernan, P. J. English-Language Hegemony in the Language of Publication and the Referential Discourse of Applied Linguists. Proceedings of the 21st World Congress of the Fédération internationale des professeurs de langues vivantes. Johannesburg, South Africa: FIPLV, 2003 (forthcoming).

Heffernan, P. J. Like a Junior High Dance: How do English- and French-Language Applied Linguists Strut their Stuff, Together or Apart? *NOTOS: Journal of the Intercultural and Second Languages Council* 3, no. 2 (2002): 12-20.

Heffernan, Peter J. (1995). Les contenus culturels dans l'enseignement des langues dans les cours de langue seconde et maternelle destinés aux élèves anglophones et francophones canadiens. Ph.D. diss., Québec, Université Laval, 1995 (2 tomes).

Jedwab, J. Social Confusion: The Decline of 'Cohesionism' in Canada and its Lessons for the Study of Citizenship. *Canadian Diversity: A Publication of the Association for Canadian Studies* 2, no. 1 (2003): 81-84.

Jensen, R. *Writing Dissent: Taking Radical Ideas from the Margins to the Mainstream.* New York: Peter Lang, 2003.

MacLeans. It's Like Being in Love: One of the World's Great Writers Reflects on His Art – And His Life. *Macleans* (March 24, 2003): 40-41.

Martel, A. Culturally Coloured Didactics: The Sociopolitical at the Heart of Second/Foreign Language Teaching in Francophone Geolinguistic Spaces. *Instructional Science: An International Journal of Learning and Cognition* 27, nos. 1-2 (1999): 73-96.

Martin, D. Dyane Adam's Anti-Anglo Crusade. *National Post*, Toronto, Ontario, Canada (March 30, 2004): A-2.

Mazrui, A. M. and A. A. Mazrui. Language in a Multicultural Context: The African Experience. *Language and Education: An International Journal* 6, nos. 2, 3 and 4 (1992): 83-98.

National Post Editorial. Pardon Our French. Toronto, Ontario, Canada (March 31, 2004): A-15.

Paulston, C. B. *Bilingual Education: Theories and Issues.* Rawley, MA: Newbury House, 1980.

Pennycook, A. Critical Pedagogy and Second Language Education. *System 18* (1990): 303-314.

Phillipson, R. and T. Skutnabb-Kangas. Applied Linguists as Agents of Wider Colonization: The Gospel of International English. In J. Pleines (Ed.) *Sprachenkonkurrenz und gesellschaftliche Planung: das Erbe des Kolonialismus Osnabrücker beiträge zur Sprachtheorie* 31 (1985): 159-179.

Phillipson, R. *Linguistic Imperialism.* Oxford: Oxford University Press, 1992.

Picard, J.-L. Politiques linguistiques dans les universités du Québec. *Affaires universitaires* (décembre 2002): 28.

Postovsky, V. A. On Paradoxes in Foreign Language Teaching. *Modern Language Journal* 59 (1975): 1-2.

Robins, R. H. and M. Uhlenbeck (Eds.). *Endangered Languages.* New York: St. Martin's Press, 1996.

Salskov-Iverson, D., H. Hansen and S. Bislev. Governmentality, Globalization and Local Practice: Transformations of Hegemonic Discourse. *Alternatives* 25 (2000): 183-222.

Schmitz, J. R. Discourse and Society Forum: Offsetting the Exclusive Use of English in International Journals. *Discourse and Society II,* no. 2 (2000): 283-285.

Seljak, D. Values: The Hidden Curriculum in Education. *Canadian Diversity: A Publication of the Association for Canadian Studies* 2, no. 1 (2003): 64-66.

Skutnabb-Kangas, T. *Linguistic Genocide in Education: Or Worldwide Diversity and Human Rights?* Mahwah, New Jersey: Erlbaum, 2000.

Swaan, A. de. A Political Sociology of the World Language System (1): The Dynamics of Language Spread. *Language Problems and Language Planning* 22, no. 1 (1998a): 63-75.

Swaan, A. de. A Political Sociology of the World Language System (2): The Unequal Exchange of Texts. *Language Problems and Language Planning* 22, no. 2 (1998b): 109-128.

The Lethbridge Herald. Afrikaans Language Fights for Survival in New South Africa. Lethbridge, AB: *The Lethbridge Herald* (July 2, 1998): A-2.

Trudeau-Reeves, F. Le savoir sans frontieres: Des scientifiques apprennent le fraçais dans les universités québécoises. *Affaires universitaires* 45, no. 3 (mars 2004): 17-19.

Van Dijk, T. A. Academic Nationalism. *Discourse and Society 5,* no. 3 (1994a): pp. 275-276.

Van Dijk, T. A. Critical Discourse Analysis. *Discourse and Society* 5, no. 4 (1994c): 435-436.

Van Dijk, T. A. Discourse Analysis as Social Analysis. *Discourse and Society* 5, no. 2 (1994b): 163-164.

Van Dijk, T. A. Discourse Studies. *Discourse and Society 9,* no. 4 (1998): 435-436.

Van Dijk, T. A. The Imperialism of English. *Discourse and Society 8,* no. 3 (1997): 291-292.

Watson, K. Language, Education and Political Power: Some Reflections on North-South Relationships. *Language and Education: An International Journal* 6, nos. 2, 3 and 4 (1992): 99-121.

Wells, G. *Dialogic Inquiry: Towards a Sociocultural Practice and Theory of Education.* Cambridge: Cambridge University Press, 1999.

CHAPTER SIX

Humanizing Global Technology

Judith A. Johnson
Yamaguchi University, Japan

INTRODUCTION

In this current period of rapid transition, there is chaos at all levels of society. However, this is not necessarily a totally negative condition. If we apply to society the chaos theory that has been useful to new discoveries in science and technology, we can expect new advancements in patterns of human organization. In fact, we all can and should take an active part in achieving this social evolution. The first step is being cognizant of the two social dynamics at work in the world: disintegration and integration. The second step is taking positive action towards furthering integration.

Disintegration is defined as the inability of old social structures and systems of thought to respond to the processes of accelerated change and growing global crisis that is happening. Integration is the individual and collective action that expresses a growing consciousness of the need for unity in all areas of life, and an awareness that this is what is needed for this age. Although these processes may at first glance seem to oppose each other, they are actually working in tandem. The essential and positive function of disintegration is to destroy the barriers that have separated human beings from each other and the rest of nature. Integration is essential to bringing unity, justice and well-being to all peoples and future generations (Anello & Barstow Hernández, 1996).

These parallel processes are influencing individual behavior and all aspects of human activity. As new knowledge, and new ways of understanding knowledge are being discovered, inappropriate and misdirected beliefs, systems and technology (which are often harmful) are being replaced. Technology affects the life of every human being, therefore, it is of utmost importance that the creators of technology are quickly involved in the rejuvenating process of integration. Assisting engineers and scientists to acquire a consciousness of the need for unity in all areas of life, will better enable them to develop and use technology in ways that will benefit all of humanity, and the world and universe we inhabit.

There are two aspects of development. Misdirected economic and industrial development trends have resulted in a global increase in poverty, violence, alienation, corruption, hopelessness and lack of high morals. On the other hand, tremendous advances in science, technology and the re-structuring of social agencies and organizations have made it possible for the masses to have greater access to knowledge, and use it to develop their capacities and improve their living conditions. Below, Bushrui (2003) gives a clear outline of the steps development must follow in order to achieve global peace and prosperity.

"The construction of a peaceful global society is thus a progressive task: first, justice is universally established; second, the unity of the planet is realized; and finally, world peace reigns supreme. The global system for which humanity should strive must accordingly renounce all forms of exploitation of one group by another; its international trade must be conducted in a manner both free and fair; and it must accord to all—workers as well as managers and owners - a share in the prosperity created. The new global order should narrow the gap between rich and poor, and grant equal opportunities to all members of the human family; above all, it should insure equality between men and women."

In this age of technology and information explosion, it is evident that scientists and engineers—the creators of technology—have a key role in achieving global unity, justice and peace. This paper offers one way of preparing this group of professionals to 'humanize' technology by contributing to the construction of the global society envisioned by Bushrui.

COURSE RATIONALE

The engineering curriculum in Japanese universities is generally lacking in courses that relate to global affairs and ethics. Even rarer is a course that combines the study of both subjects. All countries, including Japan, are experiencing turmoil and an increasing number of people are becoming confused and isolated from society. Understanding the dynamics of society will help students cope with challenges in their personal lives, enable them to assist others, help them appreciate the positive aspects of human diversity, and give them a global vision for the planet. It will give students a foundation on which to discern ethical behavior at personal, local, national and global levels.

Students will begin to consider technology from the perspectives developed *and* developing nations, understanding the need for both high- and low-tech inventions that help people survive diseases, receive an education, and live healthy and productive lives. The key role of technology in human development is giving people increased, better, safer and more equitable lifestyle options. Such a course will provide students with the opportunity to contemplate what they can do as future engineers to contribute to the goal of environmentally sustainable global human development.

COURSE OUTCOMES

Taking into consideration, the overall educational needs of undergraduate engineering students studying at a Japanese university, the course is designed with the principal goals of acquiring: 1) knowledge about major global issues, 2) feelings of connectivity to the rest of the world, and 3) essential academic, professional and social skills. Specifically, the outcomes are for students to:

- Understand current global dynamics, and global needs
- Describe their connections with the rest of the world's peoples
- Share their vision for a world based on unity, justice (equity) and peace
- Use their critical and creative thinking skills
- Practice ethical thinking and behavior
- Identify and use positive social and communication skills
- Apply research and presentation skills

Procedure:

The class is conducted over a period of one 14-week semester, meeting once a week for 90 minutes. (See the Appendix for the Course Syllabus)

Step 1. The first three weeks are dedicated to laying the foundation for the course. Students gain an understanding of why the world is in its current state of disequilibrium and what is needed to bring it back to a more stable condition. Students are led to establish a personal sense of human connection both with the people around them *and* people whom they do not see. For example, the old computer a student discarded may connect her to people in Brazil who are drinking water that has been polluted by chemicals seeping from the nearby electronics dump site, where the computer was shipped. Students become aware of the fact that technology they use today, and will create in the future, impacts people and environments in virtually every part of the world.

Students analyze the current popular social development theory, which is based on economics and leads people to believe that human development is equivalent to the possession of the most and biggest of everything. They then compare this theory with a more constructive and inclusive theory that encourages a view of the planet as one unit, making ethical decisions that result in the improvement of the quality of life of all peoples and the preservation of the environment.

Students confirm the concept that human conditions can change only when all people are able to have more than one option regarding the quality of water they drink, or the knowledge they would like to acquire. This confirmation accomplished by understanding indicators of human development, identifying and discussing actual discrepancies in living conditions and determining the reasons for the differences. For example, in 2001, the HD indicator value for the world was 0.722. For high- and low-income nations it was 0.927 and 0.561, respectively. (UNDP, 2003) In economically developed countries, a middle- or high-school education is accessible, and even mandatory for all. However, in the rest

of the world, 325 million children (183 million are girls) are not in school. people in economically developed countries have a choice between toilet color,
style and even 'intelligent' functions, while a third of the world's population
(more than 2 billion people) is living without basic sanitation. While children in
wealthy nations have access to medicine and medical care, 11 million children
in poor countries die annually from preventable diseases. In weeks 4 to 12, the
expansion of this concept is carried out by exploring separate but related aspects
of human development as an entire class, through pair and small group activities.

Step 2. In the fourth week, based on similar interests, students form thematic
research groups of 4-5 members. Themes are all related to each other, to course
content that will be studied in weeks 4 to 12, and the engineering majors of the
students. Due to the time constraints of this course, themes are pre-determined
by the teacher. Groups may not research the same theme.

Step 3. From the fifth week, students study teacher-selected theme-related materials in class, and conduct research on their topics outside of class, concurrently.
They work collaboratively, using consultation skills to exchange ideas, plan and
conduct research in various areas related to human activity. All group members
are responsible for acquiring fundamental knowledge about the general research
theme. Then, based on that knowledge, select a specific topic related to the
theme for their individual research. The end product will be a cohesive group PP
presentation that will be assessed according to the guidelines distributed to the
students in week 4.

Students are encouraged and guided to use their critical and creative thinking skills to define problems and propose viable solutions. To learn consultation
skills and build group unity, students practice following consultation guidelines
which they are instructed to apply in their groups. (See Appendix)

During weeks 5 to 12, students' preparation for and participation in in-class
activities are evaluated by the teacher, weekly. Additionally, group progress on
out-of-class work is monitored by giving students deadlines for submitting assignments for review and comments by the teacher. Students first hand in a
group presentation outline which shows the topic for which each member is responsible. A second outline shows, in greater detail, how the individual plans to
organize his or her research data. The last written assignment that is handed in is
a detailed outline of the group presentation which contains the main points of
each student's report. This is used as a handout for classmates to help them follow and take notes during the presentations.

Students are frequently encouraged to make an appointment to ask questions about the course content, or to consult with the teacher on their research
projects. When possible, a few minutes of class time is set aside for this purpose.

Step 4. In week 13, students share their findings, solutions and opinions with the
rest of the class by means of a group oral report, supported by PP (Power Point).
Since each person speaks for only 3 to 5 minutes, they are not permitted to read

from notes. The presentation is a vehicle for students to express themselves clearly, logically and convincingly about topics of import to themselves and the world. While one group is making a presentation, the rest of the class is taking notes on the handout (outline of the presentation) prepared by the group.

After all of the presentations are over, students are free to walk around the room and ask other group members for information that they need to complete their outline notes and clarify their understanding of specific points.

Step 5. The written evaluation in week 14 covers the concepts studied in the course as well as important information from the oral group presentations in week 13. The use of books, notes or dictionaries is not permitted during the test.

DISCUSSION

The course described in this paper, is presently in progress therefore no final data will be available until July, 2004. This course differs from the pilot version (Global Issues) in that more emphasis is being placed on *affective* outcomes while the emphasis of the pilot course was on research and presentation skills. The procedure is the same and the content is similar in both courses. Therefore, questionnaire results from the pilot course will be discussed in this paper.

Generally, students in the pilot course performed well on the presentations. The information was relevant and well organized and the PP visuals enhanced the presentation. The presentation outline handouts were clearly written and facilitated students' note taking. The average individual score for the group Power Point presentation (which included 10 points awarded for the group's performance) was 44.2 /50. The lowest score was 29/50 points and the highest 48/50. The questionnaire and student responses can be seen in Figures 1and 2. The Evaluation Form is in the Appendix.

Pilot course students who said that they had learned something new or interesting (Question 1) wrote that they had learned: to think about the world's problems; how to give a presentation; how to make a PP presentation; and how to explain their ideas in English. Most answers referred to what they had learned about their particular topic. Reasons cited for not having learned anything new were that reading in English was difficult, and they were not able to translate from English to Japanese.

Global Issues Questionnaire

1. Did you learn something new or interesting?
                    Yes   No
   What?
2. Was making a Power Point show interesting?
                    Yes   No
   What?
   Why?
3. Did you like working in a group?
                    Yes   No
   Why?
4. Was this the first time for you to give

   a. a presentation in English? Yes No
   b. a PP presentation? Yes No

Figure 1: Pilot Course Questionnaire

Students' responses to their group learning projects were largely positive. Some of the positive replies to what was interesting about making a PP show and why making the show was interesting (Question 2) were: learning new information, making a presentation for the first time; talking to everybody; research; using the computer; using the Internet; understanding information researched by classmates; and learning information that will be useful after graduation when they begin working.

Those who answered negatively said that: they didn't know how to use the computer; they could not use PP; and making a presentation in English was difficult. The overall response to working in groups (Question 3) was positive. Sample comments by students who said they had liked working in groups were, "I didn't have to work alone; We can share opinions; I can work with my friends; I like cooperating with other people; Knowing others' ideas is interesting; Members can talk together and work faster; Discussing is fun; Group members are interesting; Friends help me (give and take); I could make friends with other people; Several people have several ideas; I can get a lot of information; The group is important; and I have responsibilities." The negative responses were, "Some people don't attend meetings; Some members don't work hard; Everyone has his own way, so I like to work alone; My ideas didn't match the other members'; and I don't like cooperation."

Seventy-five percent of the students said that this was their first experience in giving an oral presentation in English (Question 4a) and seventy-one percent said it was their first time to give a PP presentation (Question 4b).

CONCLUSION

From the questionnaire results and the caliber of students' PP presentations, it is clear that collaborative research projects are effective in helping students learn about the conditions of the world's inhabitants, and understand the relationship between technology and human development. Students use social, decision-making, problem-solving, creative and consultation skills, and practice responsible behavior. They expand their knowledge by sharing ideas, opinions, feelings and information. Students learn how to direct and carry out their own learning, organize the knowledge they acquire, and present it to others.

After the fourth week of the course, most students could begin to discuss among themselves topics such as human potential and capacities, the process of disintegration and integration, human development indicators and the technology needs of particular countries. They could brain-storm to find possible solutions to problems they had identified. All of the presentations emphasized the responsible use of technology, for the betterment of the world's peoples. The few negative student comments reflect a continuing need to help students acquire basic social, reading and computer skills.

APPENDIX

Student Handouts and Presentation Evaluation Form

Handout 1

Technology and Human Development Syllabus

Week	*Topic*
1	Review of Course Syllabus / Review of "Classroom English"
2	The Current State of the World / Moral Issues
3	Eco-Economy and Human Development
4	Technology for Human Development Part 1
5	Technology for Human Development Part 2
6	Technology for Human Development Part 3
7	Education
8	Global Hunger / Health Issues
9	Gender Equity
10	Environmental Issues
11	Economic Issues
12	Communication Issues
13	Oral Presentations
14	Written Evaluation

Handout 2

Research Assignment

1. Your assignment is to browse the Internet to look up information on your (1) group theme and (2) individual topic, organize the data.
2. Using the information, make a Power Point presentation (with handouts) to the class. Identify how you can contribute to this aspect your topic) of human development as an engineer.
3. Hand in an outline of your presentation.
4. Hand in a Research Log – a list of the information;
   title and URL of the main information used in your presentation.
   You must review a minimum of 6 sites.
5. Hand in the group Power Point show.

Assessment of the Presentation

You will be evaluated on your:
1. Presentation – (group and individual performance)
   — Preparation (Were you ready?)
   — Can you talk about the topic without reading notes?
   — Clarity and effectiveness of the presentation (Were you interesting, convincing and well-organized?)
   — Does the content show that you understand your topic and its importance to the use of technology in human development, well? Does it include relevant and accurate data?
   — Are the visual aids you use effective?
   — Are handouts organized well and easy to understand?
2. Outline of your presentation (may be the same as the handout)

Note:
Your presentation should include graphs, charts, pictures and other figures that will help the audience understand your topic and the data/information you are discussing. Use a specific case study or example, if you think it will help clarify the point you want to make.

Handout 3

Research Themes and Sample Topics

Environment
  Health
  Buildings/Housing
  Living Areas
  Human Needs
  Low-tech/Local Solutions
  Public Works
Communications
  Computers
  Satellites (Land-Sat)
  Microwave
  Natural Disasters
  Education
  Health
Eco-Economy
  Agriculture
  Energy
  Transportation
  Living Areas
  Natural Disasters
  Natural Resources

Hunger
  Genetically Modified Organisms
  Indigenous Foods
  Education
  Gender Equity
  Satellites (Land-Sat)
  Low-tech/Local Solutions
Health
  Environment
  Genetically Modified Organisms
  Gender Equity
  Education
  Medical Technology
  Communications

Note: These are sample topics. Whether you select one of the topics, above or choose another topic, you 1) should research the topic from different perspectives and then 2) decide on the information you think is most important to human development.

Handout 4

Consultation Guidelines

BASIC RULES
We must express our views with:
1. **Courtesy**
2. **Dignity**
3. **Care**
4. **Moderation**

THREE STEPS IN MAKING DECISIONS

1. UNDERSTAND THE PROBLEM / TASK
    A. Search the necessary information
    B. Bring together all information, opinions and principles, and make sure all members have the same understanding.

2. DECIDE ON A SOLUTION
    A. Everyone must share their ideas for a solution.
    B. Agree on a solution, unanimously if possible, but if not, the majority opinion is followed.

3. PUT THE DECISION INTO ACTION
    A. Everyone must wholeheartedly accept and follow the decision (no criticism in or out of the meeting once the decision is made!)
    B. Monitor the decision to insure that it is working properly.
    C. Even if a decision is wrong, if it was reached in unity and harmony, the group can learn from the error and work together to find a better solution.

Handout 5

Individual Presentation Outline

Name :_____

Student #_____

Class: _____

Day: _____ Period:_____

Group Theme: _____

Topic:_____

I.   Introduction/ Definition

II.   Main points of discussion

1.

2.

3.

4.

III. Conclusion / Suggestion

PowerPoint Presentation Evaluation Form

Name	Group 10	Prepared 10	Content 10	Organized 5	Interesting 5	Handout 5	PP Slides 5	To-tal 50

REFERENCES

Anello, E. & Barstow Hernández, J. (1996). *Moral Leadership*. Santa Cruz, Bolivia: Universidad Nur.

Brinton, D.M., Snow, M.A. & Wesche, M.B. (1989). *Content-based Second Language Instruction*. New York: Newbury House.

Bushrui, S. (2003). The Ethics of Globalization: A Bahá'í Perspective [On-line]. Available: http://www.onecountry.org/e151/global_ethics.htm . (Last accessed: 25 April, 2004)

Hutchinson, T. & Waters, Alan. (1987*). English for Specific Purposes, A Learning-centred Approach*. New York: Cambridge University Press.

Johnson, J. A. (2002). *Using Interactive Software for the Independent Study and The Need for Teacher Training*. Globalizing Yamaguchi University, First Steps: A Language Center for Functional Integrated Language Education.(pp. 47-54).Yamaguchi, Japan: Yamaguchi University Language Center Group.

Johnson, J. A. (2003, April). Education—The Journey to Moral Leadership and Moral Citizenship. *Centre for Development of Teaching and Learning Brief*, Vol. 6, No. 4, 10-12

Johnson, J. A. (2003, June) Teachers— Catalysts of Social Development. *Association for Bahá'í Studies-Japan Newsletter, Volume12, .10-12*

Johnson, R. T., & Johnson, D. W. (1986). 'Action Research: Cooperative Learning in the Science Classroom'. *Science and Children*. Vol. 24, .31–32

Panitz, T. (1996). *A Definition of Collaborative vs Cooperative Learning* [On-line]. Available: http://www.lgu.ac.uk/deliberations/collab.learning/panitz2.html (Last accessed: 25 April, 2004).

Panitz, T. (1997). 'Collaborative Versus Cooperative Learning: Comparing the Two Definitions Helps Understand the Nature of Interactive Learning'[On-line]. Available: http://home.capecod.net/~tpanitz/tedsarticles/coopdefinition.htm (Last accessed: 25April, 2004).

Skehan, P. (1998). *A Cognitive Approach to Language Learning*. Oxford: Oxford University Press.

Slavin, R.E. (1989). 'Research on Cooperative Learning: An International Perspective'. *Scandinavian Journal of Educational Research*. Vol. 33, No. 4, pp.231–243.

UNDP Website. Human Development Report 2003 [On-line]. Available: http://hdr.undp.org/reports/global/2003/ (Last accessed: 25April, 2004)

Vygotsky, L. (1978). *Mind in Society: The Development of Higher Psychological Processes*. Cambridge: Harvard University Press.

CHAPTER SEVEN

The Sound Approach to Effective Global Communication in English: Leveling the Playing Field

Michael Leo Higgins
Yamaguchi University

INTRODUCTION

There seems to be a growing need and impetus towards the adoption or creation of an International Auxiliary Language (IAL) to assist the process of bridging cultural and communication gaps between peoples of differing language groups (Chew, 1989). However, recent calls to achieve the complete "planetization of mankind" (De Chardin, 1959) by the creation of a means of communication for people from any cultural or linguistic background to be able to communicate with other peoples around the globe, have also called for preserving each distinct language and culture from being submerged in an unknown global identity (ibid; Culkin, 1981; Higgins, 1994). In order to achieve that goal, which one international governing body has said "...would go far to resolving [problems related to achieving world peace]...and necessitates the most urgent attention..." (Universal House of Justice, 1986), the fundamental issues at stake need to be identified and addressed and practical steps need to be taken to accomplish the establishment of, and gain the approbation of the world for, an official International Auxiliary Language.

Without taking the time and space to review the entire history of languages and development, suffice it to say that a phonetic approach to language has been called "the last, the most highly developed, the most convenient, and the most adaptable system of writing" (Diamond, 1959).

The spread and use of simpler forms of writing, like Cuneiform, which was a prototypical phonetic alphabet that was developed as a universal written language from Sumerian pictograms and Egyptian hieroglyphs, were greatly aided by the spread of commerce throughout the ancient world, extending even into modern times. (ibid) However, religion has also played an important role, not only in the spread of language but also in the reduction and loss of language as well, through the process of socialization, education and acculturation (Crystal, 1988; Chew, 1989). It should be noted that religion is still playing an active role in the spread and use of language. In fact, the most recent world religion, the

Bahá'í Faith, which marks its beginnings in 1863, has as part of its original and basic scriptural tenets, a call for the establishment of an auxiliary world language and script while preserving and encouraging the first or native language (See Bahá'u'lláh, 1978; Chew, 1989). This is the first time in religious history that a global language has been mandated by scripture, and as such, holds great importance for sociolinguistics.

Currently, while there are between 2000-4000 languages spoken in the world, only 130 languages are recognized as being significant. Of these, there are only twelve written languages that are spoken by more than 100 million people, and only six of these languages are used as the official working languages of the United Nations.

In researching the need for and the possibilities of an IAL, the history of the various attempts to develop artificial languages was examined and three of the most recent and well-known attempts (Esperanto, Loglan, and Glosa) were studied in greater detail (Chew, 1989, Higgins, 1994; Clark, R., 1990; Cresswell, 1987; Large, 1985, Payne, 1984). It was easily determined from this research that none of them have achieved as great a success, as deep and varied vocabulary, or as widespread use as has English. Therefore, English as a possible IAL was studied.

Although the de facto international language leader in business, science, and travel, and more widely spoken as a first or second language than any other, English still has what some consider major linguistic flaws especially in the area of phonological/orthographic agreement (Culkin, 1986). Correct pronunciation of English is one of the key factors in effective communication and literacy in English. Yet it is precisely this area wherein second language learners experience the most difficulty (Larson-Freeman, 1991). While there have been many differences of opinion over the years about the efficacy of teaching pronunciation and about how to go about doing it (Celce-Murcia, 1999; Hinofotis, 1980), some important strides have been taken in this field that should be considered by all teachers of English whether they are strictly "grammar and translation" or more "communicative" English teachers. Hinofotis and Bailey (1980) clearly demonstrated that there is a definite threshold level of pronunciation in English which if a nonnative speaker's pronunciation falls below this level, "he or she will not be able to communicate orally no matter how good his or her control of English grammar and vocabulary might be." In more specific terms, if a nonnative speaker mispronounces between three to five vowel sounds and five to seven consonant sounds they will not be understood.

In trying to address this problem of phonological/orthographical agreement and reform, the author developed a new phonetic alphabet in 1993 from a phonics program developed in the 1920s in America called the Phonovisual Method (see Higgins, 1995A) which satisfied all of the criteria set down by Noah Webster more than 200 years ago for the reformation of English spelling to be phonetically consistent, which none of the other attempts at alphabetic reform (including the International Phonetic Alphabet) can claim. Among the criteria set by Webster were that words should be spelled without using letters that have vague or indefinite sounds (e.g., substituting *sh* for the *ch* in ma*ch*ine, or *kawf*

for cough), all superfluous or silent letters (as the *a* in bre<u>a</u>d) should be eliminated, and that there should be no additions to the alphabet in the form of new
letters or diacritical markings. (Gerber, 1968) Meeting these criteria has been
difficult due to the fact that there are between 42 and 49 discrete sounds in English but only 26 letters, with 5 letters that represent 15 to 22 vowel sounds (depending on one's regional dialect). In fact, it has been noted that English is only
20 percent efficient, with spoken English having at least 40 sounds and written
English spelling them 200 different ways, whereas most of the world's alphabets
are phoneticized to the point where they are 90 percent efficient, or in other
words, they have about the same number of sounds and letters (Culkin, 1986).
Indeed, in English we have over 300 spelling rules and over 1000 exceptions.
Proper English spelling is difficult for many educated native speakers. How
much more difficult is it for non-native students and speakers of English? With
such a huge barrier to spelling and pronunciation, it can clearly be seen that even
though the de facto IAL is English, the playing field is not level, and as a result
many misunderstandings and difficulties needlessly arise.

This new phonetic alphabet, which we called "The Sound Approach," (SA)
only represents the 42 sounds found in the International Broadcast English standard; 27 consonant and 15 vowel sounds. This standard was chosen because it
represents the most "region-free" pronunciation, it has the fewest vowel sounds
to learn (15) and it was considered that most second language learners would
have greater difficulty learning to distinguish the often minor pronunciation differences found in some British (17-22 vowel sounds) and American (16-20
vowel sounds) accents.

The sounds were divided into two charts, one for consonants and one for
vowels. Each discrete sound is matched with a non culture-bound picture that
seems to be universally understood (Higgins, 1995B). The picture and the sound
are always spoken together in the classroom (e.g., "That is the '8-ei' sound.") so
that the students can make a visual association quickly and easily.

In the consonant chart, the sounds are "mapped" in two ways. First, going
down the columns from left to right, we find all of the un-voiced consonants.
The second column has the voiced consonants. The third column has the contin-
uants, and the final column on the right has the liquid or ending consonants.
Secondly, going from the top of the consonant chart to the bottom, each consonant sound has approximately the same mouth and tongue position as the other
sounds in that same row. The top of the chart finds the sounds at the front of the
mouth using only the lips. The sounds move back in the mouth as they move
down the chart. The deepest sound is the unvoiced "h" which is made in the
back of the throat. In this way, students readily relate certain sounds with others
that share similar mouth and tongue positions.

The vowel chart is organized somewhat differently, with the so-called long
vowels across the top row. The second row of sounds holds the so-called short
vowel sounds. On the third row, we find the diphthong "au" (clown – au) and
the short and long "oo" and "uu" (book – oo and moon – uu). The final two
vowel sounds are not true diphthongs but rather represent two common vowel
combinations "oil – oi" and "church – ur." Under each picture and letter combi-

nation are the most common spellings in Standard English for these sounds from most to least common. These letter combinations are totally consistent and match the sounds 100% in SA.

There are a few basic rules for sound spelling that students are taught to keep in mind:

1. There are no double consonants like "account" or "ball". Double consonants can appear in compound words like "bookkeeper" *(BOOK-kee-pur)*.
2. There are no silent letters like "dumb", "mile", or "pneumonia."
3. Each syllable of a word can be separated and spelled with a consonant-vowel-consonant, a vowel-consonant, or consonant-vowel pattern, or vowel only. (Each consonant in English has one discrete vowel sound, providing one beat of stress.
4. Unstressed vowels or "schwa" sounds can be spelled with "u", "e", "i", or sometimes "aa". For example, the word "intended" could be sound-spelled "in-TEN-ded", "in-TEN-did" or "in-TEN-dud", and the word "homonym" could be spelled "HAA-mu-nim", "HAA-maa-nim", or "HAA-me-nim".
5. Stress can be shown by capitalizing the letters that carry the stress, if the stress is known as shown in number 4 above.
6. All regular English grammar and punctuation rules still apply.

As mentioned in the "rules" above, students are taught that syllables represent a single unit of spoken language and consist of a combination of vowels (diphthongs), vowels and consonants that form one sound when combined, consonants alone (very rare except in poetry), or vowels alone. Words are divided into syllables (syllabication) according to where discrete sounds begin and end. As a rule, ending "s" or "z" sounds are tied to the last syllable. Students are taught that if they have any doubts about where to break a word into syllables, they should try speaking it out loud slowly trying to break the word into syllables at different points. If they are still are unable to determine where to break a word, then they should look in the dictionary. Students learn that even if they do not know the correct spelling, by using the sound spelling they can usually determine the most likely spelling pattern and begin looking there. If they still cannot find the word, then they are to try one of the other spelling patterns for that sound, as we have shown in the vowel chart. Breaking the words into syllables and marking the stress can be very helpful in learning the normal stress and rhythm patterns of English. Students are also advised to do this when trying to write down the pronunciation of new words they hear as it is helpful in training their listening ability to distinguish the sounds more clearly. With certain words like "masthead" *(MAST-hed)* syllabication is helpful to distinguish that the "t" and the "h" are discrete sounds and do not make a "three-th" sound, or a word like "sewer" *(SUU-ur)* where the letter "u" appears side by side three times in a row in sound spelling. It is also important to remember is that there is sometimes more than one way to pronounce a word and this can affect how a word is syllabified. For example, "chocolate" can be pronounced *"CHAA-klut"* or *"CHAA-ko-lit"* (Higgins, 2001).

These sound charts are taught through various exercises, including minimal pair work to distinguish the difference in sound and mouth/tongue positions, listening quizzes, tongue twister practice, and group work. These exercises are designed to be somewhat lively and are not intended to be used as "perfection drills" but more as pronunciation models using successive approximation (Higgins, 1995B). The initial goal was to make the students more understandable in English, not to create native-like pronunciation.

It was initially tested on Japanese university level second language learners of English. It was decided to test this phonetic alphabet on Japanese speakers because Japanese speakers of English are notoriously difficult to understand in English due, in part, to a wide phonemic disparity between the Japanese and English languages (Hatta, 1984; Higgins, 1993; Morely, 1987; Scovel, 1969). There are many sounds, both consonant and vowel, in English that have no equivalent sound in Japanese (Imai, 1980; Miura, 1987). It is also commonly assumed that non-native teachers of English cannot teach correct English pronunciation, nor can Japanese learners ever really learn to speak English correctly, partly due to the linguistic differences previously mentioned and also due to phonological filters and perceptions which have been built up through the use of the Romanization of *katakana* syllabary sounds which they are taught to believe is English, as well as the cultural notion that Japanese people are not good language learners (Goya, 1992; Miyake, 1979; Wall, 1991). In 1969 Scovel advanced the proposition that native-like pronunciation cannot be taught, and so by extension, many teachers then thought that it should not be taught at all. This combination of assumptions and linguistic characteristics made Japanese learners of English an excellent testing ground for the efficacy of "The Sound Approach Phonetic Alphabet" (SA) in overcoming these linguistic barriers.

The need for teaching phonics to Japanese students has long been recognized by native English teachers. (Wordell, 1985, Wall, 1991) However, the Japanese students are not generally taught phonics. Instead, they learn *Romaji*, the Romanization of Japanese sounds, and are taught pronunciation through *katakana* and dictionary pronunciation symbols which change from dictionary to dictionary and differ considerably from the IPA, which is itself little used and poorly understood. This limits the students' abilities in reading, spelling, speaking, and understanding English and leads to an inability to communicate in English with non-Japanese speakers of English. Thus, it was hypothesized that the training in a phonetically constant English alphabet would allow second language learners the opportunity to improve their listening, reading and pronunciation abilities in English.

Morely (1987) points out that the goal of teaching pronunciation to foreign teaching assistants or professors, foreign-born technical, business and professional people in English-speaking countries, refugees, and international business people who need to use English as their main working language, should not be to necessarily make them sound like native speakers of English. A more modest and realistic goal, Morely says, is to enable learners to get above the threshold

level so that they will be able to communicate orally without pronunciation becoming a barrier to understanding. Morely indicates that some studies have even
shown that the most improvement that can be expected in an adult (over 15
years of age) is in the 15 to 20 percent range.

However, in the initial studies done in Yamaguchi, Japan in 1993, (see Higgins, 1993) the university level groups that studied the Sound Approach Phonetic Alphabet for a minimal 10 hour period of time over the course of one semester showed dramatic and statistically significant improvement (at the .01
level) across the boards in all areas, vowels, consonants, and extra vowel inser-
tions (known as *Katakana* English), over the control groups. For example, the
English word "ball" is pronounced "bo-ru" in *Katakana*, the word "strike" is
pronounced "suu-to-raa-ee-ku," and the hamburger restaurant known as
"McDonald's" is pronounced "maa-ku-do-naa-ru-do." The vowel insertion rate
dropped by as much as 90% in some groups and overall showed an average reduction of 82%. This is one of the major pronunciation barriers faced by the
Japanese in being understood. The "l-r" confusion was also greatly reduced
(with group improvement averages being between 73% to 94%) in all treatment
groups, in some individual cases it was eliminated entirely. The same held true
for all of the common English pronunciation difficulties faced by the Japanese
with the overall improvement rate well above the 80% level, in contrast to the
previous improvement rates in studies as cited by Morely above. (Higgins,
1994) Follow-up studies in Russia have shown similar results with classes of
elementary, secondary (Higgins, 1996) and university students. While some of
the studies on Russian university students are still in narrative form and have not
been subjected to a rigorous evaluation of the objective data, the obvious improvement in pronunciation, reading ability and listening ability of the students
taught the Sound Approach has been noted with enthusiasm by Russian educators.

According to Celce-Murcia and Goodwin (1991), the methodology for
teaching pronunciation up to now has been primitive, relying on native or near
native speakers of English who present the pronunciation inductively and correct
via modeling. In both the study in Yamaguchi in 1993 and in the subsequent
studies in Russia there was no statistical difference between the rates of improvement in classes taught by either native or non-native English speaking instructors who followed the Sound Approach materials and methods. The only
difference noted, though not statistically significant, was that there were slightly
higher rates of improvement in the classes taught by the non-native teacher
(Higgins, 1996).

In 1997, a follow-up study was conducted in classes of mixed language
groups at the ESL Centre at the University of Regina, Regina, Canada. The students presented a mix of linguistic backgrounds, Spanish, Korean, Mongolian,
Mandarin, Cantonese, and Japanese. Over a four month period of time, all students who were taught the Sound Approach for 30 to 40 minutes per week, made
significant improvement over those students who used other pronunciation materials and did not receive the Sound Approach training, dropping their pronunciation errors by nearly 70% across the mix of language backgrounds. Each

class at the ESL Centre met a minimum of nine hours per week. (Higgins, 1998B)

The pronunciation of those students who study the Sound Approach phonetic alphabet shows significant and noticeable improvement well above the 15 to 20% margin noted above with other pronunciation training methods, and well above the threshold level shown by Hinofotis and Bailey in 1980. Improvement can be observed in classes that take as little as 10 to 20 minutes per week out of a 90 minute class to work on the Sound Approach materials, and if the teacher devotes 30 to 40 minutes to this work, as the results of the Canadian study indicate, then little or no reversion to former pronunciation patterns are noted in the students outside of class, in contrast with those students that have not been taught the Sound Approach, but have worked with conventional pronunciation training materials.

By teaching English phonetics through an orthographically consistent sound spelling system, the ability to "decode" English improved the students' sight-reading abilities by helping them transfer the sound-spelling system into regular English orthography. By learning, for example, that the sound symbol "ei" could be spelled in Standard English as "eigh", "a_e", "ai", or "ea", the students were enabled to read faster and more precisely. Also by concentrating on being able to hear the English phonetics more clearly, as mentioned earlier, they were able to greatly decrease, and in many cases, eliminate the insertion or inclusion of extra Japanese *Katakana* phonetics into spoken English, which is one of the greatest barriers to effective communication between Japanese English speakers and virtually any other non-Japanese English speaker in the world. This cannot but help to increase the confidence of those trained in SA to be able to speak English and be understood, as well as to correctly understand natural English that is not influenced by and filtered through the Japanese inflection patterns known as "Katakana English." This consequently allows for more effective cross-cultural communication.

Another aspect of the research this author conducted while at the University of Regina between September and December of 1997 was doing the initial research involving the application of the mathematical theory of rough sets and using the Sound Approach phonetic alphabet in the development of a data-based word spelling recognizer using the Variable Precision Rough Sets (VPRS) model. (Higgins, 1998B) The author worked with the Department of Computer Science at the University of Regina, and specifically with Dr. Wojciech Ziarko on classifying a number of English homonyms and creating decision tables for the data to be analyzed by the computer in determining the correct spelling of a homonym spelled initially in the SA alphabet. This was the first step toward creating and testing a full-scale model of a data-based spelling recognizer for use in word-processing spell checking that could function in either Standard English orthographical mode, or in a phonetic alphabet mode (Higgins, 1998B). It was found that even with a simplified grammatical protocol and generalized rule definitions, the computer was able to classify the correct spelling of a word written in SA a significantly greater proportion of the time than many spell-checking programs currently in use. (Higgins, 1998A) The research conducted so far also holds tremendous prospects for the application of SA to word-processing/computer spell checking, and even the elimination of the keyboard for computer voice recognition systems (Higgins, 1999).

CONCLUSION

The cumulative findings have shown that those who were even minimally trained in the Sound Approach phonetic alphabet did significantly better in sight reading/pronunciation tests than those who were not trained, and are further applicable to English learners in other language groups besides Japanese as a reliable introduction to the "sound map" of English which will, in one way or another, differ from the phonetic map of their native language. If adopted as a global standard for a sound-spelling guide, future newspapers and magazines could spell out the pronunciation of any foreign name from Deng Xiao Ping (Dung Shau Ping in SA) to Wojciech Ziarko (VOI-tek Zee-AAR-ko in SA) without resorting to dictionary symbols, or the present diversity of Romanized scripts. The same would also hold true for broadcast announcers and place names that seem to have such a diversity of pronunciations for the same place, that even the people who live there often cannot recognize the name of their own locality the way others pronounce it. The development of this phonetic approach to English holds great promise and many possibilities for the future, and, perhaps, will itself become the conceptual starting place for deeper studies in the development of the International Auxiliary Language and script that many see as one of the necessary keys for completing the process of world unity.

REFERENCES

Bahá'u'lláh, 1978. *Tablets of Bahá'u'lláh.* Haifa, Bahá'í World Centre.

Celce-Murcia, M., & Goodwin, J., 1991. Teaching pronunciation. In *Teaching English As A Second Or Foreign Language.* (Celce-Murcia, Ed.). New York: Newbury House.

Chew, P.G.L., 1989. "Whither the International Auxiliary Language." *The Journal of Bahá'í Studies,* Vol. 2, No. 2.

Clark, R., and Ashby, W., 1990. *Euro-Glosa: The Interlanguage for Europe and the World.* Surrey, Glosa Education Organization.

Cresswell, J., and Hartley, J., 1987. *Esperanto.* Kent, Hodder and Stoughton.

Crystal, D., 1988. *The English Language.* London, Penguin Books.

Culkin, J., 1981. "The New Age of Reason." *Science Digest,* August 1981.

_____, 1986. "From A and Alef to Zed and Omega: Making the Case for a Single World Alphabet." *TWA Ambassador,* October 1986.

De Chardin, P.T., 1959. *The Phenomenon of Man.* New York, Harper and Row: Harper Torchbooks. 1965 edition.

Diamond, A.S., 1959. *The History and Origin of Language.* London, Methuen and Co. Ltd.

Gerber, P.L., 1968. *Lessons In Language* . London, Wadsworth. "Noah Webster's Essay on Reforming the Mode of Spelling." Kinseido Annotated Version (1986). Tokyo, Kinseido.

Goya, S., 1992. "Teaching Phonics To Japanese Students." *The Language Teacher*, Vol. 16, No. 2.

Hatta, T., et al., 1984. "Orthographic Dominance and Interference Effects in Letter Recognition Among Japanese-English and English-Japanese Bilinguals." *Psychologia*, Vol. 27, No. 1.

Higgins, M.L., 1993. Teaching English To Japanese Students. *Proceedings of the Faculty of Liberal Arts*, Yamaguchi University, 1993, 27: 187-206.

_____, 1994. The Quest For A Universal Auxiliary Language: Addressing Pronunciation And Orthographic Barriers Of English. Hawaii: University Microfilms, Pp. 162.

_____, with Higgins, M.S., & Shima, Y., 1995A. The Phonovisual Method™ — Adaptation Of A Sound Approach To Basic Pronunciation Training. *The Japan Association of Language Teachers Journal of Yamaguchi Chapter*, March 1995, p. 2-18.

_____, with Higgins, M.S., & Shima, Y., 1995B. Basic Training In Pronunciation And Phonics: A Sound Approach. *The Language Teacher*, vol. 19, number 4, April 1995, pp. 4-8.

_____, 1996. A Report On The Development Of The Yuzhno-Sakhalinsk International School: The First English Language Immersion Program In Russia. *Journal of the Faculty of Liberal Arts (Humanities and Social Sciences)*. Yamaguchi University, Vol. 28. pp. 209-222.

_____, 1998A. "Spelling Recognition of Words Expressed in the Sound Approach© Phonetic Alphabet." Journal of the Faculty of Technology.

_____, 1998B ."A Report on the International Joint Research Project for Further Research and Development of the Sound Approach© Phonetic Alphabet." Memoirs of the Tokiwa Technology Association.

_____, with Ziarko, W., 1999. "Computerized Spelling Recognition of Words Expressed in the Sound Approach." New Directions in Rough Sets, Data Mining, and Granular-Soft Computing: Proceedings, 7th International Workshop, RSFDGrC '99. Lecture Notes in Artificial Intelligence 1711. Tokyo: Springer.

_____, with Higgins, M.S., 2001. The New Sound Approach Workbook. Juneau, Alaska: International Educational Initiatives, Inc.

Hinofotis, G., & Bailey, K., 1980. American Undergraduate Reactions To The Communication Skills Of Foreign Teaching Assistants. In J. Fisher, M. Clarke, & J. Schachter, (Eds.), *On TESOL '80: Building bridges: Research and practice in TESL* (pp. 120-133). Washington, DC: TESOL.

Imai, K., 1980. "Phonetics Comparison" in *Sound and Form — Comparative Study of Japanese and English, Vol. 1.*, Kunihiro, T., ed. (In Japanese). Tokyo, Taishukan.

Large, A., 1985. *The Artificial Language Movement* . New York, Basil Blackwell.

Larson-Freeman, D., and Long, M. 1991. *An Introduction to Second Language Acquisition Research*. New York, Longman.

Morely, J., 1987. *Current Perspectives On Pronunciation*. Washington, DC: TESOL.

Miura, S., 1987. *The Language of English Language Textbooks for Japanese Senior High School Students*. (In Japanese) Tokyo, Keisuisha.

Miyake, M., 1979. "Phenomenon of Vocal Sound on Loan Words." (In Japanese) In *English and Japanese*, Tokyo, Kuroshio Press.

Payne, V., 1984. "Language: Saying it for Esperanto." *Asia,* October 7, 1984.

Scovel, T., 1969. Foreign Accents, Language Acquisition, And Cerebral Dominance. *Language Learning,* 19 (3 & 4), 245-254.

Wall, P., 1991. *Literacy in the Primary Grades*. A lecture presented at Educator's Day (in March), Okinawa, Japan. In Goya, S. (1992) "Teaching Phonics to Japanese Students." *The Language Teacher*, Vol. 16, No. 2.

Wordell, C.B., 1985. *A Guide to Teaching English In Japan*. Tokyo, The Japan Times.

Universal House of Justice, 1986. *The Promise of World Peace.* Haifa, Israel; Bahá'í
    World Center.

CHAPTER EIGHT

Children at Risk in Education (CARE): A Transatlantic Partnership Programme That Develops Global Competencies through International Experiences

Jean Benton
Southwest Missouri State University

Sandra McWilliams
Stranmillis University College

INTRODUCTION

In 2002 a grant from the European Commission and FIPSE (Fund for Post Secondary Education) enabled a consortium of six universities, three in Europe and three in the United States to undertake a three-year project to develop a curriculum for student teachers to enable them to work with children at risk of failing in school. Children at risk in this project are defined as those who may fail to develop their educational potential because of social, economic and linguistic disadvantage, combined with race, ethnicity or gender difference. They include the children of migrant labour and those whose first language is not that of the school. The consortium aimed to facilitate the development of approaches and strategies to teaching failing pupils and the development and dissemination of curricular materials. The first year 2002-3 was a planning and preparation year and in 2003-4 there was a period of student outward mobility. In total fifty-four (54) students were outwardly mobile, twenty-seven (27) from the United States and twenty-seven (27) from Europe. In the final year 2004-5 there will be an intensive programme involving tutors and students in developing and disseminating curricular materials and developing a global network of interested teachers. This paper gives an overview of the project, outlines the objectives, and considers the outcomes of the project to date.

OVERVIEW OF PROJECT

Shared global concerns in education have recently focused on underachievement and the difficulties associated with the education of the children of migrant labour. Diaz (1991) reports that the major factors affecting the educational performance of migrant children including ecological (reasons for migrating), educational (absenteeism), psychological (lowered self-esteem, resulting from ridicule for being culturally different; social isolation), and economical (child as contributor to the economy of the family). Whitaker and Salend (1997) report that socio-economic difficulties of migrant school children impact upon their educational needs, especially the absence of teaching materials which reflect the economic contribution of migrant families. Henderson (1992) shows that programmes such as Migrant Home Literacy Project, can lower the school drop out rate of migrant children which ranges from 50 to 90 percent in the United States. The "No Child Left Behind" Act of 2001 in the United States has made it a priority to meet the "educational needs of low-achieving children in the nation's highest poverty schools, limited English proficient children, migratory children, children with disabilities, Indian children, neglected or delinquent children and young children in need of reading assistance." The authorisation of $410,000,000 for the fiscal year 2002, and such sums as may be necessary for each of the 5 succeeding fiscal years have been appropriated for the education of migratory children.

The educational targets set by the British, Dutch and Spanish (Kumar 1993, Lucey & Walkerdine 2000, Mortimore & Blackstone 1982, Oppenheim & Harker 1996, Purvis & Hales (Eds.) 1983) governments also reflect significant educational imperatives. These priorities unite Europe and the United States in a growing unease that a large number of young people are not meeting their academic potential through failing at school and becoming excluded from mainstream society.

The project addressed the concerns of both the United States and the European Union reflected in their national educational policies to improve educational attainment by focusing on underachievement in schools and the potential alienation of some young people. For example, the consortium included a consideration of the impact of migrant labour which has been significant in the education of some young citizens. All the participating universities recognised the difficulties associated with educating teachers to work with children in a language that is not their first language. The issue, which is one of the educational priorities of both Europe and the United States, has focused concerns about the relationship between language, cultural background and educational attainment. This, together with the growing fears about the educational standards in Europe and the United States, which is necessary in a knowledge-based economy, requires attention to be given as to how to ensure that the majority of young people can achieve their academic potential in school.

The consortium aimed to improve educational standards by developing a curriculum for teachers to enable them to work with children at risk as defined above. It drew upon the particular expertise in working with children at risk in each participating institution.

In addressing the global concerns of underachievement in schools the consortium had expertise in specific approaches to failure in schools. This expertise was shared across the institutions and was designed to improve educational achievement in both the United States and Europe. It identified disadvantage, unemployment, material disadvantage, cultural deprivation, low expectations, gender, race and ethnicity as significant variables to be addressed by educators who are concerned about failure in schools. The holistic nature of the consortium is demonstrated in Table 1.

Table 1.

Consortia Partners/ Issues	Hogeschool van Arnhem en Nijmegen	Stranmillis University College	University of Leon	Coastal Carolina University	Southeast Missouri State	University of Central Florida
Linguistic Disadvantage	X	X	X	X	X	X
Unemployment		X	X	X	X	X
Low wages		X	X	X	X	X
Material Dis-advantage		X	X	X	X	X
Cultural Difference	X	X	X	X	X	X
Low Expecta-tions	X	X	X	X	X	X
Gender	X	X	X	X	X	X
Race	X	X	X	X	X	X
Ethnicity	X	X	X	X	X	X

The significance of this consortium was that, as a holistic entity, it could address a significant 'mix' of factors that are associated with failure in schools in both Europe and the United States. Each institution has its own particular response to teaching teachers to work with failing pupils. The 'added value' of the consortium in addressing such a mix of approaches to particular types of failure in schools is the unique opportunity to address the pedagogical approaches to failing pupils in a global context. Any teacher facing a set of variables in a specific location will be able to deal with any set of issues in any location following the experience provided by the consortium.

In summary each participating institution has a high level of expertise in addressing the significant factors which taken collectively, represent a global and comprehensive approach to underachievement in schools. The programme, built around a number of theoretical and practical concerns, would provide students with good educative experiences. The programme was structured to encourage students to explore relevant content, current scientific based research, theoretical constructs, practical experience and reflective project work.

The consortium aimed to develop ways of preparing teachers to work with underachievement by facilitating the prospective teacher's global mobility to enable them to engage with specific approaches. Through sharing and exchange, they will develop a global perspective to teaching young people who underachieve in school.

The outcomes of the project were to be of two genres. On one hand a set of qualitative outcomes will prepare students to address the general issues of working outside their native culture with underachieving young people. While on the other hand a set of curricular materials will be developed to reflect the challenging nature of intervention in the education of children who fail in schools. The expected outcome would be a teaching curriculum that would effectively address the problem of failing youth.

The objectives of the programme were to:
1. Enable young teachers to understand underachievement in different school systems
2. Develop professional skills in young teachers to help them work in an international context with underachieving pupils
3. Support the professional aspirations of young teachers by helping them consider critically, teaching failing pupils
4. Encourage young teachers to consider their professional practice in a constructive and critical way
5. Facilitate the employment potential of young teachers, enabling them to draw upon their experience of working in international and multi-national contexts
6. Engage young teachers in a debate about standards in education
7. Engage in the intellectual and personal development of young teachers through the maintenance of the set of multinational high quality learning environments
8. Encourage the engagement of young people, a key intellectual and professional task in educating failing pupils
9. Encourage young teachers to develop an awareness of the contemporary issues surrounding the education of failing pupils
10. Provide opportunities in national and multi-national context for young teachers to develop core philosophical positions and professional skills on key matters associated with teaching failing pupils.

LANGUAGE IN EDUCATION

The consortium developed opportunities for young teachers to work with children whose first language was not the language of the host country. In the

United States students worked with children whose first language was not English, while, students working and studying in the Netherlands and Spain worked with children whose first language is the national language. All the institutions had experience in working with children from such backgrounds and particularly where pupils in schools come from areas, which reflect high multiple deprivation variables. The experience of working in different educational cultures hopefully will enable young teachers to develop ways of working with disadvantaged pupils that will be effective irrespective of the context.

The programme was designed to give young teachers the opportunity to experience different perspectives and value positions and to work with failing pupils drawing upon the perspectives of different experts. Students coming from different contexts in Europe would have the opportunity to study educational systems and approaches in the United States and to address the methodologies adopted in different locations to deal with academic underachievement. Likewise students who came from the United States would have the opportunity to experience different approaches associated with social class, ethnicity and gender differences in Europe. This experience would enable students to make links in methodologies and to develop approaches, which will be successful irrespective of the context in which they are working.

THE MOBILITY PROGRAMME

The programme of mobility was not entirely the same in each location, but the overall the pattern was a block of theoretical and workshop-based preparation in a host university that was specifically designed to enable students to develop an international dimension to their thinking. The theoretical context would enable students to understand and analyse the educational system in which they were working. Students were invited to compare practice in their host country with their knowledge of existing practice in their own country but in a non-evaluative matter. The programme in the first six weeks would enable students to understand the nature of failing pupils in their host location and to understand how it is 'socially constructed' within the context of the study of education and their geographical placement. Students were asked to make comparisons between their value positions and those which were articulated in their host institution.

Following the theoretical preparation and the development of the social construction of failure, students spent time and taught in schools in each location. These schools had significant numbers of pupils "at risk".

The outworking of the period of mobility proved, in each location, to be a period of intense activity for the tutors involved, both before the actual arrival of students in securing suitable placements and during the time students spent in schools. This is not the place to rehearse the myriad of detail which had to be addressed in each location. Suffice to say it placed particularly heavy demands on the tutors involved.

THE OUTCOMES OF THE PROJECT

A web site was developed and students were put in discussion groups which cut across the locations. A series of questions were posed (see Appendix I) to which students responded. Currently we are in the process of information gathering with regard to how students responded to their time in schools and apart from the subjective views of tutors involved. These postings and discussions are the most reliable information we have to assess if the objectives of the programme were met. We have included a selection of these in Appendix 2 – 'Student Voices'

As was noted above, another potential outcome was the creation of a teaching curriculum that would effectively address the issue of failing students. This will be addressed at a conference of all participating students and tutors in the academic year 2004-5.

FINAL THOUGHTS

This paper does not convey the sheer hard work which went into the planning and delivery of this project to date. Those who were most heavily committed gave so much in time and effort. It may emerge that we were too ambitious in our initial thinking and not all will come to fruition. But for us personally, this e-mail sent from a student to her group suggests some success. Next year's work will tell us more in terms of our original objectives.

> "....over the past 12 weeks I have had one of the most remarkable experiences of my life. This experience has changed the person I am. I no longer look at life in the small perspective that I had before I left, but I realise how big the world is and how much there is I still want to experience. I have also realised what an independent person I am. I think this trip was worthwhile just because of everything I learned about myself – I have definitely had a self-evaluation. I just hope I will bring back many of the things I have learned while here." (Reproduced anonymously with permission)

APPENDIX 1

The questions on the On-Line Seminar

YOUR NEW HOME AWAY FROM HOME: What's it like where you are?

THE SCHOOLS: What's it like in the schools?

CLASSROOM CLIMATE: What is the classroom climate like?

TEACHING IN YOUR SCHOOL: What's it like to teach in your school?

CHILDREN AT RISK: Tell us what you have discovered about children at risk?

APPENDIX 2 – Students' Voices

YOUR NEW HOME AWAY FROM HOME: What's it like where you are?

I'm from Florida and I've never seen snow, so seeing snow here has been absolutely awesome. The city is marvellous and it isn't too big, which is nice, especially since we take our bikes everywhere. Everyone seems to be very nice and friendly and they don't hesitate to speak English to us (our Dutch is incredibly poor). It's been very cold for me here, but I'm adjusting. I hope everyone else is doing well where they are.

SEMO is a pretty campus. The ice came last Sunday and transformed it into a fantasy world. But inside our dorms we are always kept warm and safe - we have a police station on the floor below us! My new home is going well. It is definitly a changefrom living at home but I am keeping myself amused. The local people are lovely and have bee taking good care of us. So... although I may not be at home SEMO is doing well as a substitute!

Belfast is a busy city in Northern Ireland. It is not really what I expected it to be like. It reminds me of Baltimore, Maryland. Belfast Locke is similar to Baltimore Harbour. I thought Belfast would be like what I imagined the rest of Ireland to be like. I pictured, rolling green hills with sheep and small cottages. In Belfast that is not what you will find. Here you will find polluted streets and walls covered in graffiti. My school is in Northwest Belfast (which is where many of the troubles were in the early nineties and still today). Looking at any given wall you will most likely find spray painted IRA, RIRA, UDA, etc. which is just a few of the many different para-military groups in Belfast. However, not all of Belfast is dirty. Stranmillis University College is located in a nice part of Belfast. Around our school one would find very, very expensive cars and houses. Not to far down the street is the Botanic Gardens and Queens University which is also very beautiful.

THE SCHOOLS: What's it like in the schools?

Education, in brief, nearly the exact same! They test (not as much as Americans) about everything. They track students the same as we do. The differences are found in the material -we're looking at the remedial groups and the lower level groups so of course they will appear to be behind what we're used to.

Teachers presentation of material- much more hand fed than I'm used to. They just present material and don't seem to have any attention getter at the beginning which seem to be so important says my professor from EDG 4323.

Type of class work- They do seem to have a few more worksheets than I'm used to.

Length of class- only 35-40 minutes...SOO short!

Uniforms- different since public schools in US. don't tend to have these.

Overall though, a classroom is a classroom. I was a bit nervous to be in the classrooms in an all boys school before I got there, but as soon as I saw the looks on those little lads, my fears were put to rest. They just want to have fun and maybe learn something while they're at it. They also, I feel, need to have at least 6 hours to escape the hellish reality they call home. So I'm having the most wonderful time here, learning to live in another culture, a people so different in expressing their opinion (Americans will give you their opinion without you asking. Northern Irish might not give you their opinion even if you DO ask them). Also, I heard the most wonderful quote the other day, " People are people and people come from people". I think that quote is the great equalizer which can bring battling groups together.

It seems strange to me that I've only been here 2 1/2 weeks and I already feel like I belong here. It was about a week ago that the feelings of homesickness wore off and I was able to settle in a little more. Before that, I had had grand times on the town and being a tourist. I was able to see the schools (which I ultimately think made me settle down and feel at home here), get accustomed to which stores to shop for what and in general just get used to being here. Things are great here. School is great. My flat-mates are the best- we really all get along so well! I don't know how they managed to place us SO well!

In my placement primary school many of the children come from torn single family homes. Many of the children's parents have been killed by opposing paramilitary groups or have committed suicide. Drugs are also very common in the area where my school is located.

The school I am in is in down town Orlando. It's a middle school which carries about 1300 students. I am in the Emotionally Handicapped class with an excel-

lent teacher and teacher aid. The classes are small, the maximum is 7 children per period.

The children have various background and reasons for being here, and that is what makes it very interesting for me. Problems children have here are; born substance exposed, aggressive behaviour, not a stable family background, gang members etc. The children here just seem to have a more difficult life here than they have in The Netherlands. There is a lot of pressure on them, and they already have to go through a lot when they are still young.

The teacher is really a inspiration to work with. She is calm, respectful, caring, giving and patient. She really knows how to work with these children and she gives her all every day. She tries to engage the children and the is enthusiastic. I can imagine it must be hard for her sometimes to just be teaching 2 children because the rest is suspended. But it doesn't show. She just keeps going!

The schools themselves are very well-equipped! All the teachers have their own classroom with a lot of closets, books and computers in it. The classrooms are dressed nicely and are a good learning environment!

During my placements I mostly work with he children in small groups and I observe a lot. Being here inspirers me to work with at risk children and I am learning new things every day!

It's just good to be here! I may sound a bit overreacted... but it's just true!

I'm in a Kindergarten class at an elementary school. The teaching methods are much more informal here as the students work and learn through centres.

The elementary school system runs from K (5 years) to 4th grade (10 years) and I have found the schools to be much bigger than at home. Other differences include things like clothing, the students do not wear a uniform, religious education, is not allowed in state schools, ethnic groups, Franklin has a diverse population of students mainly including white, black and Hispanics and the speciality teachers for art, music, P.E., library and computers. The teachers and students from Franklin have been fantastic and are taking great care of us all.

I'm a secondary education major (chemistry and physics specifically) and everyone else here in the Netherlands is a primary education major, so I'm the only person who is in a secondary school here. The secondary system is the Netherlands is divided into sections with high academically achieving students going to certain schools and lower students going elsewhere. I am working with the lower end secondary students. The students seem far more enthusiastic than students back home. I was very surprised here by the lack of security around schools (in Florida, you're required to bring I.D. and check in at the front office when you arrive on campus, plus you need to have a specific reason for going on campus in the first place). The students remain in the same classroom for many of their lessons and the teachers simply trade rooms. I enjoy being in this school very much.

CLASSROOM CLIMATE: What is the classroom climate like?

Our classroom has a very, "come as you are" feel to it. The teacher, Marly, is young and exciting. She is very animated and always keeps the classroom decorated with student work. She has created a very safe and welcoming environment for the students and it is evident in the way they interact with her. The majority of the students participate and really respect Marly. I've been extremely impressed with the students and the teacher.

To begin I have two different classroom climates since I teach in two different classrooms. My first class consist of first year students, which are 11 - 12 years old. They are very quiet and eager to learn the material. They also can be intimidated, so if is a very easy to control the class when it comes to behavior problems. There are 22 boys in this class, and they are at the top of their grade level. The teacher just went on maternity leave last week, but the new teacher, who is a male, is just as helpful as the first teacher.

My second-class consists of third year students. Their ages range form 13-14 years of age. They actually are a trickier to deal with when it comes to behavior problems. I do not intimidate these students. And I always have to try to do something new just to keep their attention. This group is naturally more talkative. They are below average students that have great potential but do not necessarily care about schoolwork. The teacher is very helpful but she lets me deal with them until I ask for help.

Both of these classroom climates are extreme opposite from each other. I am very grateful of that because I am getting a wide range of experience.

TEACHING IN YOUR SCHOOL: What's it like to teach in your school?

Because of class discipline issues I have found teaching here difficult. Even though we share a common language, we do not always communicate with each other. They live in a different world that I can leave at 3:00PM when I travel on two buses from North Belfast to South Belfast.

The class is divided up into three groups high ability, average, and low ability. Each group has different math and reading books. This makes teaching literacy and math difficult. Because of the wide ability level one lesson cannot be taught. Most of the time I teach the low ability math group and the average ability reading group. This meant that until recently I did not know the higher ability students very well.

Also, the students were confirmed yesterday (March 22) so a lot of classroom time has went into preparing for confirmation, which limited my classroom time.

One big difference with my teacher is that she never yells to the children. She always uses positive reinforcement. I really like the way she get the attention of all the children.

I see a lot of boys who are acting macho, but I just look further because most of the time they aren't that macho as they act. In the Netherlands they would say big talk but a tiny heart. In one of my field experiences I really had a hard time with some macho boys in class they were always fooling around in class and just didn't want to listen. I talked with my teacher and I asked him what kind of history do they have and what are their background. He told me a lot of shocking things, one child lived at a foster family he came as a refuge from Africa to the Netherlands and he saw his mom and dad being killed. This is just one of the stories, but now I know why children with a bad behaviour act like that, they just come up for themselves and have to do it on his own. So what I'm trying to say is that for every bad behaviour there must be a cause for it.

And about the set schedule is something they don't have in my school too. The children never know what they can expect. It would be much better if the children knew what they can expect.

Teaching here has given me much more empathy for the children who don't speak English. I never thought I would not be able to communicate with students in the classroom. Before coming to Nijmegen we were told we were coming to an "English speaking" school. When I arrived in the classroom I was surprised to find out only a few children spoke English. Lessons here have been modified quite a bit for the students to understand. At times it has been frustrating, knowing you could teach so much more- but just not knowing how to explain it to them. Although the students have begun to speak more and more English (or at least try to) it's still hard to teach. The students seemed to have really taken to the English lessons and are always willing to learn. The supplies that are available are pretty slim in our school. In the states you have many resources to choose from- here you are very limited.

CHILDREN AT RISK: Tell us what you have discovered about children at risk?

This Girls' High School, although in an area of high unemployment in Belfast City, performs very well. It is not a grammar school, so many of its pupils may not pursue continuing education but, while they are here, the students that I have encountered are very eager to learn. It is appalling to hear about some of the home lives of individual students, parental problems, involvement in paramilitaries, and the like, and amazing to think that they have to suffer through so much trauma and then come to school to learn.

Back in Orlando, I was employed by the Inner City Games so I was witness to inter-city Orlando students at the middle school level. I've found that there are a lot of similarities between them. There are different societal pressures, different negative influences, but they all face very similar adolescent issues. These students need to be nurtured just as much as any other child, if not more so, and they are deserving of the same education.

Being here as made me realize that as a teacher in training, you are responsible for many things: completing government standards, following school guidelines, making parents happy, and the like. Sometimes in the chaos of preparing for graduation and completing degree requirements, the students (that we're preparing to teach) can get lost in the mix. An issue that can be dealt with upon reaching it -- and I've seen the issues now. Children can be enlightening and inspiring and my students here have done so. They have prepared me more than any class or textbook on how to be a better educator and I am so thankful for this experience because of them.

I have heard the stories and the hardships of the students in my school. Yet, it amazes me how happy they are and how quickly they bounce back from things. They all have their problems, but they work well together and they look forward to seeing each other at school. I will take away the courage they taught me to have and their happiness and curiosity in every little thing.

This trip has definitely taught me a lot about at-risk students. I learned that there are many reasons that can cause children to be at risk, and they have no control over them. These students are all capable of performing just as well as other students their age, but because of some external factor, they are dragging behind. One thing that really surprised me was that some of these students had been absent from school for two or three years! I knew that these students had missed a lot of school, but I was thinking more like once or twice a week, not whole years at a time! I also learned about what is being done to help these students. Besides what I expected, such as one on one attention, there are some programs that surprised me, such as teachers going to hospitals to help ill students. Now that I think about it, I guess that would make sense. I don´t know why that surprised me. I have learned that to help these students you need time and patience. These students are usually the ones who act up in class and give teachers a hard time. This makes them the students that teachers usually don´t particularly enjoy spending a lot of time with. As the teacher, you have to know each student´s specific situation to understand where they are coming from. Only then can you act in such a way that will help the student.

REFERENCES

Diaz, J. O. (1991). The factors that affect the educational performance of migrant children. Education, 91(111), 483-487.

Henderson, Z.P. (1992). Project promotes literacy among migrant families. Human Ecology, 92(20), 4-5.

Kumar, V. (1993). Poverty and inequality In the UK: The effects on children. London: National Children's Bureau.

Lucey, L. & Walkerdine, V. (2000). Boy's underachievement: Social class and changing masculinities. In Cox, T. Combating Educational Disadvantage. London: Falmer Press.

Meighan, R. & Siraj-Blatchford, I. (1997). A sociology of educating. 3rd edition. London: Cassell.

Mortimore, J, & Blackstone, T. (1982). Disadvantage and education. London: Heinmann.

Oppenheim, C. & Harker, L. (1996). Poverty: The facts. London: CPAG.

Purvis, J. & Hales, M. (Eds.). (1983). Achievement and inequality in education. London: Routledge & Kegan Paul.

U.S. Government. No Child Left Behind Act of 2001.

Whittaker, C.R. & Salend, S.J. (1997). Voices from the fields: Including migrant farmworkers in the curriculum. Reading Teacher, 50(6), 482-494.

CHAPTER NINE

Educating for Global Citizenship and Social Responsibility

Noorjehan N. Ganihar
Karnatak University

INTRODUCTION

Citizenship education still occurs, but too often it is reduced to formal and/or ritualistic actions such as voting, paying taxes, saluting the flag, etc. The students are not being taught about authentic participatory democracy. Advocating this idea of global citizenship, the problems and possibilities were global in scope during the last years of the second millennium, which was characterized by unprecedented capitalist power. As national sovereignty gives way to the New World Order, the people most affected by the hyper-exploitation of the earth's human and physical resources are unable to protect themselves. This is why the global citizenship is needed. Obviously, this citizenship has to be within new political institutions capable of opposing global capitalism and its subjection of everyone and every place to the logic of markets and profit.

Many educators have been unable or unwilling to engage in radical critique of what is wrong and unjust in the world today. However, they provide useful educational ideas concerning what could be done. Teachers play an important role in terms of educating students for global citizenship. The teachers' accomplishments are cited so that they can learn from what is occurring theoretically and pedagogically.

PRIMARY PURPOSE OF EDUCATION

The primary purpose of education is to prepare students to become stewards of the earth and participants in democracy for global social justice. (Brosio 1994)

We can question the relevance of formal schooling to an understanding of life in an increasingly complex and interdependent world. From the observations gained from their experiences as professional educators, champions of formal schooling cite examples of misinformation in their own schooling and of widespread instances of parochialism and lack of cultural sensitivity in today's schools. Moreover, noting the obvious global dimensions of the most serious problems we face today—environmental destruction, depletion of natural resources, hunger and homelessness, disregard for the rights of ethnic minorities, children, women, and the poor - the crucial question that must be asked is, "Are teachers prepared to help their students develop the global consciousness needed to support human rights and ecological sustainability?" Sadly, the answer to this question is "No". Despite the efforts of dedicated teachers and the good intentions of policy makers who pass mandates for multicultural and gender-fair education, schooling remains parochial and insensitive to the global nature of social and environmental problems.

Today, our education system is dominated by the imperatives of the marketplace - an imperative that ignores any notion of social responsibility. Although historically the primary mission of education has been to prepare students for responsible citizenship, but in practice schools emphasize preparing workers for the global marketplace.

The emphasis should be citizen education but more specifically education for global citizenship. In this context global citizenship entails an examination of our own cultural assumptions about life and work. We in the industrial world associate survival with employment. This association is being forced on other cultures as the global economy establishes dominance. Community leaders challenge even the idea of individual human rights when these rights conflict with communal obligations and responsibilities that have traditionally served to hold the community together.

First of all, it is a shock that there are people who do not share fundamental principles that they hold dear. When reflecting on what it means to encounter people who live a life that is full of dignity and purpose, but do not value many of the material things and ideological positions that many students take for granted, there proves to be some hope for the future. One must come to the realization that commonalties do bring us together. This is the type of global consciousness that Andrzejewski (1996) says should call for education.

We must learn to respect and appreciate religions, regions, languages, cultures, beliefs, traditions, heritages and practices that are different from our own. Here we can begin to appreciate dimensions of truth and goodness that are different from our own; it is here where we begin to establish the groundwork for democratic participation and responsible action as global citizens.

We are entering a new age of global markets and automated production. The road to a near-workerless economy is within sight. Whether that road leads to a safe haven or a terrible abyss [will depend on how well we prepare for an era that follows the Third Industrial Revolution]. The end of work could spell a death sentence for a civilization as we have come to know it. The end of work could also signal . . . a rebirth of the human spirit. (Gibbrey 1991)

CITIZENSHIP EDUCATION: THE GLOBAL DIMENSION

Citizenship education should cover the following schemes of work:
1) facilitate a discussion about what is meant by 'the global dimension';
2) explore the role of the school as a global institution in a global society;
3) highlight where the global dimension is both explicit and implicit in the programmes of study;
4) provide teaching and learning ideas under the headings of political literacy, social and moral responsibility and community involvement;
5) explore teaching and learning methods;
6) suggest starting points and pathways;
7) list further sources of support and guidance.

Global Dimension of Education

Perhaps the younger generation knows instinctively what it is to be a global citizen, because that is what they are. Schools need to foster their knowledge and understanding of other countries throughout the curriculum while always remembering that the young can teach their elders.

Young people are growing up in an increasingly global context. Citizenship education needs the global dimension to equip young people with the knowledge and skills to enable them to make use of the opportunities and to deal with the threats when they can live, work and participate fully in society at every level.

The incorporation of the global dimension into citizenship education helps pupils understand issues around them such as racism, refugees, human crisis, apartheid, terrorism, asylum seekers and the impact of migration. It also helps develop a balanced and informed view of these issues enabling them to respond in active and responsible ways to what is happening in the wider world. The global dimension to citizenship education is more than learning about other countries. It is a vital part of every aspect of the school curriculum, the life of the school and its teachers and pupils. Global citizenship is more than learning about seemingly complex 'global issues' such as sustainable development, conflict and international trade – important as these are. It is also about "the global dimension to local issues", which are present in all our lives, localities and communities. It is part of
1) the jobs we do
2) the clothes we wear
3) the food we eat
4) the music we listen to
5) the people and faiths in our communities and
6) the pupils in our schools.

It affects the decisions we have to make about our everyday lives from what to buy to where to go on holiday. Furthermore the processes at work at a local level are also at work all over the world and at many different levels, highlighting the similarities and ties that exist globally.

THE CITIZENSHIP EDUCATION PROGRAMMES

The programmes of study for citizenship education provide a framework from which teachers can develop and build their lessons. This allows teachers considerable scope for devising activities in ways that are relevant and interesting to pupils and are appropriate to their local communities. They also allow teachers to build on their own experiences and interests. Within this framework there are both explicit and implicit references to the global dimension of citizenship education.

The global dimension is not only applicable where it is explicit in the framework, but is relevant to all aspects of the curriculum where it has a unifying function. Many subject areas already include a global dimension that can be made citizenship-rich by emphasizing the relevant elements – for example, looking at domestic fuel consumption in a worldwide context and discussing action those individuals can take. This means approaching the subject in ways that enable pupils to recognize its relevance to their own lives. The depth of coverage within different aspects can be varied; it can be woven into citizenship or other strands in the curriculum. It is also important that staff and students understand the links across the curriculum that contribute to citizenship education.

The key factor is that the framework provides an opportunity for teachers to develop their own programmes of work. The teacher's role is to manage the pupils' learning so that there are opportunities for pupils to make progress, participate and achieve. Active learning opportunities can enhance student motivation and underpin key learning outcomes.

The vast majority of pupils world over believe that it is important to learn about global issues at school and that young people need to understand global matters in order to make choices about how they want to lead their lives.

The School in a Global Society

Whatever else the school system in any country achieves, the bottom line surely should be that it has a highly developed sense of ethics and of global as well as national citizenship.

CITIZENSHIP EDUCATION: THE GLOBAL DIMENSION

The gateway for teachers and educators keen to explore the global dimension of citizenship education are:
    1)   What does citizenship education involve?

2) Why is it important that citizenship education has a global dimension?

3) How can teaching of citizenship education be enhanced by the inclusion of the global dimension?

WHAT DOES CITIZENSHIP EDUCATION INVOLVE?

The rationale for citizenship education is based on three clear components set out in the Crick Report (1998): Political Literacy, Social and Moral Responsibility, and Community Involvement. These components provide the basis of the QCA's schemes of work for citizenship education:
1) The global dimension to political literacy
2) The global dimension to social and moral responsibility and
3) The global dimension to community involvement

WHY DOES CITIZENSHIP EDUCATION HAVE A GLOBAL DIMENSION?

Our students are growing up in an increasingly global context. Many of us have family origins or family members in other countries. Many of us live, work and study alongside people from all over the world. More and more people are traveling for work or for leisure. All forms of culture are shaped by global influences. Each decision we make as consumers or electors has an impact on global society.

To understand the nature of citizenship, young people need to learn about their position and role in relation to the world in which they live. They also need to develop the skills that will enable them to participate fully in society at a local, national and international level.

ENROLMENT OF THE TEACHING OF CITIZENSHIP EDUCATION BY THE INCLUSION OF THE GLOBAL DIMENSION

The Global Dimension to Political Literacy

Presenting the global dimension to citizenship helps young people to understand the issues that are around them such as racism, the plight of refugees, the impact of international legislation, and effects of environmental change.

It provides young people with the knowledge and understanding to make use of the opportunities available to them and to react responsibly to these issues so that they can live, work and participate fully in society at every level.

The Global Dimension to Social and Moral Responsibility

The global dimension helps young people understand the universality of issues that are of concern to them, such as what is fair and unfair, what is right and wrong, and the importance of sustainable development. It helps them understand that they share rights and responsibilities with others around the world.

The global dimension gives young people a sound foundation on which to base and build their value system and encourages them to respect the rights and dignity of others in an interdependent world. It builds appreciation of and respect for difference in: nationalities, ethnicities, religions and cultures. It also helps young people see that individual action can make a contribution to making the world a better place.

The Global Dimension to Community Involvement

With two-thirds school children having relatives in at least one other country, the global dimension to citizenship education and community involvement is essential. It makes a positive contribution to pupils' understanding of themselves, their sense of belonging and social inclusion, and their understanding of the diverse nature of society. It helps prepare all pupils for involvement in their community and for life in a multicultural society and to recognize that we are all members of a wider, interdependent global community. The global dimension helps young people understand how action can be taken at a local level.

With the following statements from the citizenship programs of study have implications for the global dimension to community involvement.

CONCLUDING OBSERVATIONS

The advancement of Science and Technology (S&T), Research and Development (R&D), Liberalization, Privatization and Globalization (LPG), increased awareness of human rights, the spread of information and communication technology, transnational migrations, and international tourism etc., the world can truly be considered a "global village".

The global/world society which we are living in today necessitates a subsystem global education system. In the global education system, all the dimensions and components should serve the needs and purposes of the global society. The student who comes out of this education system should be a true global citizen in letter and spirit as well as should be competent to discharge the global responsibilities.

REFERENCES

Andrzejewski, J. (1996) Knowledge and Skills for Social and Environmental Justice. In *Oppression and Social Justice: Critical Frameworks*. Andrzejewski, J., Heights N., (Eds.) M.A.: Simon and Schuster, 3-9.

Blackledge, D., & Hunt, B. (1985). *Sociological Interpretations of Education*. Sydney: Croom Helm.

Brosio, R. (1994): *A Radical Democratic Critique of Capitalist Education*. Peter Lang Publishing, Inc.

Brown, P., & Lauder, H. (1996). Education, Globalization and Economic Development. *Journal of Education Policy, 11*(1), 1-25.

Brown, T. (1999). Challenging Globalization as Discourse and Phenomenon. *International Journal of Lifelong Education, 18*(1), 3-17.

Daun, H. (1997). National Forces, Globalization and Educational Restructuring: Some European Response Patterns. *Comapre, 27*(1), 19-41.

Green, A. (1999). Education and Globalization in Europe and East Asia: Convergent and Divergent Trends. *Journal of Education Policy,* 14(1), 55-71.

Rifkin, J. (1995) *The End of Work: The Decline of the Global Labor Force and the Dawn of the Post-Market Era.* New York: G. P. Putnam's Sons.

Russell, B. (1916) Principles of Social Reconstruction.. *London: Allen and Unwin.*

CHAPTER TEN

Education for Peace: Models of What is Working in Working Models

Marilyn Higgins
Yamaguchi Prefectural University

INTRODUCTION

Children in Mrs. Akabane's sixth grade class have been working on a new way of solving problems that they encounter in their class. For example, there was a drop in participation in the weekly class recreation activity. The children weren't fighting. They just withdrew and grumbled among themselves in small groups. But such "passive resistance" is a sign of deeper conflict and is sometimes even harder to resolve because the reasons remain hidden. The all-class game activity was selected by the students themselves (or, at least, a democratically elected committee of students). "So what was the problem?" the teacher wondered. She decided to try the "Conflict Resolution Bridge" exercise. The children had tried it before on other class issues and liked the way it helped them to clarify and settle issues that seemed to weigh the class down. They had settled "name calling" issues that had led to outward fighting, and they even settled a dispute with the teacher about how much homework was too much. Now this...

The teacher asked the children to write down their feelings about the class recreation period. She then asked for two representatives from among the children who liked the game activity and two from among those who did not like the game activity, to take the steps from opposite sides of the bridge toward the middle, step-by-step — expressing and exchanging their wishes, feelings and understandings on the matter:

1) "I want..."
2) "I feel..."
3) "I feel this way because..."
4) "You want, and you feel...because..."
5) "Maybe we should try..."
6) "Let's try..."

The students' responses after the activity was finished demonstrate how the lights of empathy, reason, imagination and resolve can illuminate the children's

hearts and minds" while providing them a conflict-free pattern for conflict resolution.

One member of the class game committee wrote:

"I understood for the first time that some people didn't like the way of de-
ciding the team or doing the same game. I wanted to play Keidoro (a "cops and
robbers" game), so I didn't expect that. If we had another problem like that, I
want to solve it using this bridge."

A normally shy member of the class who had not liked the game, but would
normally not voice a complaint wrote:

"At first, I was worried whether we could solve the problem truly or not,
but today we could. So I thought it is awesome."

One of the boys who had been chosen to represent the viewpoint of those
who liked the game wrote:

"Last time (we did the Conflict Resolution Bridge exercise) I only watched.
This time I thought that doing this bridge is different from just watching it. First,
I was so comfortable giving my opinion. And at last, we can understand the
other persons' feelings. I like that point best. These days, we have an opportunity to communicate with foreigners a lot. We have many problems between the
countries for example Japan and North Korea. In the future, we have to think
and solve those kinds of problems. To solve that, we have to understand the
other persons. This bridge makes us aware of how important the way to solve
problems is. This is a good way, I think."

In fact, 100% of the students responded that they were satisfied with the
outcome and looked forward to resolving other problems in this way. In the first
exercise 27 out of 30 of the students had responded positively. With practice, all
of them were won over.

Mrs. Akabane, encouraged by the effectiveness of this tool, did not stop
there. She began to pick up other tools and approaches for peace education from
a selection offered at the workshop of a small Peace Education Research Project
I began last fall in Yamaguchi, Japan. The approach of the workshops was to
first present an overview of the inter-related strategies and concepts that have
made for successful peace education projects in various places around the world.
Then the teachers began to choose and incorporate into their classrooms healing
remedies for the conflicts and contentions they themselves identified.

We'll get back to Mrs. Akabane's classroom later to see what approaches
she and other teachers have incorporated. At this point, let us take a step back
and look at the overview they were presented.

GLOBAL PERSPECTIVE

At a Peace Education Seminar held in Tokyo in February, 2003, as a training
activity for employees of JICA (Japan's version of the "Peace Corps") the Director of Peace Education for the United Nations Children's Fund (UNICEF),
Cream Wright, pointed out that peace education is needed everywhere (Wright,
2003). But its form may vary according to the needs and the setting in various

localities. He described four kinds of peace education: prevention, construction, mitigation and reconstruction. Of course, education for prevention of conflict is needed everywhere. Peace, it seems, does not "just happen." The more complex the society, the more peace and harmony must be planned for, educated for, and enabled — just like safe and smooth traffic patterns in a large city.

In fact, when systems are in the midst of rapidly changing circumstances, an added level of peace education is needed, which Mr. Wright referred to as construction. From the end of the Second World War until the present, educators in Japan have relied primarily on "prevention" strategies, which mostly have taken the form of helping children to understand the harmful effects of war. Thousands of Japanese 5th and 6th graders file through the "Peace Museums" of Hiroshima and Nagasaki every year and are given the "no more war, "no more nuclear bombs" themes by rote. They learn in "moral education" classes such stories as "Barefoot Gen" who bravely survived and vowed to work for peace though his peace-oriented family was killed in the nuclear holocaust. Never mind that the deeper causes for the war, the details of what led to the conflict that led to the bombing and the implications for the children's lives today are left undescribed even at higher levels of education. Japan considers itself devoted to peace and first and foremost the "Land of Wa" (harmony). Yet by 1986 (the United Nations International Year of Peace) the education ministry reported that up to 55% of Japanese schools were troubled by violence, bullying and delinquency (Schoppa, 1991). The increasing number and severity of violent incidents has been on the minds of educators for at least twenty years. In my recent survey of elementary schools in my somewhat rural area of central Yamaguchi, over 25% of principals who responded to the survey indicated that they have experienced serious incidents of violence in their schools in the past two years. Fully half of the schools with over 500 pupils reported violent incidents and/or classroom breakdown.

Just last summer one of the four main national newspapers, The Yomiuri Shimbun, called for "a new approach to peace education," recognizing that the post-war slogans were really fading in their effectiveness (2003). Mr. Wright's points regarding the "construction" approach seemed to elicit a positive response from the JICA personnel. After all, Japan is a country whose society is and has been in the midst of rapid change. It is no longer a "one-culture" society. Even if all of the students in a school are Japanese, there are subcultures and diversities to consider which all-to-often have been ignored or discounted in the "We-Japanese" approach to unity in uniformity. If we look at successful peace education projects throughout the world, there is at least one principle that stands out: they construct a viewpoint that recognizes the more powerful potential of unity in diversity. Education for peace begins with appreciation of differences and builds toward a culture of inclusion that embraces both similarities and uniqueness.

If conflict exists, Mr. Wright notes, mitigation skills are needed. He noted that education for peace projects around the globe include ways to teach conflict-free conflict resolution to children. In some places, it is the children who then teach it to the adults in their families and communities. Those taking roles as mitigators learn to develop peace-making attitudes, the knowledge that peace is possible, and the communication and logistical skills to make it happen.

But where the worst has happened and people are still "raw" from recent conflict, healing and rebuilding are needed. While reconstructing the community to deal with the basic survival needs, people who feel "cheated" or "oppressed" also need hope and perhaps new life skills, as well as a kind of peace education that enables them to take active and constructive approaches to understanding and achieving their rights. They face the challenges of learning how to negotiate and eliminate barriers to discrimination, and skills for consensus building with the very people who they may feel have harmed them. The "majority" culture, many of whom may feel little connection to the conflict, or may be quite reticent to get involved, also needs education. New awareness must be developed, and a reconstruction of attitudes or societal views that they may have unwittingly inherited so that ingrained or traditional "structural impediments" or so-called "structural violence" can be overcome.

DOES PEACE EDUCATION WORK?

When challenged by participants of the JICA conference about whether we know that "peace education" actually works, the UNICEF Director for Peace Education had to admit that he was not sure. We see examples of success and examples of failure. He had not seen clear research. After all, he noted, that systematic lines of reporting are not well set up (even with the UN and its agencies) and those who are in the trenches don't often have the where-with-all to do the counting and reporting as well. The point was well taken, and led this researcher to the library of the United Nations University in Tokyo to do a bit of digging into whatever statistics and information could be found.

I'm happy to report that the news looks good. I found a fair array of positive reports from various projects around the world. In addition, Nevo and Brem report in a chapter called "Peace Education Program Evaluation" in Salomon and Baruch's book Peace Education, (1999) that 80% to 90% of nearly 80 peace education programs they studied in various parts of the world were effective, or at least partly effective in achieving their aims. Those that enhanced "pro-social orientation" reduced violence; projects focusing on "political and social efficacy" reduced delinquency; projects that promote "value-oriented attitudes" and "tolerance of diversity" reduced stereotyping and ethnocentricity. In other words, when pro-social skills and inclusive attitudes are conscientiously taught there is a corresponding decline in violence, anti-social behavior and harsh, divisive attitudes. The projects that failed to achieve their goals could be seen to have one or more of the following flaws: their methods relied more on "didactic" (one-way learning) rather than participatory methods; their goals were not suited to the actual time frame or scope of their project (in other words, they may have expected too much too soon); or their statistical designs or reporting methods were not actually well-matched to their situation. I'm quite certain that in the past five years, other researchers have been finding similar results. (See Christie, Wagner and Winter, 2001)

For many of us, the potential effectiveness of peace education is a matter of faith that grows from positive experience. The question is what kind, where, when, how? But if data on whether or not it works is needed for the skeptical, I believe it is out there for the gathering.

What was most interesting to me as I investigated various projects to get a closer look was that many of the most successful projects have evolved in the most difficult and even violence-prone areas of the globe: Israel, Boznia-Herzagovina, racially divided areas of Los Angeles, even parts of Australia challenged by increasing ethnic and cultural diversity. This may be due to the shear contrast they present and the natural motivational opportunities within the environment. Another interesting point about successful projects is the consistency with which the same interweaving list of strategies came up again and again.

FOUR PRINCIPLE PEACE EDUCATION STRATEGIES AND SOME PROGRAMS THAT MODEL THEM

Toh Swee Hin (1997) summarized four effective principle strategies within the integrated framework of peace education programs: First, he mentioned the need for a holistic framework that tries to clarify inter-relationships between and among the root causes of "peacelessness, conflict and violence." He also noted that, "peace education cannot...be limited to the very marginalized and oppressed." "Allies for transformation" and "points of potential influence" may be found among the advantaged, governing and elite sectors of society as well. If I were rewriting that last sentence, I would say, "must be found." If peace education is to be a unifying process it must include everyone.

An example of such a strategy is demonstrated in the Education for Peace project (2003) being carried out in Boznia and Herzegovina (BiH). The government of BiH invited experts in non-violent conflict resolution and peace education from a European university, and with grants from various concerned countries including Luxemburg and Japan, they have endeavored to create a "culture of peace" in areas that have long been divided by ethnic violence. Three years after beginning this program in six schools, the atmosphere of these schools has changed dramatically. And in what seems a miracle to the local residents, Bosnian, Serb and Croat teachers enjoy getting together in each others neighborhoods for coffee and to share ideas on their mutual projects.

The primary approach of this EFP project first trains teachers to implement an integrated curriculum applied across all subjects in the every classroom. The traditional curriculum is infused with the principles of unity in diversity, and the focus in all areas is directed toward the nature of peace and conflict. Although the teachers were the first to be introduced to how to bring this sense of unity and integration to all parts of the curriculum, the total program required universal participation of all students, all parents, all staff, teachers and administrators within the locality of the schools who adopted the program. As BiH is an area still suffering the results of recent intercultural conflict, a reconstruction approach is also needed and a "culture of healing" is being created between the three main ethnic groups, the Bosnians, the Serbs and the Croats. Participants are asked via initial questionnaires to reflect on how highly educated people from an advanced society could commit such terrible acts; whether they believed people can change; whether they believe peace is possible, and whether religions such as Christianity and Islam which are based on principles of love and peace can explain such acts of aggression on the part of their followers as have been perpetrated by all sides in the recent conflicts. They are asked how their children, whose parents had been involved in war atrocities, might grow up differently. Tough choices are given: do they want their children to grow up amidst more war and violence, or are they willing to commit themselves to trying an alternative path to peace by using peaceful means? With these thought-provoking and challenging questions in mind, meetings are gradually arranged in which even still-skeptical parents and children from the three conflicting ethnic groups can begin to "hear" each others' stories (both negative and positive) and recognize the unity of the problems they are all facing.

The integrated curriculum approach helps the teachers to do two things: 1) to see the relevance of the subjects they are teaching to the process of reconstruction, and thus to inspire a greater enthusiasm and optimism in themselves and their students; 2) to recognize that teaching involves not only the passing of skills and knowledge, but also attitudes (over which they have more control that they had previously realized). The teachers are taught to recognize the opportunities to teach "peace building principles" in relation to every subject. For example, if the topic is cooking, is it possible to leave the baking soda or yeast out of cookies or bread just because you personally don't like the flavor of the ingredient by itself? What would be the result? In biology, what are the effects on a garden or orchard that admits only one type of plant? In arts, what if we limited ourselves to only one or two colors, one or two musical notes, or one or two building materials? In math, what happens to formulas where even minor parts of an equation are dropped? How do order and diversity play a part in every aspect of life?

The arts play a vital role in this program to promote and enhance interactive links between individuals, the communities involved, and the schools. Periodic festivals, theatrical events, art shows, etc. based around peace-building themes enable young and old to contribute their unique talents and participate together in positive cross-cultural events. The program is systematically integrating people, communities and locations, infusing new skills and attitudes, most importantly a new sense of hope, empathy and determination.

After only one year of the program, the results, in terms of community feeling and reduced violence, were such that the BiH Ministers of Education requested that the EFP program be introduced to all schools in Bosnia. It has taken time to gear up for that, however. At present, one hundred and three schools are involved in the program.

I am told by a photojournalist (Higgins, 2004), who recently visited the area, that not all of the schools are uniformly successful at grasping and implementing the spirit of the project. Some schools take longer than others to over-come their sense of "exclusivity." He cited the example that there are maps on the walls of some schools that exclude the districts of the other ethnic groups (similar to the weather maps in the US that stop at the Canadian border, as if there is no weather over there.) But even in these schools, there is an intention of compliance — even if it means that they will "fake it until they make it!" Even minimal attention makes a difference to many of the children. More complete attention creates great differences and a compellingly attractive atmosphere that teachers do not want to retreat from.

An integrated educational approach focusing on the inter-relatedness and unity of all things, and including as broad a spectrum of players as possible in the peace education project is the first important key, then.

The second point that Toh Swee-Hin makes is that "peace education emphasizes the crucial role of values formation through its pedagogical processes." He goes on to say, "Clearly, peace education needs to be very explicit about its preferred values, such as compassion, justice, equity, fairness, caring for life, sharing reconciliation, integrity, hope and active nonviolence." No "value free" pretensions in this process!

Some examples of this "values formation" orientation can be seen in "The Children's Enrichment Program" in Los Angeles California(2003). Attention to "Habits of the Heart" is one of five aspects of its "Full-Circle" approach to learning. The other aspects are "enriched academics" (an integrated educational approach), conflict resolution skills, arts enrichment, and community service. The "Habits of the Heart" element draws heavily on the Virtues Project (Popov, 2000) and its five strategies for teaching and using the language of virtues to empower children and adults to bring out the best in themselves and others. I have heard a few experts in moral education speak disparagingly at what they called "a bag of virtues" approach. I think that such skepticism may be understandable if the teaching methods for the virtues are limited to "didactic" (one-way, or authoritarian) approaches, and if there is no integration of the mere words to the whole experience of the children. However, character education in the model adopted above involves a kernel of direct teaching surrounded by and enriched in a nurturing environment of participatory learning opportunities focusing on what such virtues look like when they grow in actual fruitful practice, as well as what circumstances may appear when they are lacking. For example, in "The Children's Enrichment Program" which is located in the heart of an area of Los Angeles marred by racial tension and riots in the past decade, one of the "values" encouraged (among such virtues as courtesy, respect, tolerance, empathy, helpfulness, etc.) is "tenderness." The lesson plans in this program are linked to activities and service projects that empower students to exercise "enlightened altruism" in their own surroundings. In the unit related to "tenderness" children study biological life cycles, then students go to visit homes for the elderly. In their chances to demonstrate their powers of "tenderness" they are transformed from viewing themselves as among the "deprived" to persons rich in personal power. The children also relate their experiences with their own family and community experiences with gardens, pets, babies, handicapped people,

and so on. You may not be surprised to learn that the "musical" experience offered during this unit is singing the popular song, "Try a little tenderness!" in a
light-hearted and whimsical way.

In my small project in Japan, some Virtues Project approaches have also
been introduced. The necessity of connecting the abstract "universal" principle
to concrete "everyday" experiences of the children is stressed. The teachers involved were stirred by this, and even more pleased when they began to put it
into action. Mrs. Akabane, for example, took a list of virtues she had noticed
were also related to the "moral education" stories she had been dutifully introducing to the children each week. She asked the children to first do a dictionary
exercise defining each of the words. I was not surprised based on my long experience in Japan, that a number of the "values" which we have learned to take
for granted (such as trustworthiness, dignity, or even generosity) could not be
defined by the children in practical terms. It is not that these qualities do not
exist, but they are not "named" or noticed by most people in this culture at this
time. Mrs. Akabane asked her students to identify examples of the virtues from
the lessons they had been reading. The light began to dawn. Then she asked
them to carry out a daily reflection exercise in which three students were fea-
tured and the class would be asked to mention the virtues that these students had
displayed during that week with examples of where/how they noticed them. The
students began noticing that their own virtues were recognized and valued by
others. This "inspired" and "empowered" them to demonstrate even more of
their positive qualities and to comment more freely on the virtues they notice in
their classmates. Mrs. Akabane said that the "dry" moral education curriculum
suddenly came to life for the students and for her. Even another teacher in the
project, who had had a great deal of trouble with her class, found that working
directly with the virtues had a visible turn-around effect on her students.

The Virtues Project approach (Popov, Popov & Kavelin, 1997) is being implemented in classrooms, community groups, families, businesses, government
agencies, and even prisons in over 80 countries of the world. Its approaches
have a "simple elegance" that make them relatively easy to integrate as a thread
into any on-going educational experience whether personal, in the family, in the
school, the workplace or the community at large

The third "important pedagogical principle of peace education" mentioned
by Toh Swee-Hin is the "strategy" of dialogue. He points out that such strategies that use dialogue cultivate "a more horizontal teacher-learner relationship in
which both…educate and learn from each other." A good example of this is the
Conflict Resolution Bridge activity mentioned above. It was first introduced to
me by Teresa Langness who started the Children's Enrichment Program. Dr.
Langness could hardly contain her enthusiasm about the effectiveness of this
exercise particularly for upper elementary school children. She first introduced it
to her students in her after school program using "hypothetical" examples. Before she could try it out with "real" problems the students had taken the Bridge
to the playground themselves to solve problems that they were encountering,
without the teachers' assistance. She then began to hear from parents that children were teaching the method to them as a way to solve problems in the family.

Toh Swee-Hin's point about teacher-student relationships is well demon-strated by one of Mrs. Akabane's experiences using "the Bridge" to dialogue with her students about homework assignments. She was concerned that the children were getting lax about their homework. By employing the bridge exer-cise she learned that the students were exhausted by longer school hours on par-ticular days of the week. They well understood and appreciated the need for homework, but had found themselves unable to keep up especially on the long school days. Mrs. Akabane agreed to reduce the number of homework assign-ments and the time they would take on the "long days," and the students prom-ised to do their best to do and turn in their assignments all through the week. Both the students and the teacher were pleased, and amazed by the results. "I didn't think we could change the teachers' mind," said some of the children. "I didn't realize how much the students actually felt their responsibility for the homework," said the teacher.

From my personal observation of classrooms, I must say, there is something magical about an environment in which the teacher and the students are jointly engaged in the process of communication in their mutual learning activities. The Conflict Resolution Bridge provides one approach to resolving issues that have become divisive. Although it is basically a "two-sided" approach there is room for wider consultation. For example, when Mrs. Akabane's class does the exer-cise as a formal procedure, she engages the entire class by passing out a work-sheet on which each student writes his or her own response to each question as well as what the viewpoints and feelings of the children on the bridge. When they reach Step 5 ("Maybe we could...") the participants on the bridge turn to the class to ask for ideas. It's a brainstorming step. After a few, or even several ideas are given by people in the class audience (with the teacher playing the part of secretary by writing the ideas on the board), the students on the bridge offer their own ideas for solution before proceeding to Step 6. They choose one or two of the solutions offered that they believe would work ("Let's try..."). Teach-ing "consultative" approaches to multi-dimensional problem solving can happen in a number of activities and within structured lesson plans. Even in math classes, just because there is one right answer does not mean there is only one right way to get there. I observed a math class in Japan where students in small groups were asked to solve a particular problem. Six groups came up with four different ways to solve the problem and they discussed the merits and demerits of each approach. In many cooperative educational activities, consultation skills emerge somewhat naturally. It is often effective to teach children ways to facili-tate consultation in group projects that require some level of participation of every member of the group.

"Consultation" is considered one of the elements of the "roof" which pro-tects the "House of Peace" in the creative "Peace Pack" lesson series by Geor-gina Sounness and Terri Turner (2003) that is used in upper elementary Baha'i Classes in many schools in Western Australia. These are lessons given as part of the "religious education" portion of the curriculum. The Baha'is teach the fun-damental history and teachings of all religions to those who take this course. After that, a "Peace House" is made demonstrating how the teachings found in these various traditions can work together for building a peaceful world. The roof tiles, tied with threads of "virtues" found in the sacred texts of the various spiritual traditions, are added to a "Peace House" lesson-by-lesson. In addition to the skill of consultation," the protective roof tiles include concepts of "world citizenship," "independent investigation of truth," "elimination of prejudice," "equality of men and women," "oneness of religion," and "respect for the environment," among others. These are elements of the house that has "love" at its base, and "unity" for its walls. Through this broad and diverse lesson series, students learn to respect a diversity of cultures, recognize the organizing principles that make peace possible and learn how to communicate in fair, friendly and effective ways.

Toh Swee-Hin's "fourth vital principle" is what he calls "critical empowerment" — or developing a "critical consciousness that actively seeks to transform the realities of a culture of war and violence into a culture of peace and nonviolence. In the peace education projects I have studied or observed, this consciousness is developed and enhanced primarily in two ways: 1) through service to the community, and 2) through the use of the arts.

In the Children's Enrichment Project in Los Angeles, low self-esteem and hopelessness about their future abounds in the surrounding neighborhoods and within the schools. The arts provide an immediate way for students low in academic or verbal skills to communicate their impressions, feelings and ideas. Even for students whose academic skills are high, the arts have a salutary effect on their overall communication skills. The arts of various kinds provide ways for people across age groups and cultural barriers to communicate in nonthreatening ways, and are additional avenues for building feelings of success.

Student in the CEP program also gain confidence in their future when teachers and facilitators listen carefully to students' hopes and dreams. Members of the community who have occupations and professions that students have expressed interest in are invited to come and meet the students. Some examples include veterinarians, doctors and nurses, civic leaders, artists of various kinds, and so on. People representing these occupations are asked to speak with the children about how the skills and topics they learned in elementary school, junior high school, and high school are applied in their professional and daily lives as adults. Students begin to see their school experiences as part of a path toward the "power to serve" and the "power to achieve." Students are then invited to take part in various kinds of service projects that connect to these professions. The projects often include some form of arts including speaking, dramatic and artistic presentations. For example, children wondered about how the math they had to learn in school could be of benefit for them if they wanted to go into a profession using art. A police artist was invited in to give the children a demonstration of how his work involves the use of proportions and geometry that he had learned while in school. The children practiced making portraits using his "proportional drawing" methods and decided to do a project in which each child in the group made a larger than life portrait of a "missing child" from the police files. When the portraits were done, the children displayed the portraits in a community parade that was covered by local TV stations. Imagine their exultant feelings of efficacy when a child who had been missing was actually found through their efforts.

It is sad to think that the problem of "missing children" is part of these children's reality, but it is encouraging to see the creative ways that the threads of an approach to education that integrates their academics to empower them to work with others can effectively change their reality for the better. These are examples of the "critical empowerment" mentioned by Toh Swee-Hin.

It should be noted that the CEP project has been going for almost a dozen years since the riots in their neighborhood in 1992. Results of the program showed 80% of the participants in the after-school program increased their ranking in national reading, and math tests. 100% of the children participating in the summer programs increased their interest and abilities in reading, and other areas of study, and 85% of them improved their math performance. The ratings for behavior and global awareness are unanimously high.

The "Full Circle" approach is now beginning to be implemented by a number of schools in their regular programs. It is one of the integrated educational programs being investigated by teachers in China who are looking for innovative approaches that balance physical, social and spiritual education.

SUMMARY AND CONCLUSION

Before I came across Toh Swee Hin's overview, I had written my own list of "common threads that create the warp and woof of successful peace education endeavors"(Higgins, 2004). These threads included:

1) "A universal view of mankind as a whole made up of a diversity of cultures with a common desire to live in harmony." This corresponds to the holistic approach. Holism in the curriculum also comes through in point number four below.

2) "A universal ethic which recognizes the need to develop our sense of dignity, our nobility and the practice of such positive 'habits-of-heart' as tolerance, justice, truthfulness, peacefulness, love, service, and excellence." This corresponds to Toh Swee Hin's second point about explicit values.

3) "A universal appreciation of our uniqueness and diversity from the individual to cultural level that can be expressed in positive ways from the earliest years ...through arts (including sports, crafts, and creative technologies) and through education." Along with the next point,

4) "A universal appeal that makes academic achievement a door to advancing abilities for service to society," covers what I believe Toh Swee-Hin refers to as "critical empowerment." That is to say that truly integrated education empowers students to expand consciousness, and add value to their personal and social realities. (Elements in the curriculum are not felt to be just "dry bones" left over from a skeleton of no longer viable traditions.)

5)   "A shared power to communicate in such ways as to create lasting bonds
     of friendship and to solve problems and conflicts in a way that rein-
     forces, rather than continues separation or erosion of social relation-
     ships." This clearly connects with Toh Swee Hin's third point on the
     importance of "dialogue."

Focusing on these strategies is not to neglect the motivating factors that
provide content and direction to various peace education programs. As has been
pointed out by Toh Swee-Hin, some educators are motivated by a human rights
approach, others by inter-cultural understanding, or international issues, and
many are inspired by the overarching spiritual traditions that educate and promote unity of soul and spirit. I find myself inspired by all of these. There are so
many ways to work for peace. I leave you with this thought from the Writings of
the Baha'i Faith (1976):

> *"Bend your minds and wills to the education of the peoples and kindreds of the
> earth, that haply the dissensions that divide it may, through the Most Great
> Name, be blotted out from its face, and all mankind become the upholders of
> one Order, and the inhabitants of one City...Blessed is he who mingleth with all
> men in a spirit of utmost kindliness and love."*

REFERENCES

Wright, Cream, "Peace Education." Presentation at the JICA Seminar on Peace Educa-
    tion, Tokyo, February, 2003.
Schoppa, Leonard, "Education Reform in Japan: Goals and Results of the Recent Reform
    Campaign" in Beauchamp, Edward, Windows on Japanese Education. Westport, Ct.,
    Greenwood Press, 1991, pp. 51 – 75.
    http://www.people.virginia.edu/~ljs2k/educate.txt
"Peace education needs review" Editorial, The Daily Yomiuri, Friday, August 15, 2003,
    p. 8
Nevo and Brem, "Peace Education Program Evaluation" in Salomon & Baruch, Peace
    Education. Lawrence Erlbaum, 1999, p. 275.
Christie, D., Wagner, R., and Winter, D.(eds.) Peace, Conflict and Violence: Peace Psy-
    chology for the 21st Century. Prentice Hall, 2001.
Toh Swee-Hin, "Education for Peace: Towards a Millennium of Well-Being." Paper for
    the Working Document of the International Conference on Culture of Peace and
    Governance (Maputo, Mozambique, 1-4 September, 1997).
    http://www.peace.ca/educationforpeace.htm
Education for Peace. A Community Development Program of Landegg International
    Univsity, Switzerland, Landegg InternationalUniversity, 2003.
    http://www.efpinternational.org/
Shannon Higgins (freelance photojournalist), telephone interview on his trips to Bosnia-
    Herzegovina and visits to the EFP project sites, February and April 2004.
Langness, Teresa, Making Peace, A Full-Circle Learning Conflict Resolution Supple-
    ment. Los Angeles, California, Children's Enrichment Program, 2003.
    http://www.childrensenrichmentprogram.org
Popov, Linda, The Virtues Project Educator's Guide. Torrance, CA: Jalmar Press, 2000.

Popov, Linda, Popov, Dan, Kavelin, John, <u>The Family Virtues Guide</u>. New York: Plume, Penguin Books, Ltd., 1997. http://www.virtuesproject.com

Sounness, Georgina and Turner, Terri, <u>Peace Pack</u>, A Programme for Baha'i Classes in Schools. Australia: Spiritual Assembly of the Baha'is of East Freemantle, 2001.

Higgins, Marilyn, "Education for Peace: Successful Multi-Cultural Programs from Around the World May Hold Keys for Peace Education in Japanese Schools." Bulletin of the Faculty of International Studies, Yamaguchi Prefectural University, No. 10, March 2004.

Baha'u'llah, "Gleanings from the Writings of Baha'u'llah, Wilmette, Illinois: Baha'i Publishing Trust, 1976, pg. 333.

CHAPTER ELEVEN

'Education for All' – Problems and Perspectives in the Light of Globalization

Geetha Janet Vitus
Karmela Rani Training College, India

INTRODUCTION

"Everyone has the right to education. Education shall be free, at least in the elementary and fundamental stages. Elementary education shall be compulsory. Technical education and professional education should be made generally available."(Universal Declaration of Human Rights, 1948, Art. 26).

More than five decades after the Universal Declaration was adopted, no one would dare to deny that all children and young people have the right to basic education. All are aware that expansion and improvement of the education of children and youth, in order to meet their basic learning needs is in the interest of individuals and societies. Education leads to creativity as well to improved participation of the learner in the social, economic, cultural and political life of the society. Education is a prerequisite not only for the full exercise of the individual's rights, but also for understanding and respecting the rights of others. Education through its influence on attitudes and behaviours and its positive impact on health, productivity, protection of the environment, family planning and child care can transform the cultural, social and economic life of people.

Education as it is today is expensive and the world economic crisis which imposes dramatic reduction in investment and expenditure has led to the demands for heightened accountability and financial stringency. As a result there has been an acute shortage of a skilled work-force which has hampered the economic and social development of countries around the world. If the capacity of people to shape and improve their own lives is the measure of development, then basic education for all is surely a necessary condition as well as a human right. Developing countries deeply affected by the economic recession and growing debt burdens after the 1980's were generally unable to maintain the pace of educational expansion in view of the cost of education for the development of skilled labour among other reasons.

In response to the sorry state of affairs the executive heads of UNESCO, UNICEF, UNDP and the World Bank convened "the World Conference on Education for All – Meeting Basic Learning Needs (Jomtein, Thailand, 1990). Its task was to draw attention on the importance and impact of basic education and to forge global consensus committed to provide basic education for all, which resulted in the birth of both the "World Declaration on Education for All" and the Framework for Action to meet the basic learning needs.

Today we are experiencing the impact of globalization on education. After a decade of the "World Declaration on Education for All", issues that continue to be raised are, have we achieved the target of educating all? Have we met the basic learning needs of the learners? Has globalization been a boon or bane in this direction? To what extent has the concern for human rights in education been achieved in the context of globalization? This paper examines the "Problems and Perspectives of Education for All in the light of Globalization".

GLOBALIZING EDUCATION FOR ALL

There are many definitions on globalization. "Globalization presents the apparent paradox of stimulating competition between universities, while at the same time calling into being a much richer and more variegated problem-based collaborative environment amongst them." (Michael Gibbons, 2001)

"Internationalization at the national, sector and institutional levels is defined as the process of integrating an international, intercultural, or global dimension into the purpose, functions or delivery of postsecondary education." (Knight, 2003, as cited in 'Globalization' by Scholte, J.A)

In order to compete towards progress and development in a global economy, students at all levels need to have a global perspective. Globalizing education for all implies a better place to live, in terms of the environment, social justice and the promotion of cross cultural understanding. This has become a challenge to educators. How are they to provide education for culture maintenance while at the same time promoting effective learning of modern knowledge. Despite its important relationship to the economy, education cannot be reduced to a vehicle geared solely for employment, growth and efficiency. Culture is an essential ingredient of any learning process. A child's respect for his or her own culture and language is the foundation of self respect and tolerance of others. If attitudes such as 'trust', 'hope', 'respect' and 'optimism' are nurtured during infancy and the early years of schooling they will lay the foundation of personal development crucial for later life and for establishing positive attitudes to others. Education has a vital role to play in helping human beings to improve their relationships with their environment and indeed in contributing to the ultimate sustainability of the planet.

A country should be able to ensure that all its citizens are given the opportunity starting from the earliest stages of education to gain an understanding of science and technology and the capacity to put them to appropriate use and develop them to meet collective needs to be truly independent. Sound basic literacy and numeric skills and at a higher level, problem solving and abstract reasoning abilities will be cornerstones of scientific and technological advance.

Education for all requires systematic analysis of learning needs. According to the vision of UNESCO, science and technology rather than being taught as separate subjects, should be integrated into the teaching of basic communication and the skills of numeric linked to health and environment themes. The "World Declaration on Education for All", Article 1.1, sets out its scope in clear terms. To quote, "Every person-child, youth and adult-shall be able to benefit from educational opportunities designed to meet their basic learning needs".

Education for all is increasingly seen as a life long experience, more attention will need to be given to non-formal education for youth and adults especially through the media, with better links between the formal educational system and non formal programs. Learning in the classroom should be linked with the learning in the school community and the family. The key to success will lie in the quality and training of the teacher educators who will themselves be responsible for the training and retraining of the millions of teachers throughout the world. They in turn will equip students in the classroom to make the world a better place to live.

BENEFITS OF GLOBALIZING EDUCATION FOR ALL

Education has been conceived as a tool to promote national development as well as international understanding. Globalization and economic integration are perceived in terms of opening of a nation's economies as well as a process of integrating science, education, technology and culture. As a consequence the globalization of education has been going through many modes. To list a few:

1) Educational institutions operate in foreign lands by granting franchise or agreements with the educational institutions of the host countries;
2) Establishment of campuses of foreign universities in host countries;
3) Establishment of the Centres by the governments and programs offered by their universities;
4) Operation of virtual campuses by using satellite and the information superhighway. Students can benefit through e-learning.

The benefits of globalizing education can be categorized under the Academic Aspect, the Professional Aspect and the Social Aspect:

A. Academic Aspect:

It has resulted in better use of machines, gadgets and greater output, extended the dimensions of passing on of information and knowledge from one country to another in the context of intellectual culture. It has created a level of excellence in students that is directly reflected in their achievement and there is more demand for it in all countries.

B. Professional Aspect:

It has the built-in scope of producing qualified employees for economic development to benefit their society. It can also enable the young graduates to provide
better and expert service to their society. It can produce a large number of qualified technocrats in every field of activity so that no country should suffer from
lack of qualified manpower. The third world countries can provide relatively
good quality education at an affordable cost to all the Anglophonic countries.

C. Social Aspect:

This aspect can help create better understanding of the impact of advancement in
all fields of development, in the society. It has broadened goals of general education to prepare students with attitudes and capabilities for life long learning.
By globalizing education for all we can create better learners, thinkers, commu-
nicators and performers.

   We can also say that by globalizing higher education the overall quality of
higher education can be improved. It will promote the understanding of at least
one other culture. It can increase understanding of the global system. It provides
opportunity to examine the organizational needs of international education. It
also will motivate universities to revamp curricula to reflect the need for international needs. It will bring universities together to build consortia to enhance capabilities. It will promote co-operation and interdependence with institutions in
other countries. Thus, by globalizing education for all we are creating citizens
for a globalized world. Students will be able to locate information from a variety
of sources, identify underlying values and investigate the variety of information.

   One of the long-term benefits of globalizing education for all is to create a
safer, healthier, more peaceful, more just and sustainable world in which to live.
We can also study the global problems and various strategies for addressing
them and can generate a renewed sense of hope and optimism. We can provide
meaning to the curriculum by practicing active citizenship whether through personal changes, service learning, grass root –organizing or by a myriad of other
activities. By globalizing education for all, educators and policy makers alike
have an opportunity to dramatically change the nature of education regardless of
our discipline or portion in the educational system.

SCOPE FOR TOTAL QUALITY MANAGEMENT

In globalizing education for all, there is a scope for total quality management in
education. To support globalization education institutions are paying increasing
attention to 'internationalization which is the process of integrating an international or intercultural dimension to the teaching research and service functions
of the institutions. Cotemporary society is considered a knowledge society, and
the UN agencies including the World Bank and UNESCO have declared that
economies are built not only through physical capital but on the foundation of

information learning and adoption, the basic parameters of higher education. Higher education is provided with new opportunities in terms of increased accessibility of information and knowledge due to innovations in technology.

One of the flows of globalization is people. They move to work or study and this means that they want their study and qualifications accepted in the countries in which they move. The General Agreement of Trade in Services (GATS) puts a requirement on its signatories that they facilitate the trade in services. This can mean that the signatories are required to accept the competence of a consultant educated in another country.

The second half of the twentieth century will go down in the history of higher education as the period of its most spectacular expansion. But it is also the period which has seen the gap between the industrially developed, the developing countries and in particular the least developed countries with regard to access and resources for higher learning and research. Sharing knowledge of international operation and new technologies can offer new opportunities to reduce the gap. This can materialize only by total quality management in education. For quality management in education we need accurate, up-to-date information on the nature and status of institutions and the meaning of the qualifications they offer. The main difficulty might prove to be the manual step of keeping the information complete and current.

As institutions internationalize their curricular or their research links or offer courses abroad or enroll foreign students, these activities should be subject to an internal quality assessment process. By the same token, external quality assessment agencies must be able to assess the nature and effect of these internal processes. Where competence in Quality Assessment in this area does not exist, it must be developed. Quality Assessment also has to be internalized. In 1995 the Global Alliance for Transnational Education (GATE) was established to address issues relating to the quality of educational offerings that cross national boundaries (Woodhouse, 1997 a). But now GATE has changed its structure.

Quality in education is a multidimensional concept, which should embrace all its functions and activities, teaching and academic programmes, research and scholarships, staffing, students, building facilities, equipment, services to the community and the academic environment. Internal self-evaluation and external review conducted openly by independent specialists with international expertise is vital for enhancing quality. Independent national bodies should be established and comparative standards of quality recognized at an international level should be defined. Quality also requires that higher education should be characterized by its international dimension: exchange of knowledge, interactive networking mobility of teachers and students and international research project, while taking into account the national cultural values and circumstances.

To attain and sustain national, regional or international quality, certain components are particularly relevant, notable among them are the careful selection of staff and continuous staff development, in particular through the promotion of appropriate programs for academic staff development. These would include the teaching / learning methodology and mobility between countries, between higher education institutions and between the higher education institutions and the world of work, as well as student mobility within and between countries. The new information technologies are an important tool in this process owing to their impact on the acquisition of knowledge and technical know-how.

ECONOMIC DEVELOPMENT AS A RESULT OF
GLOBALISING EDUCATION

The global economy grows and is enhanced as a result of globalizing education for all. More qualitative curriculum enables the students to seek job in any part of the world. We are now living in an industrial world and associate survival with employment. This association is being forced on other cultures as the global economy establishes dominance.

One of the most visible manifestations of globalization is the emerging 'borderless' higher education market. The huge increase in the worldwide demand in higher education (the budgetary and capacity problems of many nations to meet this demand) and the opportunities created by new communication technologies and the internet have shaped an environment in which profit-minded providers can successfully expand the supply of educational services. Many European and American Universities take initiatives to reach out their educational provision to this international higher education market by active recruitment of international fee-paying students to home institutions by establishing branch campuses for franchising and twinning agreements with local institutions or via distance education and e-learning and other transactional activities. But globalization is more than a flow of economy.

With commodification and the corporate takeover in education, what has resulted is economic growth. Commercial concerns look constantly for new markets and areas of activity. "It is time to recognize that the true tutors of our children are not school teachers or university professors but film makers, advertising executives and pop culture purveyors" (Benjamin R. Barber quoted by Giroux, 2000:15). There are many ways of making money from formal education, "but the most widespread is the use of school as an advertising medium".

High ideals tend to fade-away as state provided finances decline and the state encourages closer partnership between education and industry. The prevention of education and the exploitation of learners that we have catalogued here is a matter of profound concern. We have witnessed a fundamental attack on the notion of public goods, and upon more liberal ideas of education. Learning has increasingly been seen as a commodity or as an investment rather than as a way of exploring what might make for the good life or human flourishing. The market ideologies the teachers and educators have assimilated in their curricula have required them to embrace corporate sponsorship and intervention, which has resulted in the degradation of their work to such an extent as to question whether what they are engaged in can rightfully be called education. It has been said that globalization has changed the lives of the people of our era faster and more unpredictably than any other phenomenon. Globalization has given hundreds of people the opportunity to achieve a standard of living incomparably higher than ever before. But it has likewise driven many into economic distress and insecurity.

Global development needs global ground rules. To enable us to make our world develop in a more equitable way we must be able to many variables at the same time. States have an important role and we must strengthen their opportunities to create favorable conditions for people and companies to operate in. At the same time the fundamental factors for sound, socially just economic development should be created.

HUMAN RIGHTS FROM THE GLOBAL PERSPECTIVE

Human rights are linked to environmental issues in a global perspective. Capitalist imperialism over the whole world has already resulted in the destruction of land, water and people on a massive scale. Educators must acknowledge these occurrences. They should also prepare their students to consider a possible response. A global citizenship is needed to protect ourselves from the hyper-exploitation of the earth's human and physical resources by super powers. This citizenship must be within new political institutions capable of opposing global capitalism.

If globalization is a fact of life, so is human diversity. The management of national, cultural and religious diversity is a high priority for the United Nations and national policy makers of the century. As more and more people are brought together by the integration of markets in the wake of globalization and continual advances in telecommunication and transportation, many individuals encounter confusion and conflict in adjusting to a multicultural experience that for them is new. Inspired by the UN Charter or perhaps the inspiration behind it, human rights are significant in helping the international community deal with the dilemmas arising from a real or imagined clash of cultures and protecting the dignity and the worth of human person.

The age of globalization is simultaneously the age of interdependence. Leaders must motivate ordinary people to participate in plans "to promote social progress and better standards of life in larger freedom, to practice tolerance and live together in peace with one another and to unite to maintain international peace and security". This is a major challenge of international policy makers.

Democracy cannot guarantee human rights but human rights cannot be protected without it. The UN Commission on Human Right affirms "the indissoluble links" between the principles underling the Universal Declaration of Human Rights and "the foundation of any democratic society". The protection of the human person is a top priority of the United Nations; human rights are interwoven into all aspects of its work and cover a broad spectrum of issues – political, economic, social, cultural and individual. They are universal rights and represent the consensus of the international community. They do not exclude any culture or region and are flexible enough to be relevant to diverse cultures.

The Vienna Declaration of 1993 clearly stated that the significance of national and regional particularities and various historical, cultural and religious backgrounds must be borne in mind. The challenge for the international community is to help national authorities where necessary. In Article 26 of the Universal Declaration of Human Rights 1948, it is stated that 'Every one has the right to Education". By globalizing education everyone is given the right for education, an education that will enable them to understand the universality of the human rights, how they enhance respect for cultural and social diversity. A cursory look at some international human rights instruments bring out this reality. Among them are the Universal Declaration of Human Rights, the Convention on the Rights of the Child, the International Convention on the Elimination of all forms of Racial Discrimination and the Declaration on the Elimination of all forms of Intolerance and Discrimination based on Religion and Belief.

Education can play a great role in bringing about an awareness of human rights in the people. Also educators can train administrators, legal and judicial officials in the art of good governance. It is they who formulate and implement legislation on human rights and preventive development in their respective countries. Education in its broadest sense can contribute to the forging of a culture of peace within and between countries. Without peace, there can be neither development nor accommodation of diversity.

'Democracy' and 'Human Rights' are the two security issues in the new millennium. Human Rights is the security of the human beings implemented through democratic institutions they can simultaneously safeguard "the inherent dignity...equal and inalienable rights of all members of the human family...." as the foundation of freedom, justice and peace in the world'.

ANALYSIS OF THE SITUATION

The investigator prepared an Attitude Scale which included statements reflecting the four areas as related to the Benefits of Globalization, selected for the Paper. The four areas were:

Aspect I: Benefits of Globalizing Education for all - Statements 3, 6, 7, 8 and 20;

Aspect II: Scope for Total Quality management in Education - Statements 13, 14, 15 and 18;

Aspect III: Economic Development and Globalizing Education-Statements 5, 9, 10, 17, 11, 12;

Aspect IV: Human Rights from the Global Perspective - Statements 1, 2, 4, 16 and 19.

The three point attitude scale gave a choice of Agree (A) Disagree (D) and Un-Decided (UD) for which the respondents had to mark their choice by putting a check mark in the appropriate column. The total sample taken was 50 persons, including eminent scholars in the field of education, students of education and social workers.

Table showing the Statements and the Responses and Percentages

Sl. No	Statements	Responses & their percentages		
		[A]	[D]	[UD]
1.	In the global sense, the right to education and the right to learn constitute a vision rather than a reality	30 60%	20 40%	---
2.	Democracy and human rights are the security issues in the new millennium	45 90%	5 10%	---
3.	Globalising education has a vital role to play in helping human beings to improve their interrelatedness and contributing to the ultimate sustainability of the planet	37 74%	8 16%	5 10%
4.	An international community can help to create an environment that might make it easier for states to implement human rights norms	31 62%	13 26%	6 12%
5.	An undesirable aspect of consumerism may grow as a result of globalisation in the field of education.	31 62%	12 24%	7 14%
6.	We can provide education for all by globalizing it.	10 20%	35 70%	5 10%
7.	Globalizing education help the learners collaborating to create a window on the world	35 70%	10 20%	5 10%
8.	By globalizing education we can make it an essential element in nation building.	23 46%	21 42%	6 12%
9.	Globalization of education has resulted in raising the cost of higher education.	31 62%	19 38%	--
10.	By globalizing education there is the threat of the demise of the physical community and its replacement by virtual community.	25 50%	15 30%	10 20%
11.	Globalization of education will result in the loss of indigenous cultures and the relentless imposition of western values.	35 70%	13 26%	2 4%
12.	The drastic reduction in funding of public universities as well as the falling population of traditional 18-20 years old students in the western countries is the critical factor forcing administrators to look for global markets in education	30 60%	10 20%	10 20%
13.	Globalization is changing the fundamental conditions of an educational system	40 80%	--	10 20%
14.	Global educators are the new colonizers inventively spreading their own view of the world on to developing nations.	28 56%	21 42%	1 2%
15.	We should re-examine our educational philosophies based on the impact of globalization on education.	40 80%	10 20%	---
16.	It is necessary to have some global ground rules for globalizing education for all which will enable us to make our world develop in a more equitable way.	28 56%	19 38%	3 6%
17.	The voice of teachers is silenced, the voice of 'industry' cultivated and education policy is driven by market forces	28 56%	15 30%	7 914%
18.	One of the most visible manifestations of globalization is the emerging 'borderless' higher education market.	33 66%	17 34%	---
19.	Internationalization and globalization lead to an erosion of the national regulatory and policy frame works in which universities are embedded.	23 46%	17 34%	10 20%
20.	Globalization provides opportunities for international understanding and solidarity	40 80%	5 10%	5 10%

RESULTS AND INTERPRETATION OF THE DATA

1. As per the percentages calculated, it was noted that the first aspect, namely, benefits of globalization of education for all, 74% were of the opinion that globalization has a significant role in improving inter-relatedness of people and sustainability of the world. 70% agreed that it is a window on the world, and international understanding, i.e., 80 % and it can also help toward nation building to the extent of 46 %. However, the percentage was low, i.e., 20% for the agreement on the provision capacity of globalization towards education for all.

2. With regard to total quality management through globalization, it was agreed by 80% that globalization would bring about the fundamental conditions of the educational system and it will also develop new colonies for the development of education, namely, 56% and the suggestion that was agreed upon was that we have to re-examine our educational policies in this context, 80% and that border-less education ahs come to stay, 66 %.

3. Looking at the relationship between development and globalization, it was noted that consumerism would grow with globalization, 62 %, and consequently the cost of education, 62 %. On account of border-less education and virtual universities there would be a threat to the physical community, 50 %, loss of indigenous cultures, 70 % and drastic cut in the funding of education by state agencies, 60 %. The greatest consequence would the silencing of the voice of the teachers and cultivation of the voice of the industry, 56 %.

4. As per the factor on human rights and globalization, human rights will turn out to be a myth rather than a reality with globalization, 60 %, hence the major issues to be tackled would be democracy and human right since the twenty first century, 90 %. With the global village it would be the responsibility of the global community to create an environment conducive to human rights safeguards, 62 % and the need to have global ground rules in this direction, 56 %. However, the only indication was that the national regulatory and policy frameworks in which universities are embedded would not be affected just to a very great extent, 46 %.

FINDINGS OF THE STUDY

1. The percentages obtained for each item indicates that even though there are seeming benefits for globalizing education for all, the disagreement of 70% of the total sample on statement number 6 clearly indicates that providing education for all by globalizing it is only a vision rather than a reality. However, we can arrive at the conclusion that globalization provides opportunities for international understanding and solidarity.

2. Regarding the second aspect, the statements and the percentages obtained of those who agree to the views clearly indicates that there is scope for total quality management in education, re-examining our educational phi-

losophies based on the impact of globalization of education. Global educators can provide quality education through a 'border-less' higher education market.

3. The percentages obtained for the statements regarding the third aspect indicates that there will be relentless imposition of western values, most of which are industrialized values which in turn will result in the economic growth of many countries driven by market forces. But many developing countries feel that it widens the gap between the rich and the poor.

4. For the fourth aspect, the percentage obtained in favour of 'agree' for the statements indicate that globalization provides opportunities for international understanding and solidarity. 90% of the total sample agreed that 'Democracy and Human Rights are the security issues in the new millenium.

CONCLUSIONS

There are many benefits of globalizing education for all. Who could deny the importance of a safer, healthier more peaceful more just and sustainable world in which to live? By globalizing education for all, our students can study about global problems and the various strategies for addressing them. They can generate a renewed sense of hope and optimizing nature of the problem. By introducing a global curriculum based on science and technology to preserve the earth rather than destroying it, education could teach active skills in influencing the direction of policies and practices. By globalizing education for all, institutions can meet the students' demands for global citizenship, compete in a global economy, have a global perspective in making the world a better place in terms of the environment and social justice in order to promote cross cultural understanding.

The advocates of borderless education have an economic view of education but their opponents have a socio-cultural perspective, which aims at the development of the human being. A fine human being is one who excels in the values, ideals, etiquette and a code of conduct cherished in the socio-cultural milieu. We have to equip the young generation of this era with the knowledge of the challenges of globalization and the means to meet it, so that equality of opportunities can be provided, poverty systematically reduced and economic growth achieved.

We have also to remember that even after all development in the field of science and technology we still have women and girls for whom education is myth. That is why on 9th April 2003 halfway through Global Action Week 2003 (6 to 13 April) over 1.3 million people (students, teachers, celebrities, governmental officials) from over a hundred countries converged in universities, schools, community halls etc., took take part in what was going to be 'The world's biggest lesson. Around the world, lessons were taught simultaneously by luminaries and ordinary people alike. The event was devoted to raising awareness of the importance of education of girls and women and its direct impact on the health, economic development and poverty reduction of the family.

REFERENCES

Andrezejewski & John Alessio (1999), 'Education for global citizenship and social responsibility'

Behar S.C. (2004), *"Internationalization of Education: Two Perspectives"*; University News, Vol 42 (04) Delhi

Development Gateway Foundation : Useful set of pages on the Knowledge economy + plenty of other resources.

Gnanam, A (2003), *"Transnational Providers and the Indian Education Market"*, University News, Vol 41(46) November pp. 4-7.

Held. D and A. McGrew (2000), *"The Global Transformations Reader, An Introduction to the Globalization Debate"*, Cambridge : Polity Press.

Joshi, J.P. (2003), *"Globalization; A Need for Change in Educational Management System"* University News Vol. 41 (20) Delhi

Mason, R. (1998), *'Globalising Education Trends and Applications"*, London : Routledge

Scholte, J.A (2000), *'Globalisation'* New York : St. Martin's Press, Inc.

Seitz, J. L (2002), *"Global Issues – An Introduction"*, Oxford : Blackwell Publishers Ltd.

Singh, A.Z, (2001), *"Diversity, Human Rights and Peace"*, UN Chronicle 2(36)

UNESCO Publication (1991) *"Education for All; Purpose and Context"*, Paris, UNESCO

UNESCO Publication (1992) *"Education for All; An Expanded Vision"* Paris, UNESCO

UNHCR (1999) 1998 "Global Report". Geneva : United Nations High Commissioner for Refugees, available at http://www.unchrch.

Vlasceanu, L & Welson, L. (2000), *"Transnational Education and Recognition of Qualifications"*, Bucharest : UNESCO/ CEPES

Wolferen K.V. (2000), "The United Nations and the Conceptual Challenges of a Globalizing Economy" UN Chronicle 2(66)

www.infed.org/biblio/globalization.htm

www.uvm.edu/-dewey/monographs/glomono.html

CHAPTER TWELVE

Equitable Sharing of the World's Information Resources Via The Internet: How ready are Higher Education Teachers in some Nigerian Universities?

Alice E. Asim
University of Calabar

INTRODUCTION

Human migration from place to place is as long as human history. Reasons behind such migration span the whole of Maslow's hierarchy of needs: food, shelter, belongingness, and self-actualization among others. When people move as a result of war, famine, earthquakes or other natural and man-made disasters, sympathy is evoked. On the other hand, when intellectuals considered as the best brains necessary for sustainable development of any nation migrate in a seemingly peaceful time, it calls for concern. The migration of the best brains from a country drains it of its essence of existence: the best human resources.

The phrase 'brain-drain' captures this phenomenon of migration of not just anybody, but of professionals often from less developed countries (LDCs) to developed countries (DCs). Brain drain has become a problematic issue for universities who need to retain teachers in order to maintain the status of centres of excellence in the face of dwindling economy. Global recession and a reduction in per capita expenditure in universities may be an antecedent for brain drain among its professionals. Intellectuals have their skills to trade in for good pay and better working conditions. However, since they may be unaware of a means of divulging themselves physically from the skills to be marketed, they sometimes migrate physically to where their skills can be marketed.

Brain drain is a global issue (Porter 2004). Wyss (2004) describes it as global poaching and reports that Jamaica lost 2000 teachers between 2000 and 2002. Using Jamaica as an example, she succinctly described the effect of brain drain when she wrote that the country was "haemorrhaging nurses and teachers". This points to the fact that global information sharing through brain drain may be beneficial to global economy but can adversely affect other countries. Edokat (2004) reported that in a survey of University teachers in Cameroon, 89% of them were in the affirmative when asked whether if given the opportunity they would move abroad. Asked what measures can be adopted to stem possible migration of teachers, the answers included a complete review of the salary situation, providing good working conditions such as computers, offices for lecturers, small sized classes, laboratory equipment, and libraries among others. Ezeife (2004) pointed out that since 1983, Nigeria has lost in excess of 5,000,000 of her best and brightest. As far back as 1995, 21,000 Nigerian doctors were known to be practicing in the US alone (Anekwe, 2004). Ezeife sees brain drain as a legitimate commercial asset for export in the face of crushing unemployment coupled with a dearth of social infrastructure. He concludes by saying that the country has no viable option. I do not agree that there is no viable option; the problem may be lack of awareness on how intellectual skills can be marketed without a destabilizing effect on the home country of the intellectuals. The presidential committee on Brain Drain set up in 1998 by the Babangida administration concluded thus: "In our work on brain drain, we realized that the major problem is the economy, particularly the devaluation of the Naira and inflation". Consequently, the country lost the ability to pay its top specialists competitively (Anekwe, 2004). In the face of dwindling resource allocation to the universities which has led to strikes by its teachers calling for a better funding of universities, brain drain will likely increase. Hence the urgency for a search of viable options, which is the focus of this paper.

Africa in particular (Porter, 2004) gave 17 bibliographic listings of online resources on brain drain affecting Africa. In the summary of an e-mail discussion on 'brain-drain', it was reported that the total loss to Africa across all professionals is about 4 billion US dollars per year. The loss of the educational investment alone costs poor countries 500m US dollars per year, according to one source cited in the discussion.

VARITIES AND DANGERS OF BRAIN DRAIN

Migration of intellectuals can be transverse or circular and it happens under different guises. Some young academics go to the UK and US for postgraduate studies and somehow remain there. Some senior academics that go for post doctorate fellowships or sabbatical leave manage to end up in other institutions where remunerations are better. Other academics continue to seek openings where job-related requirements fit their abilities and interest. When they succeed, brain drain follows. Depending on their work values, some groups of academics may not particularly care what they do as long as the salary and benefits are good, thus the job migration.

Different forms of brain drain have different implications for both the receiving and losing institutions/countries. In terms of intellectual competition, there are, of course, respective advantages and disadvantages. On the other hand, brain drain may end up as brain waste when preferences for the kinds of rewards to be gained from work are not prioritised. The waste is more evident when brain drain results in a surplus in one country and a dearth in the other. Frustration may result when intellectuals drift into occupations that under utilize or do not use the skills they trained for. Under such a circumstance, brain drain may be linked to "self trade" which may be considered as slave trade under another cloak. The difference being that self-trade is voluntary on the part of the person that allows him/herself to be traded. A new dimension to this self-trade becomes evident when such intellectuals show willingness to accept wages that are not on par with what their counterparts who are citizens of such countries receive. Such institutions or countries become centres of excellence to the detriment of the professionals' country of origin.

TEACHING RESPONSIBILITY AND INTERNET UTILITY IN HIGER EDUCATION IN NIGERIA

Nigeria has 36 states and a Federal Capital Territory with a total of 53 Federal, State, and Private universities. Enrolment into these institutions has been increasing astronomically during the 56 years of university existence in Nigeria. As of March 2002, student enrolment was in excess of 526,780 with a teaching force of 20,214 teachers (NUCVIHEP, 2004). The traditional roles of the university include teaching, research, and dissemination of existing and new information, as well as community service, and a storehouse of knowledge. Considerations of academic staff for promotion are based on their contribution to these functions (University of Calabar, 2002). These requirements explain why only the best in a graduating class in Nigerian universities are often offered automatic employment. The intention is to maintain the culture of excellence in the ivory towers through choosing and picking only the brightest and best.

The role of the university and the quality of its graduates in sub-Saharan Africa has come under sharp criticisms in the face of shortage of funds and the attendant brain drain. However, concern about raising the quality of education is a global issue resulting in about 20 world conferences related to education between 1990 and 2000 (Obanya, 2002). The low rating of sub-Saharan Africa on several indicators of basic and higher education in areas such as access, gender equity, inclusion, quality and achievement has been of particular concern (Shabani and Okebukola, 2004). The Conference of African Ministers of Education (MINEDAF), the African Union (AU) and the New Partnerships for Africa's Development (NEPAD) are addressing this concern in terms of capacity building – targeting teachers and managers, according to them.

Nigeria as the giant of Africa has made a commitment through its National Universities Commission (NUC) to improve the quality of teaching and learning in higher education in Nigeria. Under the able leadership of the Executive Secretary, Professor Peter Okebukola, NUC has initiated the Virtual Institute for Higher Education Pedagogy (VIHEP). The institute, which started functioning in September 2003, has II modules, spanning September 2003 to July 2004. Participation in this Internet-based course, though not mandatory, is free for all academic staff in Nigerian tertiary institutions (NUC, 2003).

As one of the imperatives for revitalizing education in Africa in the height of world conference recommendations, Obanya (2002) had suggested a functional inter-African cooperative. Acting on this imperative, the Nigerian NUC and UNESCO Harare Cluster Office have entered into a partnership meant to build/strengthen the capacity of teachers and other personnel in educational institutions in sub-Saharan Africa in critical areas of national and regional needs as identified through the machineries of AU, MINEDAF and NEPAD (http://www.viheaf.net/body_index.cfm). Registration for the courses is free though access to Internet is crucial for participation. The module on HIV/AIDS Education spanning March to May 2004 is on for this Virtual Institute for Higher Education in Africa (VIHEAF).

Both viheaf and vihep require access to the Internet as the prerequisite for participation thereby bringing to the fore the importance of Internet-based skills. Various researchers have looked at the import of Internet in higher education worldwide (e.g. Mahroum, 2004), in Africa (e.g. Okuni, 2004) and in Nigeria (e.g. Jagboro, 2003). The Internet can be described as an excellent legacy bestowed on humanity by man's ingenuity in Information Technology (IT). Asserting to the utilitarian value of the Internet as a tool for teaching, Polevchak and Ofori-Attah (2004) observed thus, "the Internet contains information from all academic areas and all parts of the world that can be used by anyone".

One of the conclusions drawn at the International Conference on Nigerian Higher Education Reforms using IT held on 26th and 27th September 2002 in Abuja was that, "Nigeria has come of age in its capacity but must seize the moment to utilize its human resource" (Nigerian Computer Society, 2002). The main focus of the conference was to assess the level of the use of IT in our educational system as well as consider the areas of curricula development. In attendance were representatives of the Nigerian Computer Society (NCS), Computer Professionals Registration Council of Nigeria (CPN), Education Tax Fund (ETF), National Open University of Nigeria (NOUN), Institute of Software Practitioners of Nigeria (ISPON), University of Jos (UNIJOS), and Fountsuam Foundation. The fact of this conference indicates urgency for higher education reform using IT. Experts in IT do know that computer mediation through the World Wide Web (www) can act as a catalyst for research, teaching and learning in higher education.

As financial resources dwindle, institutions of higher education seek to cut manpower overhead through reduction of traditional lectures, thus the increased need for internet based curricula. Suggested uses of the Internet in Higher Education include placing syllabi and assignments online; developing web sites and courseware for teaching and to facilitate students' research; computerizing classroom presentations to enhance or replace lectures and discussions; using e-mail and online discussions (synchronic and asynchronic) to improve communication with traditional students on campus and/or to reach new students at a distance. Beyond this, remote access to digitised libraries and databases can enhance or replaced on-campus resources, both for coursework and for original research (Atieh 1998; Connick 1999; Harknett and Cobane 1997).

In his presentation during the International Association of Universities (IAU) World Conference on Higher Education in 1998, Henrik Toft Jensen, Rector, Roskhide University had this to say: 'I would like to draw your attention to the fact that information distributed via new ICTs is to a large extend created in North and West and not in South and East". As a panacea, he was of the opinion twinning and networking of universities in the North and South and in the West and East are as important and necessary initiative. The reason for his suggestion was partly to create close institutional collaboration in the discussion of the investment in and use of information technology, and partly to improve opportunities for the South and East to contribute to the knowledge and information used in IT. Furthering his argument on the need to move from traditional to virtual through new IT, he opined that one benefit of using ICTs in higher institutions, is that it would help limit the amount of brain drain and brain waste. One cannot but agree with him that many are the benefits of ICT for higher institutions particularly the Internet. It is also important to observe that a myriad of factors may also hamper the derivation of benefits of the Internet. Collaboration among universities is not entirely new, the outcome had been bodies like Association of African Universities (AAU), the Association of European Universities (CRE) and the Association of Universities of Asia and the Pacific (AUAP), and International Association of Universities (IAU).

STATEMENT OF PROBLEM

Both regional and national intentions are commendable but what is the standing of higher education teachers in regards to ICT skills necessary for participation in global information sharing? Are there constraints to the acquisition and utilisation of these Internet-related skills? Against this background, this study investigates the following:

1. Whether University lecturers in the sample have access to the Internet.
2. To what extent they exhibit independence in Internet use.
3. Whether they frequently use the Internet
4. Whether they are aware of Internet-based collaborations as evident in Virtual Institutes
5. To what extent they face constraints in Internet usage.

METHODS

Instrument

Subject readiness for global information sharing via the Internet was assessed through a 44-item structured questionnaire eliciting, among other things, information on respondent demographics, personal and departmental access to Internet, awareness of and participation in virtual institutes and collaborations, and constraints to Internet access.

Sample

A random sample of one thousand, six hundred and seventy (1,670) consisting of one thousand, two hundred and twenty (1,220) males and four hundred and fifty (450) female university teachers were used for the study. The teachers were drawn from the faculties of Science, Arts, Social Sciences, Law, Education, Management Science, Agriculture, Engineering, Environmental Studies, Basic Medical Sciences, and College of Medicine and Surgery of two (2) Federal Universities and one (1) State university in South Eastern Nigeria.

Procedure

Six hundred (600) copies of the questionnaires were administered in each of the three (3) universities through contact persons in the different departments over a period of 3 weeks. Out of the one thousand eight hundred copies, one thousand, six hundred and seventy (1,670) were retrieved giving a return rate of about 93%.

Data Analysis

Simple percentages were calculated for the different indicators assessing readiness for global information sharing via the Internet. Frequency counts as well as the computed percentage are presented in tables 1 to 5.

RESULTS AND DISCUSSION

Access to the Internet

The respondents were requested to check either 'yes' or 'no' on the five indicators of access to the internet as given in table 1.

Table 1. Percentages in each category of indicator showing access to the Internet

Indicators	Category	Groups					
		Male		Female		All	
		Count	%	Count	%	Count	%
Ownership of an e-	YES	950	77.9	340	75.6	1290	77.2
mail address	NO	270	22.1	110	24.4	380	22.8
Ownership of a	YES	470	38.5	220	48.9	690	41.3
personal computer	NO	750	61.5	230	51.1	980	58.7
Institutional Inter-	YES	1010	82.8	370	82.2	1380	82.6
net Service	NO	210	17.2	80	17.8	290	17.4
Faculty Internet	YES	70	5.7	40	8.9	110	6.6
Services	NO	1150	92.3	410	91.1	1560	93.4
Departmental	YES	30	2.5	10	2.2	40	2.4
Internet Service	NO	1190	97.5	440	97.8	1630	97.6
Total		**1220**		**450**		**1670**	

Frequency counts and percentages were computed for each category of responses for males, females and all respondents pooled together. Based on percentages, 77.2% of all respondents owned an e-mail address, more males (77.9%) than females (75.6%). Over half of those sampled (58.7%) had no personal computers. In terms of institutional link to the Internet, 82.6% of the respondents were from institutions, which were linked to the Internet via a V-SAT. Only 6.6% of the respondents belonged to faculties with Internet access and even fewer (2.4%) with departmental Internet connectivity. The findings give an indication that Internet access is basically for e-mail more than for other uses. Though 2 out of the 3 institutions sampled were connected to the Internet, faulty and departmental lack of access may deprive university teachers from information sharing and instructional enhancement through the use of computer telecommunication technology in the delivery of higher education (Noble, 2004). The bottleneck may be connected to the high cost of providing Internet service.

Results agree with findings by Busari (2003), which showed that more than 99% of teacher trainers in institutions of higher learning in Lagos state Nigeria mainly use ICT for e-mail purposes. Jagboro (2004) also found that the highest access to Internet usage was for e-mail (69.86%) followed by research material (53.42%) in Obafemi Awolowo University, Ile-Ife, Nigeria.

Frequency of Access to the Internet

Indicators for frequency of access to the Internet were considered as a combination of Internet-based activities as well as Virtual Institute-based activities as given in table 2. Frequencies of performing the activities listed in table 2 were considered in three categories, 'Never', 'weekly', and 'monthly'. This was informed by the fact that any university teacher who had information to share or who was a participant in any Virtual Institute collaboration would frequent websites more than others.

Percentages in table 2 indicate that a high percentage of the participants never had access to teleconferencing (90.4%), online discussion (75.4%), accessing virtual classrooms or libraries (83.8%) or taking tests or examinations online (84.4%). Considering the fact that these activities are at the core of Internet-based information sharing, the implication is that these groups of university teachers are yet to be ready for global information sharing. However, hope is not lost because about half of them do send e-mails regularly (50.3%) and also check their e-mails weekly (58.7%), and these are also important.

Since lack of awareness had been implicated in participation in virtual collaborations, it is hoped that when awareness of the potentials of global information sharing via the Internet is created, more teachers would be ready to share in the benefits.

Table 2. Percentages in each category of indicator showing frequency of access to the Internet

Indicators	Category	Groups					
		Male		Female		All	
		Count	%	Count	%	Count	%
Sending e-mail	Never	200	16.4	90	20.0	290	17.4
	Weekly	630	51.6	210	46.7	840	50.3
	Monthly	390	32.0	150	33.3	540	32.3
Downloading a document	Never	420	34.4	210	46.7	630	37.7
	Weekly	540	44.3	170	37.7	710	42.5
	Monthly	260	21.3	70	15.6	330	19.8
Surfing the web	Never	460	37.7	190	42.2	650	38.9
	Weekly	420	34.4	140	31.1	560	33.5
	Monthly	340	28.9	120	26.7	460	27.5
Teleconferenc-ing	Never	1130	92.6	380	84.4	1510	90.4
	Weekly	50	4.1	30	6.7	80	4.8
	Monthly	40	3.3	40	8.9	80	4.8
Checking e-mail	Never	220	18.0	190	42.2	410	24.6
	Weekly	740	60.7	240	53.3	980	58.7
	Monthly	260	21.3	20	4.4	280	16.7
Participating in online discus-sion	Never	940	77.1	320	71.1	1260	75.4
	Weekly	210	17.2	80	17.8	290	17.4
	Monthly	70	5.7	50	11.1	120	7.2
Making Internet calls	Never	830	68.0	290	64.4	1120	67.0
	Weekly	180	14.8	100	22.2	280	16.8
	Monthly	210	17.2	60	13.3	270	16.2
Accessing vir-tual class-rooms/libraries	Never	1060	86.9	340	75.6	1400	83.8
	Weekly	100	8.2	90	20.0	190	11.4
	Monthly	60	4.9	20	4.4	80	4.8
Taking test/examination online	Never	1040	85.2	370	82.2	1410	84.4
	Weekly	190	14.8	80	17.8	260	15.6
	Monthly	-	-	-	-	-	-
Total		**1220**		**450**		**1670**	

Independence in Internet Use

Independence in Internet use was considered as per indicators in Table 3 where respondents had to indicate whether they could do any of the Internet-related activities without assistance, minimum, or maximum assistance.

Respondents needed assistance in all the indicators, some minimum, others maximum. For the purpose of this discussion, those needing assistance have been pooled together (i.e. minimum assistance + maximum assistance).

Table 3. Percentages in each category of indicator showing independence in Internet use.

Indicators	Category	Male		Female		All	
		Count	%	Count	%	Count	%
Typing on computer	No assistance	440	36.1	140	31.1	580	34.7
	Minimum assistance	360	29.5	130	28.9	490	29.3
	Maximum assistance	420	34.4	180	40.0	600	36.0
Sending an e-mail	No assistance	460	37.7	120	26.7	580	34.7
	Minimum assistance	350	28.7	120	26.7	470	28.1
	Maximum assistance	410	33.6	210	46.6	620	37.1
Accessing a website	No assistance	290	23.8	100	22.2	390	23.4
	Minimum assistance	290	23.8	90	20.0	380	22.7
	Maximum assistance	640	52.4	260	57.8	900	53.9
Downloading a document	No assistance	330	27.1	130	28.9	460	27.5
	Minimum assistance	320	26.2	70	15.5	390	23.4
	Maximum assistance	570	46.7	250	55.6	820	49.1
Printing a document	No assistance	450	36.9	140	31.1	590	35.3
	Minimum assistance	300	24.6	100	22.2	400	24.3
	Maximum assistance	470	38.5	210	46.7	680	40.7
Checking an e-mail box	No assistance	540	44.3	150	33.3	690	41.3
	Minimum assistance	250	20.5	130	28.9	380	22.7
	Maximum assistance	430	35.2	170	37.8	600	36.0
Designing a website	No assistance	20	1.6	20	4.4	40	2.4
	Minimum assistance	90	7.4	70	15.6	160	9.6
	Maximum assistance	1110	91.0	360	80.0	1470	88.0
Total		**1220**		**450**		**1670**	

In terms of typing on computer, 65.3% needed some form of assistance while 65.2% would only send e-mail successfully when offered assistance. To access a website, 76.6% of the respondents would gladly receive some assistance while 72.5% would have to be aided to download a document from a website. For a basic activity like printing a document, 65% of them would require assistance to successfully execute this. Assistance in checking an e-mail box would be required by 58.7% of the respondents and nearly all the respondents (97.6%) would not design a website unaided.

Since access to the Internet was mainly for e-mail purposes, and institutional and departmental access to Internet was low as indicated in Table 1, activities like designing of websites, downloading and printing of documents would necessarily need assistance. These activities are at the core of information sharing via the net and needing maximum assistance here means; these teachers are yet to be ready.

AWARENESS OF AND PARTICIPATION IN VIRTUAL INSTITUTES OR COLLABERATIONS

The indicators for assessing awareness of and participation in Virtual Institutes or collaborations via the Internet were as given in table 4.

Table 4. Percentages in each category of indicator showing awareness of and participation in Virtual Institutes or Collaborations

Indicators	Category	Groups					
		Male		Female		All	
		Count	%	Count	%	Count	%
Awareness of National Universities Commission (NUC)	YES	570	46.7	230	51.1	800	47.9
Nigeria's Virtual Institute for Higher Education Pedagogy NUCVIHEP	NO	650	53.3	220	48.9	870	52.1
Current participa-	YES	80	6.6	70	15.6	150	9.0
tion in NUCVIHEP	NO	1140	93.4	380	84.4	1520	91.0
Interest in further	YES	930	76.2	360	80.0	1290	77.2
participation in NUCVIHEP	NO	290	23.8	90	20.0	380	22.8
Awareness of NUC-UNESCO	YES	230	18.9	120	26.7	350	21.0
Harare Cluster Office Collaboration (VIHEAF)	NO	990	81.1	330	73.3	1320	79.0
Current participa-	YES	50	4.1	60	13.3	110	6.6
tion in VIHEAF	NO	1170	95.9	390	86.7	1560	93.4
Total		1220		450		1670	

Less than half of the sample for this study (47.9%) was aware of the National Universities Commission (NUC) Nigeria's Virtual Institute for Higher Education Pedagogy (NUCVIHEP). This lack of awareness may not be unconnected with information dissemination and official bureaucracy in getting the notice to university teachers. Participation in NUCVIHEP is low (9.0%) and this may not be unconnected with the Internet based nature of the programme. This finding is as should be expected since teachers had ranked lack of Internet at their faculties and departments high as a constraint. Thus where such provisions are lacking there is a more likelihood of non-participation even for those who may be aware.

Awareness of Africa regional collaboration is more dismal as less than a quarter of the respondents (21%) indicated awareness. As could be predicted, only 6.6% of respondents were participants in the first quarter module of the NUC – UNESCO Harare Cluster Office collaboration (VIHEAF). This low percentage could be attributed to the fact that advertisement for and invitation to participate was done on NUCVIHEP website. Thus, only a low percentage of participants in NUCVIHEP were fortunate enough to get such information. A case cannot be made for lack of interest as a reason for non-participation in national and regional collaborations. In the sample studied, 77.2% indicated interest to participate therefore, the lack of awareness and not interest can be implicated for non-participation. This corroborates the result of constraints to Internet access in which respondents ranked lack of interest low among other indicators.

Constraints to Internet Access

The respondents were asked to indicate whether (yes) or not (no) the indicators as given in table 5 were sources of constraints to Internet access for them.

Table 5. Percentages in each category of indicator showing constraints to Internet access

Indicators	Category	Groups					
		Male		Female		All	
		Count	%	Count	%	Count	%
Teaching/Research/ Community Service workload	YES	310	25.4	200	44.4	510	30.5
	NO	910	74.6	250	55.6	1160	69.5
Lack of computer literacy	YES	520	42.6	240	53.3	760	45.5
	NO	700	57.4	210	46.7	910	54.5
Lack of a personal computer	YES	690	56.6	170	37.8	860	51.5
	NO	530	43.4	280	62.2	810	48.5
Lack of interest	YES	50	4.1	20	4.4	70	4.2
	NO	1170	95.9	430	95.6	160	95.8
Inaccessibility to cyber café	YES	460	37.7	110	24.4	570	34.1
	NO	760	62.3	340	75.6	110	65.9
Incessant interruption of electricity	YES	700	57.4	230	51.1	930	55.7
	NO	520	42.6	220	48.9	740	44.3
Unavailability in institution/faculty/ department	YES	730	59.8	220	48.9	950	56.9
	NO	490	40.2	230	51.1	820	43.1
Non relevance to field of specialization	YES	60	4.9	60	13.3	120	7.2
	NO	1160	95.1	390	86.7	1550	92.8
Total		**1220**		**450**		**1670**	

Percentages indicate that for all respondents, it was not the lack of interest (95.6%) or non-relevance to field of specialization (92.8%) that posed as a constraint to Internet access. Teaching/research/community service (69.5%) and inaccessibility to cyber cafés (65.9%) were only marginal constraints. For about half of this group of respondents, unavailability of Internet services in the institution, faculty or departments (56.9%), lack of personal computers (51.5%), and incessant interruption of electricity (55.7%) were seen as constraints to Internet access. From the analysis, indicated constraints have to do more with physical rather than psychological work environment.

This finding is in agreement with the report by Nigerian Computer Society (2002) that access to Internet and other IT related tools of learning are very limited in all Higher Institutions in Nigeria. The report had it that about 90% of schools/colleges/universities in Nigeria is without Internet connections while less than 2% have Internet bandwidth of about 64kbps. In the same report, lack of necessary enabling infrastructures and adequate funding were identified as major constraints.

As long as the situation remains this way global information sharing via the Internet will remain a mirage for many university teachers. Brain drain would then seem a viable option in a depressed economy.

CONCLUSION

Results indicate that only a few of the respondents had access to the Internet in their faculties and departments. The frequency for sending and receiving e-mail was more than those required for actual global information sharing. On a good number of indicators of Internet-based information sharing, some form of assistance was necessary for executing them. Also negligible percentages were aware of and were participants of on-going national and regional collaborations of information sharing via the Internet. The greatest constraints to Internet access, it was discovered, were those of awareness and unavailability at the place of work rather than a lack of interest.

Thus information sharing via the Internet should be considered as a viable option to stem brain drain and its attendant destabilizing effects. More awareness has to be created for university teachers to help them market their skills via the Internet and get paid.

How do University Lecturers get paid for online courses?

Renowned scholars can put their courses online for the benefit of their students and others separated from them by geographical distances. Such courses can become models for institutions worldwide. It is reasonable to assume that materials placed on the information superhighway may with time loose the identity of their originators. These concerns have led an increasing number of American universities to assert ownership and control over the intellectual output of their faculty (Twigg, 2000; Woody, 1998).

It has also been pointed out that most of the information on the web emanate from West and North and not from South and East. This gives an indication that it may still be possible to trace information to their geographical sources. Thus university teachers who want to publish research findings, or contribute to global issues can do so through their institutions or as affiliates of a collaboration of universities e.g. Association of African Universities (AAU) etc.

As part of university service to the community, the majority of Nigerian universities provide consultancy services to organisations and businesses. A percentage of such consultancy fees are paid as honorarium to faculty members involved while the balance goes to the university.

Since the university benefits a lot from such funding agencies, they could do more in terms of attracting such consultancy programmes and reach an agreement with donor agencies in allowing the professionals to publish findings, which are not of a confidential nature. Such online publications though under the ambit of institutions, should bear the names of such teachers. This would be a way of assisting them to market their professional skills and expertise while creating an opportunity to share the world's information resources and getting paid. Another way may be through personalized websites where some form of information e.g. certain psychological tests, can only be accessed online after the payment of the stipulated fee through credit cards etc.

Necessary Considerations in Information Sharing via the Internet

Information sharing through the Internet either as research breakthrough or online courses has, ethical, psychological and pedagogical implications. Thus in packaging and marketing such information it is important to give consideration to these concerns.

Commercialisation of knowledge through the net requires a tripartite arrangement among commercial website designers, university administration and the relevant university teachers. The university may act as the institutions affiliate to the teacher in terms of quality control but the credit for any ingenuity both financial and otherwise should be the teacher's. To protect intellectual contributions websites, courseware and CD – ROMs should be patented or copyrighted.

RECOMMENDATIONS

To minimize brain drain and encourage university teachers to market their expertise via the Internet, the following are recommended:

1. Universities, schools, and departments not yet connected to the Internet should be connected; through proper funding.
2. University teachers should develop more interest in the Internet and increase their frequency of access to the Internet through diverse Internet-based activities.
3. Those who are not computer literate should as a first step equip themselves with prerequisite ICT skills.
4. The appropriate university unit should disseminate information about global collaboration on time.
5. Where courses are put online, universities do not have the moral right to get paid by private website owners. Rather the course designers (teachers) should be paid.

REFERENCES

Anekwe, M.C. Brain Drain: The Nigerian Experience 1. http://www.firstmonday.org (visited 3/25/04).

Atah, S. (1998). How to get a college degree via the Internet: The complete guide to getting your undergraduate or graduate degree from the comfort of your home. Rockline, CA: Prima Publishing. Called from nucvihep November lecture series http://www.nuvihep.net (11/15/03).

Busari, O. O. (2003). An investigation into the training status and ICT support of teacher trainers in institutions of higher learning in Lagos State. In M. A. G. Akale (Ed.)

Proceedings of the 44th Annual Conference. 17 – 23 August, 2003 at Government Science and Technical College, Abuja, Nigeria.

Connick, G. ed (1999). The distance learners' guide. Upper Saddle River, NJ: Prentice Hall. Called from nucvihep November lecture series http://www.nucvihep.net (11/15/03).

Diocaretz, M. & Kloet, J. An exploratory study of Internet usage at Higher Education Institutions in Asia, Africa and Latin America. http://www.infonomics.nl/globalequality/reports/IDEcom.pdf (visited 3/10/04)

Edokat, T. Effect of brain drain in higher education in Cameroon. http://www.uneca.org/eca-resources/conference-reports-and-other-documents/brain-drain/word-documents/edokat.doc (visited 25/3/04)

Ezeife, D.I. Brain Drain: A legitimate commercial asset for export. http://www.firstmonday.org (visisted 3/25/04).

Harthnett, R. & Cobane, C. (1997). Introducing instructional technology to International Relations. Ps: Political Science and Politics, xxx (September) 496-501. Called from nucvihep November lecture series http://www.nucvihep.net (11/15/03).

International Association of Universities IAU (1998). Thematic Debate "from Traditional to Virtual: The new Information Technologies". Speech of Herrick Toft Jensen, Rector, Rosklide University at the world conference on Higher Education. UNESCO, Paris, 7 October.

Jagboro, K.O. A study of Internet usage in Nigerian universities: A case study of Obafemi Awolowo University, Ile-Ife, Nigeria. http://www.%20study%20of%20Internet%20usage%20in%20in%20Nigeian%20universities.htm (visited 3/11/04).

Mahroun, S. Europe and the challenge of the brain drain. http://www.jrc.ec/pages/iptsreport/vo/29/english/SAT1E296.htm (visited 25/3/04).

National Universities Commission (2003). National Universities Commission Virtual Institute for Higher Education Pedagogy (VIHEP) Information Booklet. http://www/nucvihep.net.

National Universities Commission. New Technologies in teaching and learning in higher education: using the Internet for teaching and learning in higher education. http://www.nucvihep.net (visited 11/17/03).

Nigerian Computer Society (2002) September. Report of the International Conference on Nigerian Higher Education Reforms using IT. Abuja, Nigeria 26th and 27th September.

Noble, D.F. Digital Diploma Mills: The Automation of Higher Education. http://www.firstmonday.org (visited 3/25/04).

NUCVIHEP (2004) April. Students: Access and equity issues. http://www.nucvihep.net (visited 4/8/2004)

Obanya, P.A.I. (2002). Revitalizing education in Africa. Ibadan: Hodder Sturton.

Okuni, A. Higher Education through the Internet: Expectations, reality and challenges of the African Virtual University. DSE Development and Cooperation No. 2, 23-25. http://www.%20Education%20through%20the%20Internet.htm (visited 3/10/04).

Porter, C. (2004). International Network for the Availability of Scientific Publications (INASP). Summary of e-mail discussion on HIF-net at WHO: "BRAIN DRAIN" 22nd July 2002 – 3 November 2003.

Polevchak, K. & Ofori-Attah, K.D. Using the Internet as a tool for teaching http://www.ncsu.edu/teaching with the Internet.htm of 3/11/04.

Shabani, J. & Okebukola P.A.O. (2004). Welcome to Viheaf. http://www.viheaf.net/body_index.cfm (2/26/04).

Twigg, C.A. (2000). Who owns online courses and course materials? Intellectual property policies for a new learning environment, Troy, NY: Center for Academic Transformation Rensselaer Polytechnic Institute (Pew Learning and Technology Program (2000) http://www.center.rpi.edu

University of Calabar (2002). Handbook of Revised Criteria for appointments and promotions.

Woody, T. (1998). Higher Learning: Universities are facing a revolution over intellectual property as technology blurs the lines between good business and good education. The Industry Standard.
   http://www.thestandard.net/articles/articleprint/o.1454.874.00.html (June 28).

Wyss, B. Global Poaching: Jamaica's brain (1/30/04). http://www.fguide.org/econ-attrocity bulletin (visited 3/25/05).

CHAPTER THIRTEEN

Life Long Peace Education for a Culture of Peace

H.M. Shailaja
Karnatak University

INTRODUCTION

Dictionary meanings of the word "Peace" are: quiet, silence, tranquility, mental calm and serenity. Basically, peace is a state of mind where there is no agitation and/or any sort of disturbance that might compel human beings to become mentally and/or physically violent. It means that peace is a phenomenon concerned with the mental faculty of thinking and physical pursuit for activity. We can say that peace is a psychosomatic concept. Without the body, the mind can neither exist nor act.

"Peace" is a word that is uttered almost as frequently as "truth," "beauty," and "love." It may be just as elusive to define as these other virtues. Common synonyms for peace include "amity," "friendship," "harmony," "concord," "tranquility," "repose," "quiescence," "truce," "pacification," and "neutrality." Likewise, the peacemaker is the pacifier, mediator, intermediary, and intercessor. While some of these descriptions are appropriate, they are still quite limited in describing both the nature of peace and the role of the peacemaker. Any attempt to articulate the nature of peace and peacemaking, therefore, must address those conditions that are favorable to their emergence. Freedom, human rights, and justice are among such prerequisites. Also included are proactive strategies such as conflict resolution, nonviolent action, community building, and democratization of authority.

As soon as we think of the body, we have to recognize those universal forces (seen as well unseen), which promote the process of creation, protection and emancipating of life in this world. We have also to realize that inward forces too, monitor the activities of the mind. The mind is the key instrument, which plays a vital role in bringing the physical body into existence. It is at the behest of the mutual consent of the two minds that male and female meet for procreation.

The experience of the history of numerous individuals who's that mind, when cultivated in the positive direction, surely helps to reach the state of eternal peace, the highest goal of human life. But the society at large does not reflect this phenomenon as a collective social action. We all know that the perverted minds always make personal as well as social life chaotic and full of created and self-invited problems. In the present-day society we are amply witnessing this dominance socio-cultural trend. Day by day worsening socio-economic conditions of the individual, and healthy social values and norms of society, have posed a challenge before the thinking minds to find out ways and means to regenerate peace and value education in the young minds.

DEFINITION OF PEACE EDUCATION

Peace education is more effective and meaningful when it is adopted according to the social and cultural context and the needs of a country. It should be enriched by its cultural and spiritual values together with the universal human values. It should also be globally relevant. Peace education could be defined in many ways. There is no universally accepted definition as such. Here are some good definitions from peace literature.

Peace education is an attempt to respond to problems of conflict and violence on scales ranging from the global and national to the local and personal. It is about exploring ways of creating more just and sustainable futures (R. D. Laing 1978).

Peace education is holistic. It embraces the physical, emotional, intellectual, and social growth of children within a framework deeply rooted in traditional human values. It is based on philosophy that teaches love, compassion, trust, fairness, co-operation and reverence for the human family and all left on our beautiful planet (Fran Schmidt and Alice Friedman 1988).

Peace education is skill building. It empowers children in creative and non-destructive ways to settle conflicts and to live in harmony with themselves, others, and their world. Peace building is the task of every human being and the challenge of the human family (Fran Schmidt and Alice Friedman 1988).

The basic concepts embedded in the above definitions are that peace education is a remedial measure to protect children from falling into the ways of violence in society. It aims at the total development of the child. It tries to inculcate higher human and social values in the mind of the child. In essence it attempts to develop a set of behavioral skills necessary for peaceful living and peace-building from which the whole of humanity will benefit.

PEACE: AVOIDING THE WAY OF NEGATION

The peace process additionally must acknowledge and contend with its alternative - war - because of the high value status of violence. For example, while war has brought out the worst kind of behavior in humans, it has also brought out some of the best. Aside from relieving boredom and monotony, war has been shown to spawn self-sacrifice, loyalty, honor, heroism, and courage. It is well known that suicide rates decline during war. Also, war has helped to bring about significant social changes such as racial and sexual integration, freedom, democ-

racy, and a sense of national pride. Because of its apparent utilitarian value and
its ability to enervate, violence has been solidly embedded in the national psyche
of many countries. As a result, its elimination will be no easy feat.

In its most myopic and limited definition, peace is the mere absence of war.
O'Kane (1992) sees this definition as a "vacuous, passive, simplistic, and unre-
sponsive escape mechanism too often resorted to in the past - without success."
This definition also commits a serious oversight: it ignores the residual feelings
of mistrust and suspicion that the winners and losers of a war harbor toward
each other. The subsequent suppression of mutual hostile feelings is not taken
into account by those who define peace so simply. Their stance is that as long as
people are not actively engaged in overt, mutual, violent, physical, and destructive activity, then peace exists. This, of course, is just another way of defining
cold war. In other words, this simplistic definition is too broad because it allows
us to attribute the term "peace" to states of affairs that are not truly peaceful
(Copi and Cohen, p. 194). Unfortunately, this definition of peace appears to be
the prevailing one in the world. It is the kind of peace maintained by a "peace
through strength" posture that has led to the arms race, stockpiles of nuclear
weapons, and the ultimate threat of mutually assured destruction.

SOME DIFFERENT TYPES OF PEACE

One way of clearing up the confusion over terms is to define types of peace and
war. Thus, there can be hot war, cold war, cold peace, and hot peace. In hot war,
commonly called war, there is a condition of mutual hostility and active physical
engagement through such forms as artillery, missiles, bombs, small arms fire,
mortars, flamethrowers, land and sea mines, hand-to-hand combat, and the like.
The aim is the destruction of the enemy or his surrender by intimidation. The
object is to have a winner and loser. Nationalism reaches its zenith here.

In cold war, there is mutual hostility without actual engagement. Intimidation is the sole means of preventing hot war. This condition is characterized by
propaganda, war preparations, and arms races - always at the expense of human
needs. During a cold war, nationalism prevails, and the object is to have a stale-
mate where neither side will initiate aggression - nuclear or conventional - because of the overwhelming destructive capability of the retaliatory response. In
cold peace, there is almost a neutral view of a previous enemy. There is little
mutual hostility, but there is also a lack of mutually beneficial interactions
aimed at developing trust, interdependence, and collaboration. There may be a
longing for an enemy because nothing has replaced it as an object of national
concern. In this situation, isolationism and nationalism occur simultaneously.
There is no clear objective because there is no well-defined enemy. Perhaps the
current U.S. military preoccupation with Iraq's Saddam Hussein and the debili-
tating decade of sanctions against the Iraqi people are helping to relieve this
enemy deficit. The notion that "there are still dangerous people in the world" is
often used to advance the cause of military preparedness and at least some mo-
mentum toward a restoration of cold war thinking and behavior. The term

"peace dividend" that expressed post-cold war optimism is hardly verbalized anymore. Now we are (again) advancing ballistic missile defense - a variation of the Reagan Administration's Star Wars debacle and an instigator of nuclear proliferation.

By contrast, hot peace involves active collaborative efforts designed to "build bridges" between and among past and present adversaries. This involves searching for common ground and the development of new non-human enemies threats to the health and well-being of humankind and the planet. These new enemies could include human rights abuses, air and water pollution, dwindling energy resources, the destruction of the ozone layer, famine, poverty, and ignorance. Hot peace promotes - and, indeed, is defined by - global interdependence, human rights, democratization, an effective United Nations, and a diminution of national sovereignty. The object is the proliferation of cooperative relations and mutually beneficial outcomes. Hot peace thinking imagines peace and the abolition of war.

TOWARD AN ADEQUATE DEFINITION

It is difficult not to see in these "positive" approaches to the definition of "peace" radical implications for reorganization of our society and, indeed, our entire world. Genuine peace requires the advent of a new selflessness, a willingness to see our fellow humans as our brothers and sisters and - as the traditional religions have always counseled - to love them as we love ourselves.

Actions to foster a culture of peace through education:
1) Ensure that children, from an early age, benefit from education on the values, attitudes, modes of behaviour and ways of life to enable them to resolve any dispute peacefully and in a spirit of respect for human dignity and of tolerance and non-discrimination; Involve children in activities designed to instill in them the values and goals of a culture of peace;
2) Encourage revision of educational curricula, including textbooks, bearing in mind the 1995 Declaration and Integrated Framework of Action on Education for Peace, Human Rights and Democracy for which technical cooperation should be provided by the United Nations Educational, Scientific and Cultural Organization upon request;
3) Encourage and strengthen efforts by actors as identified in the Declaration...aimed at developing values and skills conducive to a culture of peace, including education and training in promoting dialogue and consensus-building;

Actions to promote sustainable economic and social development:
1) Undertake further efforts to ensure that the development process is participatory and that development projects involve the full participation of all;
2) Include a gender perspective and empowerment of women and girls as an integral part of the development process;
3) Strengthen, through development assistance in post-conflict situations, rehabilitation, reintegration and reconciliation processes involving all engaged in conflicts;

Actions to ensure equality between women and men:
1) Promotion of equality between women and men in economic, social and political decision-making;
2) Provision of support and assistance to women who have become victims of any forms of violence, including in the home, workplace and during armed conflicts;

Actions to foster democratic participation:
1) Reinforcement of the full range of actions to promote democratic principles and practices;
2) Special emphasis on democratic principles and practices at all levels of formal, informal and non-formal education;

Actions to advance understanding, tolerance and solidarity:
1) Support actions that foster understanding and solidarity throughout society, in particular with vulnerable groups;
2) Promote increased understanding, tolerance, solidarity and cooperation among peoples and within and among nations;

Actions to support participatory communication and the free flow of information and knowledge:
1) Support the important role of the media in promotion of a culture of peace;
2) Make effective use of the media for advocacy and dissemination of information on a culture of peace involving, as appropriate, the United Nations and relevant regional, national and local mechanisms.

Schools can:
- Develop a more humanistic management approach.
- Improve human relations between, teacher-student, teacher-teacher, student-student, etc.

- Help develop good attitudes in students and teachers as well, e.g. co-operation, mutual respect.
- Help healthy emotional development in students.
- Facilitate socialization through participation in interactive and co- operative learning activities
- Improve students' discipline and moral behavior.
- Develop creativity both in students and teachers.
- Improve standard of quality of teaching and learning.

CONCLUSION

Education for Peace and Reconciliation

While wars are still going on in certain parts of the world and remain the greatest threat to mankind, it is essential that we reconsider the role of education in preventing future conflicts. Teaching peace has never been an easy task, especially in those countries where people are suffering from hatred and violence.

Through various experiences, peace education and reconciliation have developed with different degrees of success in crisis countries, some of which are described in our website. No systematic evaluation has been carried out in order to assess the relevance of these experiences and the impact of their methodological approaches. This area remains as an evolving one that requires further research and reflection. A big gap remains between educational practitioners working in the field of complex emergencies, and the copious methodological contributions and curriculum development initiatives produced in developed countries on the issue of education, peace and reconciliation.

The goal of our network is to offer support to the needs of peace educators around the world. By providing information about projects already developed, references and internet links, we hope to see further implementation in this field.

REFERENCES

Bhardwaj, A.B (2002) *Peace and Value Education: A Gandhian View Point,* Gandhi Marg: New Delhi, Gandhi Peace Foundation.

Children Working For Peace Project Manual Produced By UNICEF And The Oxford Development Education Centre In The United Kingdom.

Currents: Issues in Education and Human Development Education and Peace, Vol. 3, no. 2, pp. 7-20.

Don't Let The Foozles Get The Best Of Your Classroom! *By Fran Schmidt.*

Einstein, A. (1968). *Einstein on Peace.* Nathan and Norden (Eds). (p. 371). New York: Schocken.

International Context For The Education For Peace Program And The 2002-2006 Strategy For Program Implementation In All BIH Secondary Schools

O'Kane, M. (1991-92, Winter). *Peace: The Overwhelming Task.* Veterans for Peace, Inc. Journal, Issue no.19, p. 3.

O'Kane, M. (1992). Personal correspondence*.

Peace Education: Practice Is The Best Teacher – UNICEF

Peace through Education an article by Dr. Darleana McHenry Peace Education an article by T. Barber

Reardon, B.A. (1988). *Comprehensive Peace Education.* New York: Teachers College Press.

Russell, B. (1916). *Principles of Social Reconstruction.* (Chapter 5). London: Allen and Unwin. [published in the U.S. as *Why Men Fight.* (1916). New York: The Century Co.]

Sharp, G. (1980). *Social Power and Political Freedom.* Boston: Porter Sargent.

The Nature of Peace and Its Implications for Peace Education by Leo R. Sandy and Ray Perkins, Jr.

Woolman, D.C. (1985, Spring). "Education and Peace in the Thought of Johan Galtung."

www.unevoc.de

www.global-perspective.net

www.globalvillageschool.org

www.unesco.org

CHAPTER FOURTEEN

Enhancing an Appreciation for Cultural Diversity among Pre-service Teachers and Promoting Techniques for Teaching It

Kathleen Conway
Southeast Missouri State University

The United States is becoming increasingly diverse. The percent of non-white students enrolled in K-12 public schools in fall 2000 comprised Black/African American (17.2%), Hispanics (16.3%), Asian or Pacific Islander (4.1%), American Indian/Alaska Native (1.2%; National Center for Education Statistics 2003, Table 42, p. 38). Paradoxically, the teachers who teach this diverse population are becoming increasingly less diverse. Based on a study by the National Education Association, the majority of teachers in 2000-2001 were white (90%) with only 5% being Black/African American leaving just 5% for the remaining minorities (National Education Association, 2003). Although institutions who prepare teachers make many efforts to increase the diversity of the population they are training, this is clearly not sufficient to overcome the disparity. In our program we are also working with the pre-service teachers to increase their appreciation for cultural diversity and their understanding of how it should be incorporated into their teaching strategies.

This paper describes a developmental approach used by our program to help pre-service teachers develop concepts that culminate in instructional unit plans that reflect an appreciation for cultural diversity. The goal is that the pre-service teachers will then use this knowledge to develop lesson plans that increase student learning.

The activities that are described in this paper are included among the requirements of the Department of Elementary, Early, and Special Education at Southeast Missouri State University. The university was first founded as a teacher's college in 1873 and currently enrolls approximately 10,000 students in 150 academic programs. The department of Elementary, Early, and Special Education serves students seeking degrees and certification in its title areas; currently we have approximately 800 undergraduate majors.

In our program, courses are arranged so pre-service teachers take related education courses concurrently as a unified block of courses. There are four Blocks, each having a related field experience; typically, one Block is taken during each year of preparation with pre-service teacher classroom experiences increasing in length and responsibility over the sequence. The first Block requires that the pre-service teachers observe in the field and reflect on these observations in their journal; during the second block they are then expected to prepare and teach lessons in reading, while in Block III they prepare and teach units in mathematics, science, and social studies. Finally, in the last block (student teaching) they are responsible for instruction in all areas during the entire day.

TEACHER WORK SAMPLE

An important instructional model that is used in our program is the Teacher Work Sample (TWS). Our program first piloted the TWS methodology during Fall Semester 2001. The TWS is a process that helps the pre-service teachers write a comprehensive unit and provides prompts that they use to guide their thinking as they plan and then assess their instruction. This method requires that the pre-service teachers consider socio-economic factors as well as individual children's needs and abilities that are determined through assessment strategies. The TWS includes the following seven sections: Contextual Factors, Learning Goals, Assessment Plan, Design for Instruction, Instructional Decision-Making, Analysis of Student Learning, and Reflection and Self-Evaluation. The process is further described in Appendix A: Teacher Work Sample (TWS) Teaching Processes and Indicators.

The use of the TWS has been phased into our instructional program over the past three years. During fall semester 2001 the use of the TWS was piloted in one section of Block III. It was then implemented by other instructors in Block III followed by its use in Block II and then Block I. This implementation required the development of faculty members' understanding of the process and then modifications to the existing course structure to incorporate the process of the TWS. Full implementation was accomplished during spring semester 2003. As a consequence, most of the pre-service teachers completing Block IV (student teaching) during spring semester 2004 had experienced instruction and experiences using the TWS throughout their blocks.

Of particular interest in this paper is the first section of the TWS- Contextual Factors. In this section the pre-service teachers collect information about the learning-teaching context and variation among their students in this area. Their task is to "Discuss relevant factors and how they may affect the teaching-learning process and "include any supports and challenges that affect instruction and student learning" (Renaissance Group, 2002). To meet this requirement the pre-service teachers collect data and discuss the item according to the following instructions:

- **Community, district and school factors.** Address geographic location, community and school population, socio-economic profile and race/ethnicity. You might also address such things as stability of community, political climate, community support for education, and other environmental factors.

- **Classroom factors.** Address physical features, availability of technology equipment and resources and the extent of parental involvement. You might also discuss other relevant factors such as classroom rules and routines, grouping patterns, scheduling and classroom arrangement.
- **Student characteristics.** Address student characteristics you must consider as you design instruction and assess learning. Include factors such as age, gender, race/ethnicity, special needs, achievement/developmental levels, culture, language, interests, learning styles/modalities or students' skill levels. In your narrative, make sure you address students' skills and prior learning that may influence the development of your learning goals, instruction, and assessment.
- **Instructional implications.** Address how contextual characteristics of the community, classroom, and students have implications for instructional planning and assessment. Include specific instructional implications for at least two characteristics and any other factors that will influence how you plan and implement your unit (Renaissance Group, 2002).

Not surprisingly, the information summarized in the Contextual Factors is also later used in other sections of the TWS. After its completion, the TWS is one artifact that most pre-service teachers in our program use as they develop their certification portfolio.

CERTIFICATION PORTFOLIO

Pre-service teachers in our program are required to complete a certification portfolio. This portfolio provides an opportunity for the pre-service teachers to demonstrate their accomplishment in eleven areas that the State identified in Missouri's Performance Standards for Education Professionals. These standards are identified as Quality Indicators and comprise the following categories: knowledge of the discipline, learning and development, individualization, curriculum development, instructional strategies, motivation and management, communication skills, assessment, professional development, partnerships, and technology. See Appendix B for more information about these quality indicators.

Quality Indicator 3 focuses on the pre-service teacher's understanding of how students differ in their approaches to learning; it requires that the pre-service teachers create instructional opportunities that are adapted to diverse learners. To demonstrate that they meet this Quality Indicator the pre-service teachers are expected to document how they create activities that connect with and build upon their students' culture, family, and community heritages. The Contextual Factors section of the TWS is typically used as an artifact as the pre-service teachers discuss their knowledge of this Quality Indicator. Although the final evaluation of this Quality Indicator takes place during the pre-service teacher's last semester, the developmental approach we use requires that instruction and assignments are completed throughout the Blocks prior to student teaching. This development helps the pre-service teachers prepare for this final project.

COURSE ASSIGNMENTS

Our program provides a variety of opportunities for pre-service teachers to understand diversity issues and how these should be considered when developing and using instructional materials. The activities that relate to the TWS are consistently used in a sequence of courses and provide a foundation for the pre-service teacher's development. During Block I, teacher candidates are first introduced to the Contextual Factors section of the TWS. They complete a series of assignments where they explore the diversity of the schools they attended as a K-12 student. Following the data collection assignments they then identify instructional implications of this information. Throughout these assignments, there are class discussions about the information collected and its importance. These assignments provide a foundation for the understanding of subsequent course assignments on cultural diversity.

During Block II, the pre-service teachers are assigned to a classroom in a K-6 school. They then complete the Contextual Factors assignment for the classroom they will work in. Their understanding of the diversity of their students is then incorporated into considerations as they develop the reading lessons they will use with this group of students. During Block III this process is repeated for their new field assignment. The pre-service teachers collect information about the students they will work with and then use that information in their planning and instruction as they teach units in Mathematics, Science, and Social Studies. Finally, during Block IV (student teaching) they are assigned yet another field placement. They again collect information on this new group of students and then use this information as they develop a unit in the subject of their choice. Throughout these block experiences; efforts are made to assign the pre-service teachers to classrooms with different characteristics. The diverse classrooms provide a variety of opportunities for the pre-service teacher to look at the cultural diversity of their students. Additionally, there are discussions in the college classroom, conducted by the faculty instructor, regarding the significance of the diversity they have observed. These discussions also help the pre-service teacher identify modifications that can be made to their instruction to increase the opportunities for their students to learn.

ASSESSING SUCCESS

The pre-service teacher's ability to meet the expectations for Quality Indicator 3 (assessed in Block IV) is a partial measure of their understanding of cultural diversity and how they use this understanding in their instruction. The results reported in Table 1 indicate slight increases from the first entry (Fall 2001; 63.0%) through Fall 2003 (65.8%) as the TWS was employed in more sections and blocks. However, a greater increase occurs in the results from Spring 2004 (72.4%) when compared with those previously. We suspected that this increase was due to activities related to the TWS which, at that time, was incorporated in all sections and blocks. However, caution must be employed when examining these data since other aspects of diversity are included in the rubric for this Quality Indicator. Nonetheless a trend of increasing success in completing this quality indicator was indicated by the data collected each semester at the time of the first scoring of this quality indicator. The results of full implementation are only now having an impact and are most likely the major influence on the improved results of the portfolio scoring of QI #3 for spring semester, 2004.

Table 1. Number of Student Teachers Passing Quality Indicator #3 on First Scoring

Semester/Year	#Scored	# Passing	% Passing
Fall/2001	73	46	63.0%
Spring/2002	87	56	64.4%
Fall /2002	77	50	64.9%
Spring /2003	111	73	65.8%
Fall /2003	73	48	65.8%
Spring /2004	76	55	72.4%

In summary, the data suggest that we have increased the success of pre-service teachers' successful completion of Quality Indicator #3 over the past three years. We feel that the structure of the TWS and the implementation of this requirement throughout the program is a factor in the increased success. However, it is clear that our efforts have only begun. Although we have helped our pre-service teachers identify features of cultural diversity, we still need to better help them understand what they should do with this information as they plan, teach, and assess student learning.

Appendix A. Teacher Work Sample (TWS) Teaching Processes and Indicators

Contextual Factors
The teacher uses information about the learning-teaching context and student individual differences to set learning goals and plan instruction and assessment.
- Knowledge of community, school, and classroom factors
- Knowledge of characteristics of students
- Knowledge of students' varied approaches to learning
- Knowledge of students' skills and prior learning
- Implications for instructional planning and assessment

Learning Goals
The teacher sets significant, challenging, varied and appropriate learning goals.
- Significance, Challenge and Variety
- Clarity
- Appropriateness for students
- Alignment with national, state or local standards

Assessment Plan
The teacher uses multiple assessment modes and approaches aligned with learning goals to assess student learning before, during and after instruction.
- Alignment with learning goals and instruction
- Clarity of criteria for performance
- Multiple modes and approaches
- Technical soundness
- Adaptations based on the individual needs of students

Design for Instruction
The teacher designs instruction for specific learning goals, student characteristics and needs, and learning contexts.
- Alignment with learning goals
- Accurate representation of content
- Lesson and unit structure
- Use of a variety of instruction, activities, assignments and resources
- Use of contextual information and data to select appropriate and relevant activities, assignments and resources.
- Use of technology

Instructional Decision-Making
The teacher uses ongoing analysis of student learning to make instructional decisions.
• Sound professional practice
• Adjustments based on analysis of student learning
• Congruence between modifications and learning goals

Analysis of Student Learning
The teacher uses assessment data to profile student learning and communicate information about student progress and achievement.
• Clarity and accuracy of presentation
• Alignment with learning goals
• Interpretation of data
• Evidence of impact on student learning

Reflection and Self-Evaluation
The teacher reflects on his or her instruction and student learning in order to improve teaching practice.
• Interpretation of student learning
• Insights on effective instruction and assessment
• Alignment among goals, instruction and assessment
• Implications for future teaching
• Implications for professional development

**Appendix B. Performance Standards for Education Professionals –
Missouri Department of Elementary and Secondary Education**

Quality Indicator 1.2.1: The pre-service teacher understands the central concepts, tools of inquiry and structures of the discipline(s) within the context of a global society and creates learning experiences that make these aspects of subject matter meaningful for students.

Quality Indicator 1.2.2: The pre-service teacher understands how students learn and develop, and provides learning opportunities that support the intellectual, social, and personal development of all students.

Quality Indicator 1.2.3: The pre-service teacher understands how students differ in their approaches to learning and creates instructional opportunities that are adapted to diverse learners.

Quality Indicator 1.2.4: The pre-service teacher recognizes the importance of long-range planning and curriculum development and develops, implements, and evaluates curriculum based upon student, district, and state performance standards.

Quality Indicator 1.2.5: The pre-service teacher uses a variety of instructional strategies to encourage students' development of critical thinking, problem solving, and performance skills.

Quality Indicator 1.2.6: The pre-service teacher uses an understanding of individual and group motivation and behavior to create a learning environment that encourages positive social interaction, active engagement in learning, and self-motivation.

Quality Indicator 1.2.7: The pre-service teacher models effective verbal, non-verbal, and media communication techniques to foster active inquiry, collaboration, and supportive interaction in the classroom.

Quality Indicator 1.2.8: The pre-service teacher understands and uses formal and informal assessment strategies to evaluate and ensure the continuous intellectual, social, and physical development of the learner.

Quality Indicator 1.2.9: The pre-service teacher is a reflective practitioner who continually assesses the effects of choices and actions on others. This reflective practitioner actively seeks out opportunities to grow professionally and utilizes the assessment and professional growth to generate more learning for more students.

Quality Indicator 1.2.10: The pre-service teacher fosters relationships with school colleagues, parents, and educational partners in the larger community to support student learning and well-being.

Quality Indicator 1.2.11: The pre-service teacher understands the theory and application of technology in educational settings and has technological skills to create meaningful learning opportunities for all students.

REFERENCES

National Center for Education Statistics. (2003). *Digest of Education Statistics, 2002.* Web release, June 23. Elementary and secondary education chapter. Retrieved 6/27/04 from
http://nces.ed.gov/pubs2003/2003060b.pdf

National Education Association. (2003). *Status of the American Public School Teacher 2000-2001: Highlights.* Retrieved 6/27/04 from
http://www.nea.org/edstats/images/statushighlights.pdf

Renaissance Group (2002). *The Renaissance Partnership for Improving Teacher Quality Project.* Retrieved 6/29/04 from http://fp.uni.edu/itq

CHAPTER FIFTEEN

Practice of Online Chat Communication between Two Countries and across Different Curricula

Ritsuko Saito
University of Wollongong, Australia

Noriko Ishizuka
Doshisha University, Japan

INTRODUCTION

Many benefits of computer mediated communication (CMC) in the framework of education have been reported. Some of the well-known benefits are for the participants to be able to work at their own pace and at an hour of their choosing (e.g. Sutherland-Smith, 2002); participants also feel more comfortable and confident than in face-to-face communication as they can see the text of the discourse and understand it better and cannot see the other participants and hence find the experience less threatening (e.g. Freiermuth, 2002). In addition, online chat in particular is suggested to be an ideal place for collaborative learning activities while in a traditional language class it is often difficult for all the parties to participate actively at the same time (Kitade, 2000 and Freiermuth, 2002). The aim of the activities and the target language of the participants differ from study to study. For example, foreign language education alone involves a variety of combinations: 'native speakers and non-native speakers of the target language' (Kitade, 2000), 'non-native and non-native' (Freiermuth, 2002), and 'non-native and native as volunteer' (Iwasaki and Oliver, 2003). The participants of such studies are in the same course (except the volunteer in the study of Iwasaki), and only a few studies are available with two groups from different countries and from different curricula (e.g. Walther, 1997, but not in the field of foreign language education; Cifuentes and Shih, 2001, but not with online chat). Therefore this paper is unique in the sense that the participants are in two different courses (Japanese language and English IT literacy) in two different countries (Australia and Japan). Hence both groups can be identified as either native or non-native speakers depending on which language is employed in the course of communication. Unlike the previously mentioned studies where all the participants within the same course discuss and decide on a task via online chat,

the participants referred to in this paper are required to complete their own respective tasks by cooperating online.

With regard to incorporation of the medium, the degree of CMC incorporation becomes an issue for educators when employing the medium. Although
McCarthy (1999) points out the lack of research on integration of CALL into a
curriculum, in order to utilize CMC in the best possible way, awareness and understanding of the issues and flexibility in educators' practice appear to be the
key to a better learning and teaching environment. Therefore, this study attempts
to demonstrate how online chat between two different courses from two different countries has developed over nine years and what benefits it has brought in
both parties.

A HISTORY OF OUR CHAT PRACTICE

Computer-mediated communication (CMC) between a Japanese language class
at the University of Wollongong and an English language class at Doshisha
University first started in 1995. These nine years of CMC have seen development in several aspects. From 1995 to 2000, one-on-one conversation style
(y-talk) was employed through a Unix system. Since 2001, online chat by a
WebCT system has been employed with five chat rooms, each of which com-
prises four or five students from both sides. With this shift from pair work to
group discussion, the instructors no longer have to take the trouble to rearrange
pairs when some students are absent, and the students have more active and interactive discussion in their group as they stay in the same chat room and talk
with the same people throughout the semester.

When y-talk first started, the role of chat sessions in each curriculum was
initially assumed as cultural such as the source of authentic material and the
place for "conversation" with the native speakers of English for the students of
Doshisha University and of Japanese for the students of the University of Wollongong. Although the students took initiative in discussion, online chat practice has been more structured in planning and implementing tasks as the instructors gained more experience in the use of the medium, observed students'
learning, and better understood the potential and the weaknesses of the chat use
in each curriculum. Therefore, since then both courses have afforded variety to
the content of discussion, promoting e-mail correspondence, asynchronous CMC,
outside the class, to supplement the online discussion or to prepare for a next
session of online chat. Task-based discussion is also employed on topics which
are related to or help the understanding of other class activities in the respective
coursework. Moreover, in order to keep up with current developments in the
world, the students gather online articles from the internet and exchange opinions on what is happening in each country and in the world. To sum, the use of
online chat has been better positioned in each curriculum over the years, and the
place of online chat in each curriculum will be presented next.

PLACE OF ONLINE CHAT PRACTICE IN EACH CURRICULUM

University of Wollongong, Australia

The University offers two compulsory language courses for Japanese majors in the final year (i.e. the third year). The class meets every Tuesday and Thursday for a total of five hours per week for thirteen weeks per semester. The courses usually consist of a one hour Kanji lesson and four hours of grammar. One of the grammar hours would be replaced by online chat session when it commences. Through online chat, the students practice, recapitulate, and apply what they have learned in the courses, and they prepare for a project. In the communication with Doshisha University, they are strongly encouraged to use new grammar structures and expressions learned in the course. They are also expected to ask the chat partners' opinions and discuss the theme of the project, which consists of an essay and an oral presentation. The project is designed for the students to incorporate and demonstrate their newly acquired linguistic knowledge as well as the understanding of cultural and social issues. After each session, the students are required to write a report on each chat session in Japanese and self-reflection and evaluation on their chat practice for assessment.

Doshisha University, Japan

The department of English at Doshisha University offers this one-semester selective language course for 3rd and 4th year students. The students go through a pre-registration process to be selected by their grades for 1st-year and 2nd-year writing courses. This course is designed to integrate language skills training with computer literacy training, requiring a fair level of typing proficiency as well. The class meets every Tuesday from 9 to 10:30 for thirteen weeks. There are six or four 60-min. online chat sessions each semester. Besides online chat with the students at the University of Wollongong, the course also has asynchronous communication, e-mail correspondence, with Japanese language classes at American universities such as Amherst College and Middlebury College. After the end of e-mail correspondence and online chat, the students conduct a project to create their own English web pages to develop both their own writing skills and computer skills while presenting their achievement through the website out to the world.

DESCRIPTION OF CHAT SESSION OF THE YEAR 2003

During the year 2003, an average of 22 students of Japanese of the University of Wollongong and English-major students at Doshisha University participated in a 60-min. online chat over a seven week period in the first semester and a four week period in the second semester. They first logged on to the WebCT managed by the University of Wollongong and then went to their chat room assigned in advance by the instructors. They were instructed to balance the language use (e.g. 1st half hour in English and the second half in Japanese or vise versa). Prior to the online chat session, the instructors from both sides decided on a discussion topic each week with their respective objectives and strategies. An example of this approach will be discussed later.

The general observation of the instructors and the students' reports reveals four notable roles of online chat practice over the years. The following section will explain these four functions and how they work for the students and in the respective curricula.

FUNCTIONS AND BENEFITS OF ONLINE CHAT

1. Common place for task based discussion

This section describes how online chat can provide a place to recapitulate and deepen other activities in the course. Prior to each chat session, the instructors from both sides decided on a discussion topic with their respective objectives and strategies.

One example is a discussion of a Japanese newspaper article on 'putting on make-up on the train'. The article was initially used in the class activity at the University of Wollongong (WU hereafter). The students of WU studied the article as reading material for their project as well as for language development and cultural understanding (Japanese manners). Through online chat with the students of Doshisha University (DU hereafter), the students of WU were able to deepen their knowledge and understanding of their class activity and gain a live response from the real audience.

On the other hand, the students of DU were able to see their own culture and manners from a different perspective and had a chance to improve their own skills for opinion formation, based on their own experience. One student reports: "This talk taught me that in order to carry a successful intercultural communication, English ability is not enough: knowledge of my own culture and values is also important so that we can avoid misunderstanding and stereotypes". In spite of differences in curriculum, online chat served both sides as a common ground for discussion.

2. Tool for information collection training

One task-based discussion was designed to help the students of DU improve their skills for gathering information on the internet and also catch up with current issues in the world. They were given a task to access websites and choose an online article that would interest the students of WU. Then they sent the article of their choice prior to the online discussion to each member of the group, while every one was supposed to read the articles and be ready for the discussion. In this way, they were encouraged to take more active roles in the online discussion, creating interesting and meaningful contexts of their own. They had to keep up with the latest developments in world events and learned to communicate knowledgeably with their chat partners.   In the spring semester, many groups exchanged different articles on the war in Iraq and compared each government's reactions and gained an objective and outside view on their own country's policy.   This kind of communication practice with the real audience provided the students with training for computer literacy and opinion formation. Moreover, through this task, the students of WU had an opportunity to further develop their social and cultural knowledge and language learning strategies by reading the articles and asking about unknown words and expressions and also by exchanging their thoughts.

3. Place for collaborative learning and forming a learning community

A first benefit, particularly for the students of DU, is that the students were able to gain a live response from the real audience, which they could have hardly achieved through conventional language learning. As Hicks summarizes (2000), this more learner-centered cross-cultural setting could provide the students with contact with the world outside of the classroom and reduce the Japanese traditional language focus on form and grammar.   This also makes a collaborative and less threatening learning environment for Japanese students who have been so used to homogeneous classroom settings (Hata, 2003).   Thus, online discussion meets "individual needs by allowing students to work at their own speed, avoid pronunciation problems, and read before responding" (Sutherland-Smith, 2002, 34).

Another benefit of online discussion is that Australian students and Japanese students both as second language learners and as native speakers of their chat partners' target language can form a language learning community.   This learning experience proves that "learning is inherently a social dialogical process in which learners benefit most from being part of knowledge-building communities in class and outside of school" (Jonassen, 1995, qtd. in Opp-Beckman, 2002, 4). For one task-based discussion, the students exchanged tips for learning foreign languages.   Some students also learned to see their native language from a new perspective by listening to how their chat partners coped with difficulties in learning the target language. One student writes in her assessment of the discussion:

> . . . from my partners' remarks, I discovered how difficult it is to learn Japanese. . . . When I said it is easier to write or read English than to speak it, she said it is the same for the Japanese language as well, except Chinese characters. It seems that Chinese characters are very difficult for my partners.   Responding to the question, "How do you remember Kanji?", I told them that it is an ideograph, so each character has its meaning.   Then they said they found the meanings of Kanji easier to remember than the different readings.   It seems more difficult to remember the Japanese reading of Kanji and the Chinese reading of it.   I can see it is more difficult to master how to read Chinese characters than to remember the meanings of Kanji. There are thousands of Chinese characters, while there are only 26 letters in the English alphabet.   I was surprised at this fact.

Another student writes:

> Through the chat sessions, I came to re-think about my language, Japanese.
> While I tried to write the right and clear Japanese to them, I realized that even I,
> who have lived in Japan for 21 years, do not know very well about what the
> correct and beautiful Japanese is.

It was also beneficial for both Japanese and Australian students to do online chat
in two languages, since the chat serves them as a meaningful and collaborative
native speakers/non native speakers interaction. The students gained peer cor-
rective feedback and new vocabulary or idioms. It is also a text-based discourse,
which enables the students to carry discussion without any fear of missing any
words: they can just scroll down the screen to see a comment made earlier and
view the conversation (Freiermuth, 2002). One student writes that she could feel
more comfortable than she does in face-to-face conversation as "talking" via the
computer screen is slower, and she can understand her chat partners' opinions in
depth, and at the personal level. As Murray (2000) analyses, there are both
features of oral and written language in CMC. The students took advantage of
the speech-in-writing characteristic to gain new vocabulary or idioms or ask for
the right expression from their chat partners who were the native speakers of
their target language. On these occasions, their writing on the screen often
included mixed languages in simplified syntax. In addition, online chat is si-
multaneous communication, by which students can get a reply immediately from
their chat partner. One student writes:

> Since you cannot see the person's reactions or gestures and so on, I felt the bar-
> rier that arrives from the own cultures and the importance of the "words" itself.
> Grammars are important but in this case, I thought that the motivation of want-
> ing to know each other by using the words you know were important. When
> [the partners] didn't understand what we were saying they simply asked us. We
> can do the same thing. There are a lot that we can study from the real spoken
> language itself and not only from the written texture and grammar. I have en-
> joyed this way of communicating very much.

4. Place of self-enlightenment

This practice of cross-cultural communication also served as an occasion for
self-enlightenment. In the course of online chat sessions, the students on both
sides became not only chat partners for language training but also friends.
Even though they were talking online with their chat partners a thousand mile
away, they felt so close to them. One student reports:

> Even though [my chat partners] live thousands of kilometers away from here,
> we can be easily connected by just entering the chat room. In this room, there
> is no room between us. I think the most wonderful thing about chat is that it
> enables us to feel like sitting on the same sofa.

Thus, it is not only a tool for language learning, since students reflect their personal concerns by sharing similar interests and problems. Generally for junior and senior students in Japan, career planning is one of their biggest concerns. In spring semester, senior students are engaged in job hunting, while in fall semester, junior students start to look for their future career. One student said that she was cheered up by exchanging opinions about careers and by observing her chat partner's positive thinking toward his future career.

No doubt the online chat experience has enriched the students' learning and broadened the curricula. The following section will summarize key points to a successful and lasting relationship between the two different curricula.

KEYS TO ONGOING SUCCESS

As previously mentioned, online chatting has been a vehicle for improving language skills and also for personal development. In addition, online chat has offered supplementary and valuable aspects in each curriculum. Five key points (learner-centeredness, needs assessment, flexibility, communication in target language/native language, and time zone) will be briefly summarized here.

Learner-Centeredness

Both instructors value a learner-centered practice in the respective courses. Richards (2001, 117) explains that a learner-centered approach involves educational philosophies that stress "the individual needs of learners, the role of individual experience, and the need to develop awareness, self-reflection, critical thinking, learner strategies and other qualities and skills that are believed to be important for learners to develop". Thus the instructors identify online chat as a tool for making class activities more learner-centered, and, in practice, the online chat has made a great contribution to curriculum design.

Needs Assessment

Needs assessment is important to design and to improve a course. This means that, in order to design an appropriate course, an instructor must both know and meet the needs of the students. Ideally, this also helps improve the teaching and learning environment. Furthermore, in relation to outcomes, needs assessment helps "increase motivation and self-esteem by recognizing students' interests and abilities and valuing their own assessment of what they need to learn" (Robinson and Selman, 1996, 23). In reality, it is often difficult to fulfill needs assessment appropriately due to time constraints and resource availability. Online chat practice, however, has resolved some of these difficulties. For example, both students and instructors have appreciated the authenticity and practicality of the language used, the skills learnt, and the knowledge acquired in the course in addition to the interactive links provided with other parts of the course. With regard to the latter point, for example, students have found it easier to apply what they have learnt in traditional classes when talking to the chat partners.

Good Communication and Flexibility

Once online chat has its place in a course, it is helpful to be aware of the place in the partner's course and its relationship with the other parts of the course in order to find a common ground where both parties can benefit. Through regular communication between the instructors, each instructor could seek some ideas which are beneficial for both parties and set a topic for discussion which could bring a multiplier effect. An idea for a discussion topic sometimes arises from a conversation on what the students did in class such as a simple description of a learning activity before a given chat session. Needless to say, that flexibility enables instructors to implement such an idea in each course as well as to cope when a computer breaks down.

Communication in Target Language/Native Language

One of the target languages (Japanese or English) is always a language that the participants are currently learning at the respective universities. Therefore, language development was a foreseen benefit. Also the similarity of the courses, both in humanity discipline, has probably helped most with regard to organizing a learning activity which could be beneficial for both parties.

Time Zone

The time difference between the two countries is only one hour. It has certainly made the scheduling easier for the instructors so that they could fit the respective courses in the university timetable. Doshisha University students cannot seek online chat partners in Europe or North America because of the large time differences.

These points have certainly helped the instructors to position online chat in each course. Hence, a successful and lasting practice between two different curricula from two different countries has been realized.

DISCUSSION

While the medium has provided a unique learning place and brought benefits to the courses, there are shortcomings which are sometimes inevitable and issues to be aware of. Although the following does not necessarily apply to both courses, some issues will be discussed here, which are mismatches with the medium and technical support.

Mismatches with the medium occur at various levels. Inefficient skills, personality, and conversation domination exemplify this point. Avoiding mismatches is very important to improve students' satisfaction, motivation, and positive attitude. There is a possibility that the conversation could be dominated by others especially when the typing skill is inefficient (McCarthy, 1999 and Luke, 1996). Although the instructors monitor student interactions, conversation domination might need to be examined if CMC-related skills are to be developed further. The skill development in particular will be more important for the students of WU as the online chat session moves to a new site this year where they can type Japanese scripts (*Hiragana, Katakana,* and *Kanji*).

On-going technical support is essential for delivering a successful chat session including maintaining and securing appropriate computers and software. Student registration from other courses and countries in particular would not be possible without such support.

With regard to language and skills development, the level of achievement has been only assumed by the completion of assessment as the chat interaction is not directly assessed. Thus for future study, analysis of actual interaction (i.e., of text) might be useful in order to further understand student learning behavior in the medium and to improve the courses.

CONCLUSION

This study attempted to demonstrate how online chat between two different courses from two different countries successfully continued over nine years and has been beneficial to both parties. Four notable roles of online chat practice developed over the years have been presented. The roles are task based discussion, information collection, formation of learning community, and self-enlightenment. Such roles demonstrated that the use of online chat has enriched the students' learning as well as the curricula. In addition, some key points to a successful and lasting relationship between the two different courses were identified. Thus, online chat has been better positioned in each curriculum, and the overall chat sessions and respective courses have improved over the years. Some issues and future directions were also discussed.

Lastly, this paper hopes to have suggested how the medium might be more widely applied in education, and also to have presented some ideas of co-operative teaching, collaborative learning and cross-cultural understanding across different curricula. Although some of the key points for a successful relationship mentioned earlier might be peculiar to the particular case, online chat might be a place for consideration in the curriculum if a course seeks one or more roles mentioned above. Potential chat partners outside the course work or in a different country could make a greater contribution to deepening and developing collaborative learning.

REFERENCES

Beauvois, M.H. 1992, 'Computer-Assisted Classroom Discussion in the Foreign Language Classroom: Conversation in Slow Motion', *Foreign Language Annals*, 25, no.5, pp. 455-464.
Cifuentes, L. & Shih, Y. D. 2001, 'Teaching and Learning Onlines: A Collaboration between U. S. and Taiwanese Students', *Journal of Research on Computing in Education*, Summer, vol. 33, no. 4, pp. 456-474.
Freiermuth, M.R. 2002, 'Internet Chat: Collaborating and Learning via E-Conversations', *TESOL Journal* 11.3, pp. 36-40.
Hata, M. 2003, 'Literature Review: Using Computer-Mediated Communication in Second Language Classrooms', *Osaka Keidai Ronshu* 54.3, pp.115-123.
Hicks, S. K. 2000, 'Using Computer-Mediated Communication in a Writing and Speaking English Class to Enhance the Language Learning Experience', *Kyôto Tachibana Joshi Daigaku Gaikokugo Kyôiku Kenkyû Sentâ Kiyô* 9, pp.59-69.
Hiltz, S.R. 1986, 'The "Virtual Classroom": Using Computer-Mediated Communication for University Teaching', *Journal of Communication*, Spring, pp.95 – 104.
Iwasaki, J. & Oliver, R. 2003, 'Chat-Line Interaction and Negative Feedback', *Australian Review of Applied Linguistics*, November, pp.60-73.
Luke, C. 1996, 'ekstasis@cyberia', *Discourse*, vol.17, no.12, pp.187-208.
McCarthy, B. 1999, 'Integration: the sine qua non of CALL', *CALL-EJ Online*, vol.1, no.2 September (www.lerc.ritsumei.ac.jp/callej/index.html)
Murray, D.E. 2000, 'Protean Communication: The Language of Computer-Mediated Communication', *TESOL Quarterly* 34.3, pp.397-421.
Opp-Beckman, L. 2002 'Africa Online: A Web- and Content-Based English Language Teaching Course', *TESOL Journal* 11.3, pp. 4-8 and pp.21-26.
Ramzan, Y. & Saito, R. 1998, *Computer-Mediated Communication in Foreign Language Learning: A Case of The Students of Japanese*, The 15th Annual Conference of the Australasian Society for Computers in Learning in Tertiary Education, AS-CILITE '98 Conference Proceedings, Wollongong. pp.585-592.
Richards, J.C. 2001, *Curriculum Development in Language Teaching,* CUP, Cambridge. Ch.5.
Robinson, J. & Selman, M. 1996, 'Assessing Needs and Negotiating to Curriculum', in *Partnerships in Learning: Teaching ESL to Adults,* Pippin, Toronto. pp.22-35.
Sutherland-Smith, W. 2002, 'Integrating Online Discussion in an Australian Intensive English Language Course', *TESOL Journal* 11.3, pp.31-35.